The Renminbi Rises

Also by Chi Lo

ASIA AND THE SUBPRIME CRISIS: Lifting the Veil on the Financial Tsunami

CHINA AFTER THE SUBPRIME CRISIS: Opportunities in the New Economic Landscape

PHANTOM OF THE CHINA ECONOMIC THREAT: Shadow of the Next Asian Crisis

THE MISUNDERSTOOD CHINA: Uncovering the Truth behind the Bamboo Curtain

THINKING THE INEVITABLE: China's Economic Superpower Aspiration in the New Paradigm

UNDERSTANDING CHINA'S GROWTH: Forces That Drive China's Economic Future

WHEN ASIA MEETS CHINA IN THE NEW MILLENNIUM: China's Role in Shaping Asia's Post-Crisis Economic Transformation

The Renminbi Rises

Myths, Hypes and Realities of RMB Internationalisation and Reforms in the Post-Crisis World

Chi Lo

palgrave
macmillan

First published 2013 by
PALGRAVE MACMILLAN

Palgrave Macmillan in the UK is an imprint of Macmillan Publishers Limited, registered in England, company number 785998, of Houndmills, Basingstoke, Hampshire RG21 6XS.

Palgrave Macmillan in the US is a division of St Martin's Press LLC, 175 Fifth Avenue, New York, NY 10010.

Palgrave Macmillan is the global academic imprint of the above companies and has companies and representatives throughout the world.
Palgrave® and Macmillan® are registered trademarks in the United States, the United Kingdom, Europe and other countries

ISBN: 978–1–137–34624–7

This book is printed on paper suitable for recycling and made from fully managed and sustained forest sources. Logging, pulping and manufacturing processes are expected to conform to the environmental regulations of the country of origin.

A catalogue record for this book is available from the British Library.

A catalog record for this book is available from the Library of Congress.

To Yee

Contents

List of Illustrations

Tables

Figures

Preface

The world economy has been relying on two currencies to lubricate the flow of global trade and finance, until recently that is. Together, the US dollar and the euro account for some 90% of global foreign exchange reserves and about two-thirds of worldwide foreign currency trading. Since its inception[1] in 2002, the euro has grown to 25% of global reserves and accounted for some 12% of global trade settlements. Despite this significant growth of the international use of the euro, the US dollar remains by far the most important international currency in the world economy.

But the world has changed, with a newcomer to the global monetary system since the turn of the millennium. That newcomer is the renminbi (RMB), or Chinese yuan. The rise of the RMB is both an indicator and a result of the evolution in the global macro landscape that shifts economic weight from the developed markets, led by Europe, Japan and the United States (or the G3), to the emerging markets, led by China. There are three structural changes creeping through the global system over the past decade that have created an opportunistic environment for the rise of the RMB. They include the weakening of the US dollar's global influence, the uncertainty of the euro's fate and the structural decline of the Japanese yen (JPY).

With these changes in the global economy, many experts foresee a movement towards a multi-polar currency system in the future in which the yuan will play a bigger role. China has also taken the initiative to promote the international use of the RMB as a trade settlement currency since 2009, and develop an offshore RMB market primarily based in Hong Kong. More offshore centres are expected, with Singapore, London and Taipei as the front-runners to be the next offshore RMB centres.

However, global economic development since the US subprime crisis in 2008 has challenged the multi-polar view. The European debt crisis has threatened to develop into a source of severe global instability. A growing need for structural adjustment in the Chinese economy and possible contagion from Europe have raised new questions about the path and pace of RMB internationalisation. Finally, despite persistent fiscal challenges, the dollar has continued to play the role of a safe-haven currency for global investors.

No one knows when the world can get away from the US dollar's dominance, even when the dollar's global role has been eroded by the emergence of the euro and, most recently, the Chinese yuan. But it is certain that the global importance of the RMB has to rise to be commensurate with China's growing economic weight in the global economy. What is amazing is that China has not followed the conventional path of currency internationalisation, which argues for capital account liberalisation before the currency achieves reserve currency status. The yuan is now held by some central banks in their official reserves, despite its partial convertibility and China's closed capital account. Thus, by definition, the RMB is already a reserve currency, though its share in the global official reserve allocation is negligible.

RMB internationalisation will be the most important structural change, or catalyst for change, for China in the coming decades. It will have global implications because it will be one of the most important developments for the global monetary system. The increasing weight of China in the global economy makes it necessary for the world to think about including the Chinese currency in the official reserves and the major foreign currency league. Welcome to the RMB; the global league of G3 currencies (euro, yen and the dollar) should probably be redefined to G4, including the RMB in it soon.

All these changes have generated big excitement in the global community and financial markets, which see new business opportunities in RMB-denominated products and new investment scope in Chinese assets for foreign investors. For the first time, the world is looking seriously for exposure to Chinese assets, and governments are mulling the future role of the RMB in the global monetary system. Market players have jumped onto these themes with a lot of hypes, leading to extreme and erroneous predictions for the RMB internationalisation process and the corresponding policy and financial market development.

To be fair, research on RMB internationalisation is very difficult because the event has been unfolding fast, with frequent shifting regulations and changing market environment. Thus, structural factors are difficult to pin down for analysis. Most of the research in the financial markets is typically sales-driven extrapolation of some initial trends without serious investigation into the structural underpinning of the events. Forecasts and analyses typically come and go within a few months, or even weeks, without consistency.

Thus, the research culture in the investment community of the RMB internationalisation subject has mostly been data driven and trading orientated, with short-term views shifting according to market noises.

But this kind of research is not helpful for understanding the structural development of this important subject, nor is it helpful for designing long-term business and investment strategies. All this is certainly unsatisfactory for understanding such a crucial development from academic, business and investment, and policy perspectives.

Meanwhile, academic research on this subject has mainly focused on extending previous work on currency internationalisation and capital account liberalisation to the yuan. This makes yuan internationalisation an uninteresting subject, which it is not. Like in the implementation of many other structural reforms, China's push for RMB internationalisation has in many aspects not followed the conventional path of development.

For example, the yuan has become a reserve currency before capital account and currency convertibility. But the conventional path should be making the capital account convertible first before achieving the reserve currency status. Even on the international trade aspect, which is the starting point for RMB internationalisation, China seems to have put the cart (trade settlement) before the horse (currency convertibility) successfully so far. Despite the RMB's inconvertibility on its capital account, it has already exerted strong influence on the global trade patterns, and effectively displaced the influence of Japan in the global goods markets.

All these are new, unconventional, developments of RMB internationalisation that are different from other currency internationalisation experience. They deserve more rigorous research. So far, academic research has yet to cover these issues, and financial market research has ignored these unconventional developments. In China, there is a lot of policy research (in the Chinese language) on RMB internationalisation, but there is no conviction on the road map for finding the means to get to the end. The Chinese government has not engaged in any discussions on the sequencing for internationalising the yuan. Outside China, there is also some policy research on the subject, but these studies lack the understanding of China's constraints and local characteristics and the market elements, which are important in shaping the analysis, outcome and policy prescriptions. After all, this research is not readily available to the public.

There are also a lot of market noises, myths and hypes that obstruct fundamental and structural analyses. For example, many banks' forecasts of the growth offshore RMB deposits and trading volume have been dead wrong (and quite surprisingly, they have repeated the mistakes over and over again). Some are making bold predictions, such as the RMB being the most traded currency in the world in just a few years, China's capital account being made convertible and the RMB being free-floating soon, without serious research and rigorous thought.

Some believe that growing foreign trade with the rest of the world would be sufficient for China to deepen and broaden the internationalisation process for the renminbi. This is a myth. The JPY's internationalisation experience has proven this wrong. Others have argued that the removal of capital controls and the opening up of domestic capital markets would be sufficient to internationalise the RMB. So the development of an offshore market would play no role in the process. This is another myth. There is no evidence for successful currency internationalisation without an offshore market. In fact, such arguments reflect the confusion of financial liberalisation with currency internationalisation.

Then there are market irregularities in and between the offshore and onshore RMB markets on the path of internationalisation. Academics lack an understanding of them and are, hence, handicapped in the research on the subject. Meanwhile, the market players seek to avoid discussing them so as to protect/prolong their profitable opportunities that are wrapped under market inefficiency.

Most crucially, there has been insufficient systematic research on the structural realities behind the RMB internationalisation exercise. No one has openly questioned the credibility of the RMB as an international currency. This kind of analysis and thinking are clearly absent in Chinese circles because they involve questioning the authorities, something the Chinese culture forbids. Critical analysis also involves exposing the political and structural flaws, incentive incompatibility problems, rent-seeking distortion and moral hazard in the Chinese system. Everybody ends up taking the process of RMB internationalisation for granted. This results in partial analysis.

Political reform is an important element behind RMB internationalisation because political support has become an imperative force to push deeper structural reforms, which are in turn the ultimate underpinning for a globalised RMB. All the efforts on political and structural reforms boil down to gaining international trust for the Chinese administration that stands behind the RMB. But these issues have not been discussed so far.

So there are gaps in both financial market and academic research on the subject of RMB internationalisation. This book takes a critical thinking approach, questions the ability of conventional wisdom and the status quo to fill these gaps and corrects the hypes and debunks the myths surrounding China's currency globalisation efforts. It also seeks to identify the hidden trends by examining the structural fundamentals behind China's political setting for analysing and projecting the RMB internationalisation process.

The cruel realities behind the yuan internationalisation process are the political and structural fault lines of the Chinese system, which most analysts have tried to avoid discussing. Exposing these flaws and understanding them are crucial for identifying the correct policies and steps to make RMB internationalisation succeed. By questioning the credibility support for the yuan and discussing the internal conflicts, political flaws and systemic distortions, the book brings to surface the taboo issues in China and hopes to contribute to fuller understanding of the issues affecting this policy ambition of China.

Acknowledgements

All economic data, data estimates and figures used in this book are created from the databank provided by CEIC Data Company Limited. Founded in 1992 and acquired in 2005 by ISI Emerging Markets, CEIC has built its reputation on delivering accurate and comprehensive economic, industrial and financial data for economists globally. In particular, it has the most comprehensive economic research data on Asia and some of the emerging markets. CEIC implements meticulous measures to ensure the accuracy of its data, which is maintained by experienced researchers who aggregate data from close to 2,000 primary sources.

List of Abbreviations and Terms Used in the Book

AUD	Australian dollar
BIS	Bank for International Settlements
BoP	balance of payments
BRL	Brazilian real
CAD	Canadian dollar
CBRC	China Banking Regulatory Commission
CD	certificate of deposit
CNH	offshore deliverable RMB market (acronym for Chinese yuan Hong Kong)
CNY	onshore deliverable RMB market (acronym for Chinese yuan)
CPI	consumer price index
DM	developed markets
EM	emerging markets
EUR	Euro
FDI	foreign direct investment
FX	foreign exchange
G3	group of three countries
G7	group of seven countries
GBP	Pound sterling
HKD	Hong Kong dollar
HKMA	Hong Kong Monetary Authority
IBF	International Banking Facilities in the United States (for handling offshore USD business in the domestic market)
IDR	Indonesia rupiah
IMF	International Monetary Fund
INR	Indian rupee
IPO	initial public offering
JGB	Japanese government bonds
JOM	Japan offshore market
JPY	Japanese yen
KRW	Korean won
LGFV	local government financial vehicles
MYR	Malaysian ringgit
NDF	non-deliverable forward market

NDRC	National Development and Reform Council
NEER	nominal effective exchange rate
NPC	National People's Congress
ODI	overseas direct investment
OTC	over-the-counter market
PBoC	People's Bank of China. It is the central bank of China
PHP	Philippine peso
PTM	pricing-to-market
QFII	Qualified Foreign Institutional Investor
Redback	Nickname for the RMB in the financial markets
REER	real effective exchange rate
RMB	Renminbi, the Chinese currency. It is also called the yuan locally
RQFII	RMB Qualified Foreign Institutional Investor
RUB	Russian ruble
SAFE	State Administration of Foreign Exchange
SGD	Singapore dollar
SME	small and medium-sized enterprise
SOE	state-owned enterprise
CHF	Swiss franc
THB	Thai baht
ToT	terms of trade
TWD	Taiwan dollar
USD	US dollar
WMP	wealth management products
Yuan	local name for the RMB

1
Renminbi Shakes Up Global Currencies

For more than a decade, when the foreign exchange market has talked about the three major global currencies, or the "G3," it has been referring to the US dollar (USD), the Euro (euro) and the Japanese yen (JPY). These three currencies account for over 70% of all foreign exchange (FX) transactions in recent years. However, there are seismic structural shifts unfolding behind the G3 and the emerging markets, giving rise to some distinctive trends that are conducive to the rise of the Chinese renminbi (RMB),[1] or the "redback," as market players sometimes call it, to challenge the global dominance of the G3 currencies.

The unfolding structural trends behind the G3 currencies are 1) the weakening of the USD's global influence, 2) the uncertainty of the euro and 3) the structural decline of the JPY on the global stage. Meanwhile, even with a closed capital account, the economic, financial and political influences of China and the RMB on global markets have increased substantially. The world should seriously think about adding the RMB to the global currency trio, and redefine the group as the "G4" – USD, euro, JPY and RMB. RMB internationalisation seems to be an inevitable development in the global markets.

These structural changes are part of a larger evolution in the global macro landscape that is shifting the weight towards emerging markets (EM) and away from developed markets (DM). While the world is watching the rise of the RMB, the financial market has developed the expectation that Beijing might be freeing the currency soon to meet its currency internationalisation objective, breaking its long-held obsession with exchange rate control. Such an expectation turned euphoric in late 2011 when the RMB was allowed to appreciate against the USD by almost 1% in just a week. The sudden appreciation happened again in October 2012, just a few weeks before the US presidential election, when the redback was allowed to rise by over 2% against the USD within two weeks.

Despite the RMB's sudden moves, such expectations are wrong, in my view, because Beijing's FX policy is closely tied to its export policy. China's export policy is indeed a social policy for maintaining systemic stability. A sluggish RMB policy with limited trading flexibility is instrumental for achieving that goal. As long as such a fundamental backdrop to the RMB policy is not changed, Beijing is unlikely to make any significant shift in its FX policy, despite its intention to internationalise the yuan. So contrary to the market's euphoria about freeing RMB trading soon to help speed up the RMB internationalisation process, we should expect a change in the RMB regime to proceed slowly.

Structural change drivers

What moves the currency markets and shifts the relative importance of the currencies boils down to the long-term valuation of the currencies and shifts in countries' balance of payments (BoP). Let us review these forces and see how they change the underlying structures of the G3 currencies and create a constructive environment for the rise of the RMB.

Valuation

One of the crucial rules governing FX markets is that if a currency is not overly manipulated by policymakers, it should revert back to some mean, or fair value, over time. Some economists see this fair value in terms of Purchasing Power Parity (PPP),[2] which was popularised by the *Economist* magazine's Big Mac Index (The Economist 2012). Such longer-term FX mean reversion has solid economic logic behind it.

When a currency appreciates to a certain point for a sustained period of time, its host country's exports will lose competitiveness. *Ceteris paribus*, sustained currency appreciation becomes a drag on growth. Meanwhile, the stronger currency helps curb the country's inflation. The change in the outlook towards slower growth and lower inflation tends to create investor expectations of monetary loosening by the central bank, thus reducing the expected yield on the currency. The change in expectations and actual growth-inflation dynamics often leads investors to cut exposure to assets denominated in that currency. This, in turn, cuts demand for the currency and generates FX depreciation that eventually move the currency back to its fair value. The story goes in the opposite direction for a currency that has experienced sustained depreciation.

While some argue that these cycles often average five to seven years, empirical evidence also shows that the mean-reversion process could occur more quickly than that, especially when over- or undershooting of the currency against its fair value becomes extreme. However, a currency's fair value is not fixed over time. Structural changes in underlying economies, which affect macro variables such as terms of trade (ToT), inflation and interest rates, can increase or decrease a currency's fair value. Macroeconomic development in recent years suggests that such a shift may be happening today for some currencies, with a bias towards higher fair values for certain commodity currencies and emerging market (EM) currencies, and a lower fair value for the USD.

Balance of payments

While valuation helps one to understand whether a currency is under- or overvalued in a longer-term context and, hence, its influence on the global markets, balance of payments flows (BoP, or cross-border trade and capital flows) help determine the demand for the underlying currency in the shorter- and medium term. Until the late 1990s, when portfolio flows became a significant FX driving force, cross-border trade flows were the key driver of currency movement and the relative weight of the currency (in terms for its importance) in the global markets. A country like the United States with a chronic current account deficit would sell USD to buy foreign currency for purchasing imports. *Ceteris paribus*, such flows weighed on the dollar, especially relative to currencies where the respective country ran a current account surplus.

However, recent years have seen a shift in BoP flows. While trade still matters, global capital flows have become the dominant factor driving the currency markets. A reduction in regulatory hurdles and greater availability of information (including media coverage of global markets and economies, and the Internet) have made many investors more willing to look overseas for asset and risk diversification. This, in turn, complicates the currency demand and supply dynamics. Hence, one needs to know what drives cross-border capital flows in order to gauge the rise and fall of a currency both in terms of its value and its weight of global importance.

With these issues in perspective, let us look at the structural changes underlying the G3 currencies to see how they give rise to an international backdrop that is conducive to the rise of the redback in challenging the global dominance of the G3 currencies, especially the greenback (USD).

USD dominance weakening

The USD is in a league of its own in the FX markets. Its dominance in the global system will remain for many years to come, but the degree of this dominance will weaken gradually. The US economy is by far the largest in the world, accounting for almost 30% of global GDP in 2009. The USD, meanwhile, continues to be the most traded currency in the world FX markets, accounting for 45% of all currency transactions in 2010. This "critical mass" in the global market is part of what creates the dollar's "reserve currency" status. Given the significant amount of global trade and financial transactions done with the United States, central banks around the world try to hold a correspondingly large amount of US securities (typically Treasury bonds) in their reserves as a need for external settlement and a protection against BoP shocks.

This reserve currency status and the size and composition of the US economy and capital markets have made the dollar unique. Consider trade flows within the BoP. The United States is a country of consumers, with private consumption accounting for some 70% of GDP. When US growth is robust, Americans spend more and buy more from overseas. This is manifested in the chronic US current account deficit, which has lasted 31 out of the past 39 years. But this is also a natural way to internationalise the USD, as a current account deficit means more dollars are sent overseas to pay for imports than are received from US exports. These offshore dollars, in turn, have created deep and diversified offshore FX and dollar asset markets. All else equal, the chronic current account deficit should be a drag on the dollar's value.

That said, as noted earlier, currency trends reflect capital as well as trade flows. Here the dollar story gets more complicated. Historically, the US investor base has exhibited a strong home bias – i.e. American investors have tended to be heavily focused on investing in US assets. This bias has faded somewhat in the last two decades, thanks to market globalisation. Today when the US economy is doing well, Americans put relatively more money to work overseas. This exacerbates the dollar drag from the widening trade deficit, leaving the dollar weaker during growth periods and stronger during economic slowdown.

In an economic slowdown, the trade deficit shrinks and capital is repatriated back to the United States, providing a support for the dollar exchange rate. Data going back to the early 1970s show that annual percentage changes in US real GDP and changes in the trade-weighted dollar exchange rate have a negative correlation of 0.24. In other words, for almost 25% of the time, good US growth has been bad news for the dollar exchange rate, and vice versa.

In addition to its chronic current account deficit, America's huge debt burden (US household debt is over 100% of disposable income, while its public debt is approaching 100% of GDP at the time of writing) should also be instrumental for keeping the USD weak for a prolonged period. This is because low interest rates are needed to prevent a debt blowout that would derail the economy from its sustainable path. Low interest rates certainly weigh on the dollar, as they encourage investors to look outside dollar-denominated assets for higher returns. If unresolved, the huge US debt problem will also erode international confidence in US sustainable growth and hurt demand for US assets, including the USD.

Meanwhile, structural changes are taking place in many emerging economies, including China, that are attracting an increasingly diverse array of investors. Rising income and demand growth in many emerging markets are creating greater and sustained demand for natural resources. These changes are contributing to a positive ToT shock in commodity-exporting countries. A country's ToT are a ratio of its export prices to import prices. Improving ToT suggest that exports prices were rising faster than import costs so that they contributed to a positive growth force.

For commodity currencies, both trade and capital flows are supportive of boosting their long-term fair values. Many investors are trying to gain more EM exposure, demanding EM currencies by selling USD. Even many central banks are trying to increase their EM currency exposure and reduce the share of USD assets in their FX reserves, albeit at a very slow pace. International Monetary Fund (IMF) data show that the average share of central banks' FX reserves denominated in so-called "other currencies" had risen to 5.1% by 2011 from 1.8% in 2007, while the share of USD in these FX reserves had gone down to just over 60% from almost 90%.

The main beneficiaries from these structural changes will be EM currencies and commodity currencies. This new-world order for key emerging markets could risk pushing the fair value of the USD lower, and reinforcing the need for strategically diversifying away from the US currency. The impact of these EM currencies on the USD's fair value could be significant, as commodity and EM currencies now account for over 51% of the weights in the USD trade-weighted basket (Figure 1.1). This is not to say that the dollar would be on a one-way depreciation trend. There will still be periods of dollar strength due to its safe-haven status, as witnessed during the Lehman crisis in 2008 and the on-going

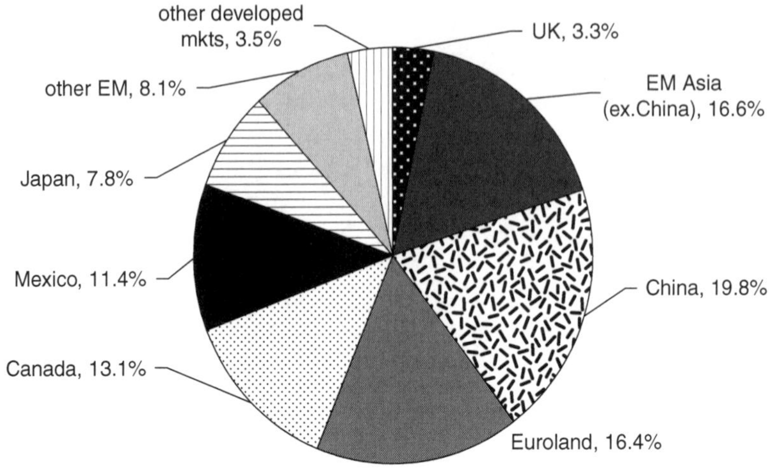

Figure 1.1 USD trade-weighted components (end-2011)
Source: US Federal Reserve.

Euro-debt crisis that started in 2010. Rather, the point is that diversifying out of the USD is becoming a secular trend that will erode its global dominance over time.

Euro uncertainty persisting

Since its inception in 1999, the euro has faced numerous stumbling blocks, including rules without adequate enforcement mechanisms. Specifically, the 1997 Stability and Growth Pact, created in preparation for an integrated Europe with one currency, said that European Monetary Union (EMU)[3] members needed to keep budget deficits within 3% of GDP and the debt-to-GDP ratio within 60%. Countries that broke these rules were supposed to be warned and then sanctioned. But for many years, peripheral countries in the spotlight since late 2010, when the Euro-debt crisis broke out, have run budget deficits and debt-to-GDP ratios many times higher than the Pact allows. Even the EMU's core country, Germany, has run fiscal deficits more than 3% of GDP for 5 out of the 12 years since 1999 without the EMU authorities taking action.

Thus, the euro has never gained much international confidence in its sustainability. Milton Friedman, the Nobel Laureate, once said before the launching of the euro that the new euro would not last for more than a decade. Well, it is now more than a decade and the euro still stands, albeit with increasing cracks that have generated even more dire predictions for its demise. The on-going Euro-debt crisis only aggravates the fears of a euro break-up (Van Overtveldt 2011).

Solving Europe's crisis will probably require even greater integration than currently exists and a stronger ability to oversee member states and enforce economic stability rules. But getting from here to there will be very difficult, as many European states fear that giving up more sovereignty to supranational bodies will erode their centuries-old local cultures. It is extremely unlikely that the EMU authorities could strike deals behind closed doors to force more integration because the political process takes place in a real-time world with transparency, wide media coverage and swift dissemination of information through high-speed communication systems.

Given the options of a failed Europe or of greater integration, Europe may ultimately opt for the latter. If that is the case, it would be crucial for the survival of the euro. Some market analysts are arguing that some five years down the road, the world might be looking at some form of a United States of Europe, with a unified bond market that could challenge the US Treasury market in terms of liquidity, and a euro that could share reserve currency status with the USD. As of March 2012, the total market capitalisation of the US Treasury bond and bills markets was US$10.32 trillion, a size that was already matched by the aggregated EMU (or Euroland, as some market players call it) government bond markets.

However, Euroland may see its composition change over time. One cannot discount the possibility that one or more current Euro members will drop out of the Union and return to their pre-euro regimes in the coming years should the toll of fiscal austerity prove too high. Meanwhile, there may be new members entering the EMU and with the aim of reaping economic scale benefits and seeking a bigger voice in global political and market matters via this currency union.

Assuming the euro survives, Euroland's BoP dynamics suggest that at least on a trade-weighted basis the euro was close to its long-term fair value. Euroland's current account, in aggregate, is basically balanced, despite some large deficits in some peripheral EMU member states. In terms of capital flows, they are likely to be volatile but, nevertheless, supportive of the demand for the euro after the dust of the financial crisis is settled in the longer term. In the short term (two to three years), it is unlikely that Euro-area growth will be strong enough to generate inflation that would require monetary tightening. Thus yield differentials are not going to boost the euro exchange rate. But longer-term demand for the euro may rise if the tail risks of a euro break-up continue to fall as politicians iron out solutions, albeit slowly and grudgingly, to the crisis.

Last but not least, reserve diversification may be a long-term factor that boosts the demand for the euro and hence its relative importance in the global markets. When central banks and sovereign wealth funds diversify out the USD as part of risk management, liquidity needs will constrain them to very large markets. After the United States, Euroland has some of the world's largest and deepest capital markets, providing an investment alternative for these sovereign and other large institutional investors.

Nevertheless, there is too much uncertainty surrounding the euro, and given the poor compliance records of the EMU member states, the structural flaws of the euro cannot be resolved easily. This will continue to drag on the euro's credibility, constrain the world's demand for it and prevent it from rising to a significant reserve currency in the medium term.

JPY structurally declining

For over two decades, Japanese GDP growth has averaged less than half of that of the developed countries, and Japanese policy interest rates have averaged around 0.63% a year. Yet over this same period, the USD has lost some 39% against the JPY. How could such weak growth and unattractive yields result in such a prolonged strength of the yen, both against the USD and on a trade-weighted basis? The yen has indeed strengthened despite multiple attempts by the Bank of Japan (either alone or in a concerted effort with the G7[4] counterparts) to intervene to curb its appreciation pressure.

Despite weak growth and low yields, what has made the yen strong appears to be Japan's chronic current account surplus, which has averaged almost 3% of GDP since 1990. It is only surpassed by that of Switzerland within the G10 countries,[5] and is in sharp contrast to other G10 countries which have run multiple-year current account deficits. A supplementary factor has been the secular decline in US Treasury yields since the 1980s (Figure 1.2). As US yields fell towards Japanese yield levels, the benefit of carry trade – by borrowing yen to fund USD-based investment – was reduced. This, in turn, weighed on the USD's exchange rate versus the yen.

Recently, there is also the influence of the Japanese investors. Similar to the United States, Japan has seen a relative reduction of home bias

Figure 1.2 US 10-year Treasury yield on secular decline
Source: CEIC.

investment in recent years. Indeed, before the 2008–9 subprime crisis, Japanese investors were increasingly allocating money through carry trades to invest in foreign-denominated bonds and investment trusts. The repatriation of those funds during and after the crisis gave the JPY an additional lift. Indeed, the yen was one of the few currencies that gained against the USD following the 2008 subprime crisis (the USD strengthened against most other currencies during the crisis as Americans repatriated funds back home and global investors took shelter in US government securities; hence, increasing the demand for USD, as global risk aversion soared).

However, the tide for the yen may be changing, albeit only slowly. On the yield differential perspective, US interest rates will eventually rise again when the post-subprime adjustment is completed although this may take many years (Lo 2009) due to the complexity of the problems and the deep structural faults within the American financial system. As for Japan, with a shrinking and aging population and limited resources, there are no compelling reasons to expect sharp growth revival to trigger inflation and a significant rise in Japanese interest rates after two lost decades.

The Japanese current account balance is turning, due to the persistent strength of the yen, a shrinking workforce and rising competition in the global marketplace. Indeed, the country recorded a trade deficit in 2011 for the first time since 1980. Together with a shrinking income surplus, the current account balance is expected to turn negative soon. Meanwhile, the continued fading of the Japanese investment home bias will mean

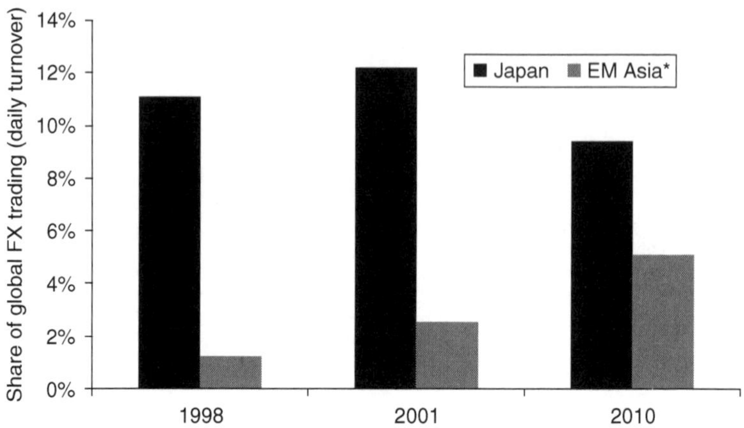

Figure 1.3 Japan's FX trading losing out to EM
Source: BIS (as of 2010).

more capital outflow in the longer term. All of these factors will reduce the structural underpinning for the JPY in the coming years, as the supply of yen will likely overwhelm demand in the global FX markets.

The relative importance of the yen in the global markets has also been fading, a trend that is likely to continue. Global currency turnover data by the Bank for International Settlements (BIS) showed that the JPY accounted for over 12% of global FX trading volume in 2001, versus about 2.5% of total volume represented by the currencies of Korea, India, China, Singapore, Malaysia, Taiwan, Hong Kong and Thailand combined. But in 2010, Japan's share had fallen to less than 10%, while that of the emerging Asia group had nearly doubled (Figure 1.3).

The fall in Japan's global influence is even more evident in the international trade area (IMF 2012). IMF data show that by 2010, China had overtaken Japan (and also Germany) in terms of its importance as a global trade partner. The rise of Chinese international trade influence is attributable to several factors. First, trade liberalisation certainly plays a central role in changing the global trade structure. Trade barriers have come down in recent years, and transport and communication costs have also been cut sharply thanks to technological advancement.

All these forces have facilitated the breaking up of production stages beyond national borders and allowed supply chains to become regional or even global. At the same time, these factors have eroded Japan's

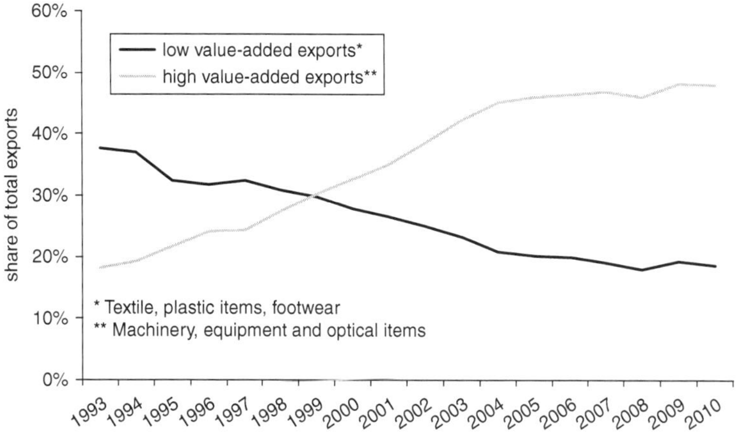

Figure 1.4 China climbing the value-added chain
Source: CEIC.

market share in global trade. China, with its tremendous manufacturing capability and advantages, has reaped huge benefits from trade liberalisation and globalisation, and has thus increased its global economic influence.

The change in the foreign trade structure itself has also aided China in moving up the global ladder at the expense of Japan. There has been an increase in the technology content of exports worldwide. China has become a major manufacturer and assembler for many of these tech products. Indeed, China's high-tech product exports have increased notably since the mid-1990s, boosted by processing trade and helped by significant contributions from Japan and other Asian countries. Overall, China has been climbing the value-added chain since the mid-1990s (Figure 1.4).

There has also been a notable shift in the roles of China and Japan as strategic export destinations for Asia, with China surpassing Japan as a more significant regional and global consumer in the 2000s. During that decade, China took in more exports from Asia than Japan (Figure 1.5), as it had more than doubled the number of its key trading partners in the region. But Japan saw the number of its Asian trading partners decline. It is amazing that a currency, the RMB, which is not even convertible on its capital account, could have such a strong influence on global trade patterns, and effectively displace the influence of Japan in the global markets.

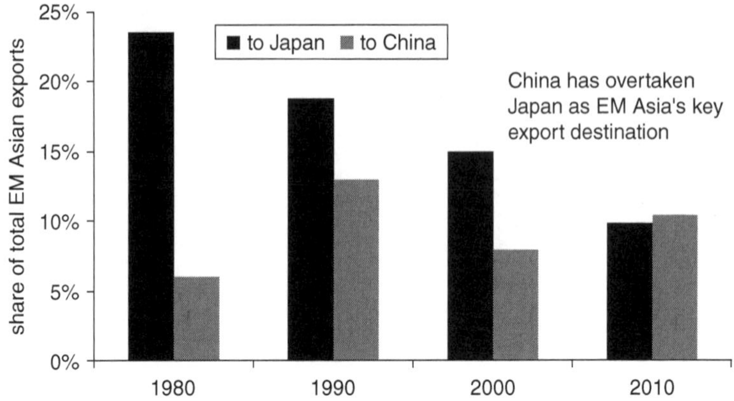

Figure 1.5 EM Asian exports to Japan and China
Source: CEIC.

In this process of climbing the global trade ladder, China does appear to have put the cart (trade settlement) before the horse (currency convertibility) successfully so far; it is a remarkable achievement for China to "eat into" Japan's export markets so quickly and decisively with a currency (the RMB) that is still non-convertible. The resultant global trade influence also increases the weight of China in the global economy and makes it necessary for the world to think about including its currency in the major currency league. Welcome to the RMB. The G3 should be redefined to be the G4, with the RMB included in it. Under these circumstances, RMB internationalisation is a natural development commensurate with China's rising global importance.

An RMB regime shift...

As the perceived influence of the RMB rises, the financial markets have begun to expect Beijing to free its currency from tight control so as to be in line with the internationalisation objective. Beijing started a soft push for RMB internationalisation in 2004, with its efforts intensifying in the late 2000s. In particular, when Beijing allowed the RMB to rise by almost 1% against the USD within a week in August 2011, it generated market euphoria that China was ready to free the RMB in order to give its internationalisation a big push.

The redback's abrupt appreciation against the greenback happened again in October 2012, just a few weeks before the US presidential election, when Beijing allowed the RMB to rise by more than 2% against the dollar within two weeks. This revived market expectations on Beijing freeing the trading for the RMB soon.

However, it is wrong to assume that Beijing's FX policy is tied to its currency internationalisation objective. Beijing has an overriding objective of economic growth maintaining systemic stability, and the RMB policy plays a central role in achieving this. This means that China's FX policy will not change easily (see below). Expectations for Beijing relinquishing control of RMB trading soon are unrealistic, and so far they have been proven wrong. Despite two abrupt jumps of the RMB exchange rate against the USD, Beijing is still maintaining tight control on the yuan's trading and is proceeding with its internationalisation at a slow pace.

Control has always been Beijing's anchor policy for the RMB. Before 1994, China had a "dual exchange rate" system with an official exchange rate that co-existed with an unofficial market rate. Between 1989 and 1994, Beijing repeatedly devalued the official rate of the RMB, which traded significantly stronger than the unofficial market rate, to increase export competitiveness.

In 1994, China unified the two exchange rates by devaluing the official rate from 5.8 per USD to the unofficial market rate of 8.7. The move ended the dual exchange rate system and replaced it with an RMB-USD peg regime. On the surface, the dollar peg was later broken in July 2005 when Beijing announced a 2.1% appreciation of the RMB against the dollar and a move to a "managed float" regime with reference to a basket of currencies.

But effectively, the RMB has still been anchored to the USD with very limited trading flexibility. This can be seen in the official trading band that Beijing has imposed on RMB trading. The daily RMB-USD trading band has been widened gradually from ±0.1% of the central rate set by the People's Bank of China (PBoC) to ±1% in early 2012. But the trading band between RMB and other major currencies is ±3.0%. Practically, the daily trading band is more tightly controlled because the daily RMB movement has rarely come close to the boundaries of the ±1% band.

Thus, when the RMB rose against the USD by 0.8% in one week in August 2011, which was the biggest weekly appreciation pace in many years, it caught the market by surprise and spurred speculation that Beijing might be about to free the RMB and allow sharp FX appreciation. The move came just after the eruption of the European and US debt crises, when the European Central Bank (ECB) rejected buying Spanish and Portuguese bonds and the Standard and Poors (S&P) downgraded the US long-term sovereign credit rating from AAA to AA+.

...Not so easy

Overall, the market's expectation of an RMB policy shift is based on the assumption that China's FX policy is anchored to the USD. But it is not. Domestic concerns weigh heavily on China's FX policy. Every year, tens of millions of poor rural Chinese pour into large cities looking for better-paying jobs. If they fail to find jobs, the country risks social instability. Maintaining fast growth to create enough jobs to preserve social stability is Beijing's top policy priority. A sharp rise in the RMB exchange rate will hurt exports, the biggest job-creation engine. So Beijing has always pursued a stable exchange rate regime, allowing only gradual RMB appreciation against the dollar.

But despite the gradual RMB-USD appreciation, the RMB's trade-weighted exchange rate, as approximated by the nominal effective exchange rate (NEER), has been falling since 2009 (Figure 1.6). This has kept Chinese exports competitive, despite the rise in the RMB against the USD. In Beijing's FX policy framework, it strives to keep a relatively stable NEER, using the RMB-USD exchange rate as an adjustment factor. Within this framework, the pace of RMB appreciation can quicken at times but also stall at other times, depending on the economic situation. The sharp RMB appreciation against the USD in August 2011 only arrested somewhat the fall in its NEER (Figure 1.6) since 2009.

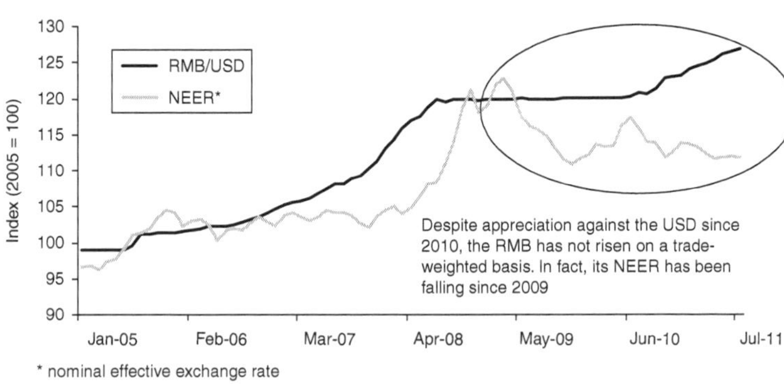

Figure 1.6 RMB's nominal exchange rate indices

Source: CEIC.

As long as the strong need for job creation remains, it is difficult for China to shift its production orientation to consumption orientation within a short period of time. Through production, the Chinese government can create more jobs. But excess production, because of insufficient domestic consumption, means that China will have to rely on exports to keep the job-creation machine going.

Massive social disorder is the single most important risk for China. There is evidence that the number of social unrest cases have been on the rise, though this may also reflect the fact the Chinese government has become more open about media reporting. The Beijing leadership would rather create more jobs through boosting exports, even by subsiding manufacturers via direct and indirect means, than risk job shortages and social unrest by freeing the RMB, allowing it to appreciate significantly.

To this extent, China's production/export policy is actually a social policy, which is designed to maintain social order. And keeping the RMB broadly stable is instrumental for achieving this goal. The essence of this social policy for economic development has been reflected in Beijing's repeated claim that the economy needs at least 8% growth a year[6] to create enough jobs for absorbing the huge labour force.

Due to this need for constant job creation, China is unlikely to move as quickly as many would like to see in rebalancing domestic consumption and exports. The domestic economic and policy backdrops behind Beijing's stable FX policy have not changed much, despite the changing global dynamics. Because economic rebalancing will take a long time to implement, this means that the RMB policy cannot be changed within a short period of time either. The Chinese authorities will continue to pursue a stable RMB policy with tight control on its trading in the medium term, and will only tolerate gradual RMB appreciation against the USD with a broad reference to a stable or weak-biased NEER.

Degree of internationalisation

The level of the exchange rate is crucial in affecting the development of the RMB's internationalisation through its impact on capital account liberalisation in China. We shall discuss this in detail in subsequent chapters. At this stage, the question is what does it mean to internationalise the RMB, and how is it done? Simply, RMB internationalisation means ownership of the currency outside of China. The degree of internationalisation thus refers to the extent of non-resident holdings of RMB and RMB-denominated assets (such as RMB deposits, stocks, bonds and other kinds of assets denominated in RMB). There are many channels through which foreign holdings of RMB or RMB-denominated assets can be increased.

First and foremost, foreigners can get hold of RMB by accepting RMB payments from Chinese importers. RMB outflow through the trade account is a form of internationalisation. It will reduce China's trade surplus and eventually lead to a trade deficit. Another way for RMB to flow out of China is through overseas direct investment (ODI) or purchase of offshore securities by the Chinese using RMB as the settlement currency. Non-residents can also acquire RMB by borrowing in RMB or buying RMB-denominated bonds, or they can convert other currencies into RMB under financial account transactions (which is very limited in scope at the time of writing).

Hong Kong is the prime offshore RMB centre in which most of the RMB's financial account transactions take place. When a non-resident changes FX for RMB, the PBoC will have to buy the FX and supply RMB at the given exchange rate in order to keep the RMB stable under its stable exchange rate policy. At the same time the FX are bought, the PBoC will have to create matching RMB deposits. This is how most Hong Kong residents obtain RMB deposits through changing Hong Kong dollar (HKD) into RMB up to RMB20,000 a day under Chinese regulations. These RMB deposits end up going back to the PBoC (Shenzhen branch across the Hong Kong borders). This clearly increases non-residents' (Hong Kong) ownership of the RMB, and hence increases its degree of internationalisation. Once they are circulating offshore, more RMB deposits can be created through the multiplier effect of RMB lending in the offshore market, propelling the process of internationalisation.

However, Beijing still retains the ultimate control on the amount of offshore RMB circulation by only allowing one bank, the Bank of China, as the clearing bank for RMB trading. This means that offshore RMB can trade in different centres, including Hong Kong, London, Singapore, Tokyo and New York, but all trades must be settled ultimately through the designated clearing bank in that centre (and it is the Bank of China in Hong Kong). As long as this restriction is not relaxed, the degree of RMB internationalisation is limited to the amount of RMB that the designated clearing bank can clear under the instructions of the PBoC.

2
A Not-so-Mighty Yuan

In the last chapter, we argued that structural changes in the global economy were eroding the dominance of the world's leading (G3) currencies, notably the US dollar (USD), the Euro (euro) and the Japanese yen (JPY), shifting the balance of influence towards the emerging market (EM) currencies. These secular trends will unfold over the coming decades. A dark horse from the EM universe that will challenge the dominance of the G3 currencies is the Chinese yuan, or renminbi (RMB). Indeed, China has been internationalising the RMB since 2009. This begs the question of the credibility of the RMB to live up to its potential global currency status.

If a currency lacks credibility, its global acceptance will be very limited. This will, in turn, frustrate its internationalisation effort. The RMB, or redback, is seen by the international community as artificially suppressed by Beijing to achieve undervaluation in the face of a large current account surplus. Some cynics have even argued that the right way to think about China's exchange rate is not to think about the exchange rate at all (Krugman 2010). Instead, they suggest, one should focus on Beijing's currency intervention to see the economic and financial ramifications.

This perception is potentially damaging for Beijing's RMB internationalisation initiatives, as it could act as an obstacle to creating interest in and demand for RMB outside of China by damaging the yuan's credibility and image. Meanwhile, the Chinese authorities' control of the RMB exchange rate (by preventing it from appreciating to the extent that market forces would warrant it) has created persistent hype and speculation in the market that the RMB exchange rate would only rise, but not fall.

China has fought back recently by arguing that, with the falling current account surplus, the yuan has moved towards equilibrium. However,

China's trade fundamentals reveal that the yuan is still far from equilibrium, despite some correction in its undervaluation. There are many more issues hidden behind an ostensible decline in China's current account surplus than meet the eye. The perception of RMB approaching equilibrium is more an illusion than a fundamental improvement as long as the trade distortions remain. Meanwhile, analysis of the micro foundation of China's capital flow shows that it would face a serious risk of capital flight if the capital account were fully open at once.

What all these factors imply is that periodic depreciation pressure on the RMB is not unimaginable. The one-way bet on RMB appreciation is gone for good. The yuan has entered a normal two-way trading paradigm, albeit still within the central bank's tightly-controlled trading band of 1% above and below the official daily set-rate. In other words, the yuan's foreign exchange (FX) trading will become more volatile. But two-way trading of the yuan is necessary for China to move towards the goal of a flexible RMB regime. Higher volatility will lead to higher RMB risk relative to its past. This will, in turn, lead to demand for a higher risk premium in the offshore deliverable RMB (or CNH) market. All this will be instrumental for RMB internationalisation and the CNH market development.

The potential risk of capital flight means that capital account convertibility, which is an essential step for full RMB internationalisation, will not move quickly. Optimists who expect fast capital account and RMB convertibility will likely be disappointed. Finally, Beijing needs to salvage the yuan's credibility to facilitate internationalisation. Pursuing a rule-based exchange regime, such as pegging the redback to a basket of currencies, to minimise government intervention may be a way to go. But what is in the yuan basket?

The rise of the redback

While China opened its current account in 1996, its capital account remains largely closed. That is, Chinese (and foreign) capital for purposes other than trade cannot move in and out of the country freely. However, Beijing has been taking small steps in recent years to liberalise its capital account. The following are the notable moves so far:

- A non-deliverable forward (NDF) market for RMB was set up in the mid-1990s. Major trading takes place in Hong Kong and Singapore, with an average trading volume of about US$4–5 billion a day (as of 2011).

- Starting in 2009, a designated number of Chinese firms could use RMB for foreign trade settlement. But this restriction was scrapped in early 2012 when all Chinese exporters and importers were allowed to settle foreign trade in RMB.
- In July 2010, China introduced a spot RMB FX market, called CNH, for delivery outside of mainland China. Hong Kong has been designated by Beijing as the CNH market for trading RMB offshore, though there is also limited trading in London and Singapore. The advent of the CNH market has also opened the door for related financial instruments, such as CNH deposits and bonds; the latter is also known as "dim sum" bonds.
- In late 2011, China allowed the usage of offshore RMB to be invested back in China as foreign direct investment (FDI). It also approved the so-called RQFII scheme, which is a quota system for RMB in Hong Kong to be invested back in the mainland stock and bond markets. The initial RMB20 billion quota was expanded by RMB50 billion in July 2012, and then by another RMB200 billion in November 2012. Also in July 2012, Beijing expanded the quota of the QFII scheme, which allows foreign investors to invest in Chinese onshore stocks and bonds by converting foreign exchange into RMB, by US$50 billion. These moves allow more RMB and foreign exchange to flow into China in a controlled manner.
- In March 2012, Beijing gave approval to Wenzhou city[1] to accelerate its financial reforms by allowing local residents to invest abroad without government approval if the amount is less than US$3 million. It also allowed private investors to invest in local financial institutions.
- In mid-2012, Beijing broadened the daily RMB/USD trading band to 1% above and below the daily benchmark rate (or the "daily fixing" in FX market jargon) set by the central bank (People's Bank of China, PBoC). This marked a step, albeit a very small step, towards liberalising RMB FX trading. The trading band was last widened in 2007 from ±0.3% to ±0.5% of the PBoC's daily fixing. Since the band widening, CNY (onshore RMB) trading volatility has increased, ending the one-way bet on RMB appreciation.

With these market changes, and against the global trade liberalisation backdrop, it is not surprising that the growth of RMB-denominated investments has been remarkable. This can be seen in the dramatic growth of the dim sum bond market in Hong Kong, which launched nearly RMB108 billion of initial public offerings (IPOs) by 91 issuers in 2011. This was up from about RMB10 billion in 2007 (Figure 2.1).

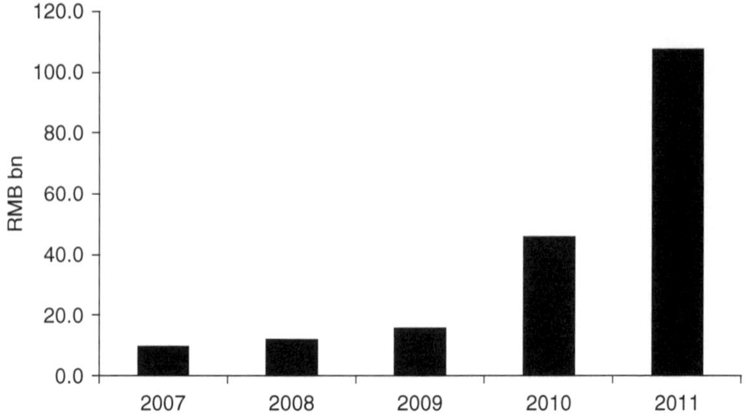

Figure 2.1 Gross issuance of "dim sum" bonds in Hong Kong
Source: CEIC, Reuters, HSBC.

Meanwhile, the outstanding amount of RMB certificates of deposit (CDs) issued by banks in Hong Kong soared from RMB5.7 billion at the start of 2011 to RMB72 billion by the end of the year.

Given these trends and the increasing usage of the RMB for international trade settlement, could the RMB grow into a reserve currency alongside the USD, or even displace it as the super currency of the world? History shows precedent for multiple reserve currencies during the 1920s and 1930s, for example, with the USD and the Pound sterling (GBP) sharing the global reserve currency role. The demand for RMB will certainly grow over time, assuming China's role in the global economy continues to grow. We shall explore these issues in the subsequent chapters. Let us first address the issues of the equilibrium value of the RMB and the potential risk of capital flight in the context of RMB internationalisation.

What RMB equilibrium?

In theory, an exchange rate reaches equilibrium when its underlying demand and supply forces are balanced so that there are no depreciating or appreciating pressures. China's falling current account surplus is a visible sign for correcting the RMB's undervaluation and, hence, a trend towards equilibrium. The same narrowing trend is also seen in the surplus of China's basic balance, a broader measure of the external accounts by adding long-term capital inflows (approximated by foreign direct investment in China) to the current account balance (Figure 2.2).

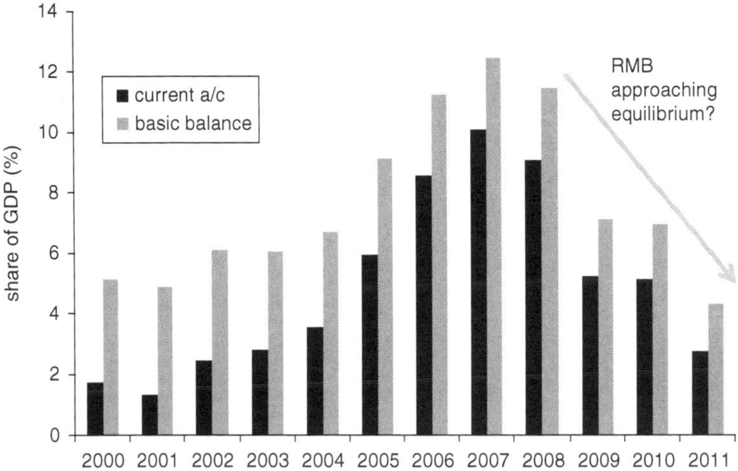

Figure 2.2 China's external surplus falling
Source: CEIC.

Figure 2.3 RMB real effective exchange rate
Source: CEIC.

Some analysts have also argued that the RMB's real effective exchange rate (REER) has been rising since 1994 (Figure 2.3), when Beijing reformed the dual-exchange rate system by devaluing the RMB by over 33% against the USD. So the distortion to the yuan exchange rate due to the massive devaluation should have been corrected, and

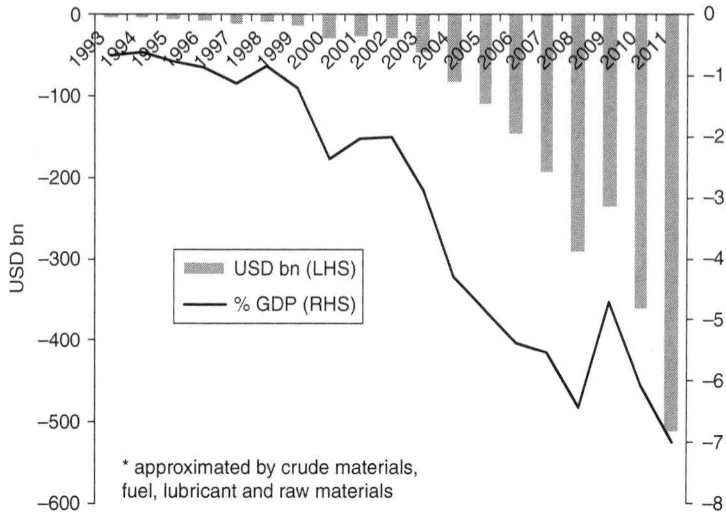

Figure 2.4 China's raw material* trade balance
Source: CEIC.

it should be approaching equilibrium in the light of falling external surpluses.

This latter argument does not make sense, in my view, because 1994 is hardly the right reference point for exchange rate equilibrium when China's economy was in chaos with rampant inflation of over 20% a year and a large trade deficit of over 3% of GDP. Fundamentally, China's "basic surplus" is still large, at over 4% of GDP. Unless narrowed further, this size of the basic surplus is hardly consistent with a stable RMB equilibrium.

Crucially, the narrowing of China's current account surplus has not been a result of a change in the trade structure that corrects China's external imbalance. The fall in China's current account surplus is an illusive indicator for the RMB approaching equilibrium. Rapid industrialisation has turned China from a net exporter of primary products and raw materials into a chronic net importer. Its raw material trade deficit has grown from less than 1% of GDP in the early 1990s to 7% (Figure 2.4). Excluding this deficit, China's current account surplus is still large at 9.7% of GDP (Figure 2.5).

The point is that China's shrinking current account (and also trade) surplus in recent years has more to do with the rise in commodity prices, which has created a negative terms-of-trade shock on its external accounts, than with a genuine change in the trade structure that

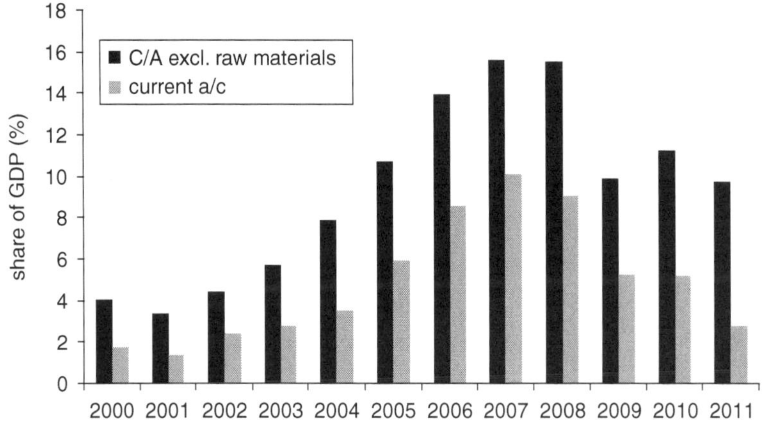

Figure 2.5 Current account adjusted for raw materials
Source: CEIC.

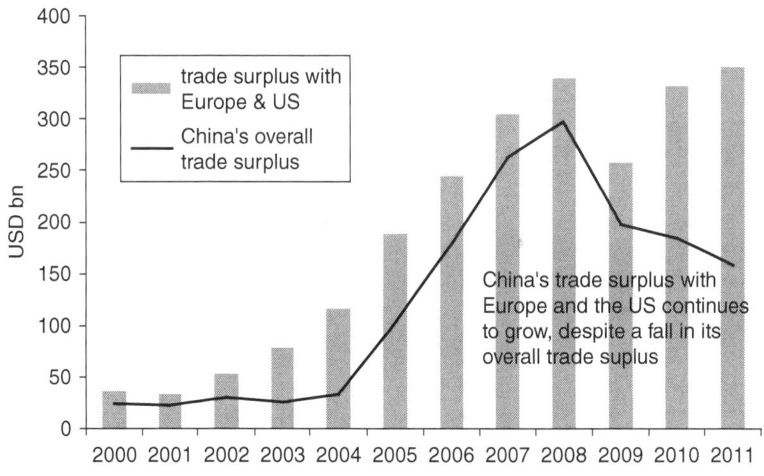

Figure 2.6 China's overall trade surplus vs. surplus with Europe and the United States
Source: CEIC.

rebalances Chinese demand towards more imports (domestic consumption). This can be seen in the fact that China's trade surplus with its two largest trading partners, Europe and the United States, has continued to rise despite a fall in its overall trade surplus since 2008 (Figure 2.6). In other words, the RMB's steady appreciation over the years has not caused a fundamental shift in China's trade competitiveness to favour imports over exports. So the sharp decline in the current account (and trade) surplus since 2007 is not really indicative of the yuan approaching equilibrium.

A regime shift underway

Under such circumstances, the RMB will continue to experience mild appreciation pressure for a while longer than many have predicted. Sustained depreciation of the yuan is unlikely yet, but its trading will become more volatile due to fluctuations in capital flows and the narrowing of the current account surplus. China is going through a FX regime shift, as Beijing moves to allow more RMB fluctuations in the coming years.[2]

Already, Beijing is relaxing the RMB's trading restrictions, albeit in mini steps. In July 2012, it broadened the daily RMB/USD trading band to 1% above and below the daily People's Bank of China (PBoC) fixing from the old ±0.5% band. This is a necessary step for China to move towards a floating exchange rate regime and internationalise its currency.

Since early 2012, after more than two years of experimenting, Beijing has finally allowed all Chinese importers and exporters to use the RMB for international trade settlement. This will help increase RMB two-way trading as Beijing becomes more comfortable with greater FX fluctuations when international RMB transaction is more prevalent. Meanwhile, the development of the spot CNH FX market has augmented the NDF (non-deliverable forward) market for RMB in providing market signals for the Chinese system. This development is a big step forward in helping to improve the market signalling problems of the onshore RMB (or CNY) market due to its manipulation by the authorities. A two-way market driven by market forces is instrumental for pushing China's capital account convertibility and RMB internationalisation, which ultimately affect Chinese asset prices.

More yuan trading flexibility will lead to greater speculative risk and arbitrage opportunities in the offshore market. Since offshore RMB trading is market driven, CNH volatility is much higher than the CNY rate. Until recently, foreign investors have been accepting the low-yield RMB because of its low volatility and the expectation of persistent currency appreciation. But this incentive has gone away with fading expectations of yuan appreciation and the expected rise in RMB volatility. The lack of hedging tools for the RMB has aggravated the decline in the demand for RMB-denominated financial products in the CNH market from time to time, notably between mid-2011 and 2012. Going forward, CNH investors will likely demand a higher risk premium on RMB products to compensate for higher volatility/risk and the loss of currency appreciation benefit.

Yuan issuers offshore have also been enjoying the twin benefits of low cost and high demand for RMB products, until recently that is. With fading expectations on RMB appreciation and rising volatility, they will likely face higher cost going forward. In other words, both demand and supply forces suggest a higher risk premium structure (relative to its short historical performance) in the CNH market until China develops better hedging tools for the RMB.

The tide of RMB turning

With all this improvement in the CNY market and progress in developing the CNH market, it is not surprising that many market players, including banks, brokers and investors, and the general public have developed an expectation of speedy capital account convertibility, arguing that this would push for full internationalisation of the RMB soon. The hype about CNH market growth and high-speed RMB internationalisation is quite significant.

For example, one of the global banks in Hong Kong predicted at the beginning of 2011 that CNH deposits in the city would top RMB1 trillion by year end (HSBC 2011). But they only ended up at RMB586 billion by the end of 2011! Another bank predicted that the RMB would be the second most traded currency in the world in just five years, by 2017 (ANZ 2012). Time will tell. But given the amount of uncertainty and political and structural obstacles surrounding the internationalisation process, and the lack of rigorous research for backing up the forecast, this will likely prove to be just another hype rather than a rational forecast.

In particular, the potential risk of capital flight will remain a key obstacle to full capital account convertibility in a short period of time. Indeed, China saw net capital outflow in October 2011 for the first time in four years (this was on an official basis; illegal capital outflow has been known for years). The offshore RMB exchange rate in the CNH market, which is market driven, has also reflected waning demand for RMB since then. All this goes against the rhetoric of excess demand for RMB due to its rising popularity.

A hypothetical analysis shows that there might even be massive RMB outflow if the capital account were fully opened today (see next section)!

This may reflect the risk of local Chinese losing confidence in their home currency. If this is the case, capital flight will be a big obstacle to the RMB gaining international confidence that would enable it to become a global currency. Indeed, there are structural reasons for rising capital flight incentive.

China's FX reserves fell by US$3.91 billion in October 2011. That was the first monthly drop in foreign reserves since 2007, and reflected net capital outflow. FX reserves fell again periodically in early 2012, reflecting periodic net capital outflow. In fact, capital inflows to China outside of the trade channel have been slowing since late 2011 due to fears about a Chinese economic hard landing and global investors abandoning Chinese and EM assets and repatriating funds to meet the liquidity squeeze back home during the European financial crisis.

The market started to doubt a sustained rise in the yuan exchange rate since China's current account dropped from the peak of over 10% of GDP in 2007 to 3% in 2011. This has weakened the argument for an undervalued RMB exchange rate and, hence, eroded the expectation for sustained RMB appreciation. The concern about the bursting of China's property bubble pulling the rug out from under its financial system and rising awareness of Chinese credit risk have only hurt RMB sentiment further.

The fact that China runs a persistent, though smaller, current account surplus suggests that the culprit for the net capital outflow might be hot money. Indeed, hot money outflow from China between August and October 2011 was the largest for the past 10 years, by my estimate (Figure 2.7). Meanwhile, RMB sentiment in the offshore CNH market in Hong Kong has also turned sour due to investors' risk aversion amid the European debt crisis and the financial scandals of Chinese-listed companies in North America since late 2010. Reduced demand for RMB has weakened the offshore (CNH) RMB/USD exchange rate below the onshore (CNY) rate since September 2011. This is the first time such a persistent CNH discount to CNY has arisen (Figure 2.8).

However, hot money flows are volatile, and the recent outflow from China was not the first time (see Figure 2.7). Short-term capital will certainly return as market sentiment and the economic cycle turn. Likewise, the CNH discount to CNY will disappear as and when the poor RMB sentiment in the CNH market changes. The point is that a temporary fall in the yuan exchange rate is becoming more common than before. But given the still strong underlying macro fundamentals, a sustained RMB depreciation is unlikely at this stage.

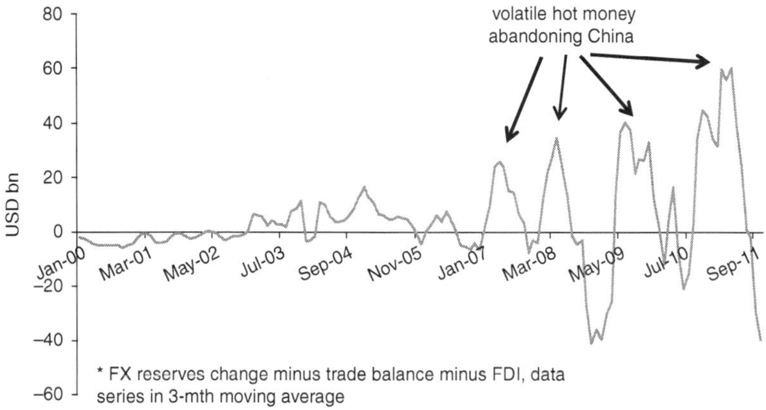

Figure 2.7 Estimated hot money flows*

Source: CEIC.

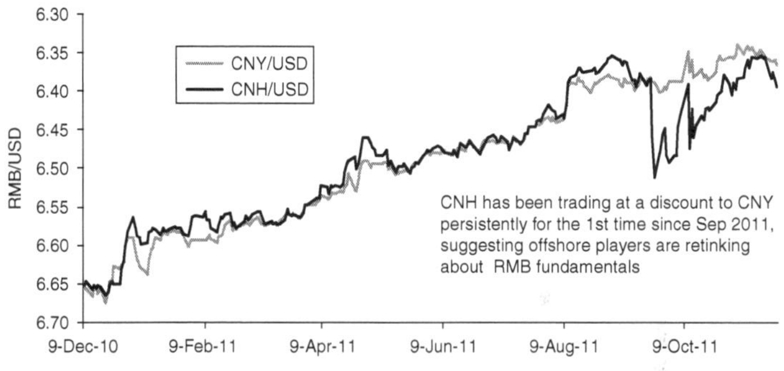

Figure 2.8 Offshore vs. onshore RMB exchange rate

Source: Citi.

Potential risk of capital flight

It is a different story when one looks at the micro backdrop for the RMB. It is crucial to note that both capital outflow from China and the CNH discount to CNY are market-driven phenomena, suggesting that players are questioning the structural fundamentals behind the RMB. So let us play devil's advocate and ask: What would happen to capital flow if China's capital account were to become fully convertible today? The worsening of China's over-invoicing problem may be indicative of an ever-increasing incentive for capital to leave the country if the floodgates were opened.

In over-invoicing, a Chinese firm will inflate the import bill by charging the import price of some commodity much higher than the actual cost. By reporting an inflated import bill to the Chinese customs, this allows the passing of capital overseas, with the foreign (exporting) entity crediting the amount of the excess payment into its Chinese counterpart's bank account outside of China.

One, though imperfect, estimate for over-invoicing is the difference between China's import values and the export values of its corresponding trading partners. In principle, after allowing for the small foreign exchange rate differences used in the different official reporting systems, they should be the same. But the data show that China's inflated imports bills had been getting larger over the years (Figure 2.9), suggesting a rising incentive of capital outflow.

This seems to run contrary to the perception of rising hot money flowing into China, until recently. Note the two sets of data do not necessarily contradict each other, because they correspond to two different incentives (or two disjoint sets, technically): one is local capital wanting to get out of China (the over-invoicing problem), and the other is foreign capital wanting to come into China (the hot money inflow issue). The players in these two sets are different and have different views on China's investment climate. Further, the over-invoicing problem has

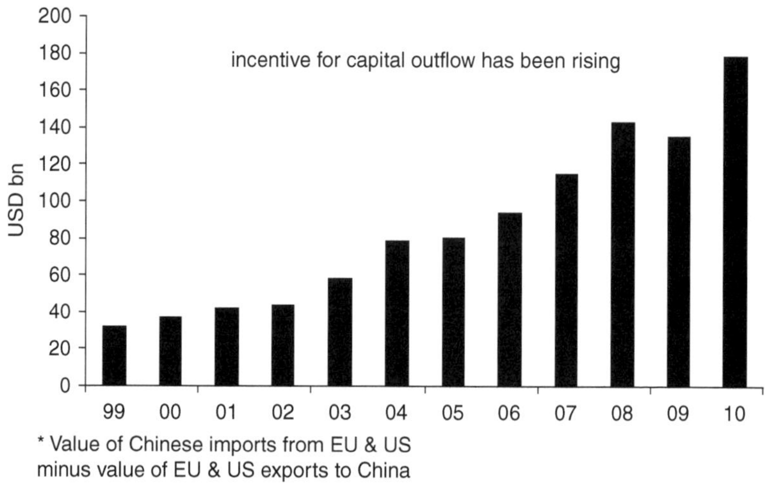

Figure 2.9 Estimated over-invoicing of Chinese imports*
Source: CEIC.

a persistent rising trend, but the hot money inflow is volatile from year to year without a steady trend (see Figure 2.7 again).

So China's closed capital account is barring capital flight from taking place. In other words, such a potential risk of massive capital outflow argues against full capital account convertibility and, hence, fast RMB internationalisation, anytime soon. In the medium term, China will likely keep its asymmetric stringent capital control, which is to allow capital to come into the country much more easily than it goes out. This practice is meant to minimise the possibility of massive capital flight that could destabilise China's financial system.

Behind the capital flight

If economic growth is supposed to enhance people's living standard and make them happier, why is there such a large incentive for capital flight? This speaks volumes about the unhappiness of the mainland Chinese eroding the micro fundamentals behind the RMB. Criticism of the government by the public has been exploding, despite fierce censorship. Local academic and media polls in 2011 showed that an average of 40% of the Chinese were unhappy about their lives; 70% of the farmers were very unhappy because of land seizure; and 60% of the wealthy were emigrating or wanting to do so.

Until recent years, most Chinese had faith in their national leaders and accepted the post-1989 (i.e. post-Tiananmen incident) social contract in which the Party provided rising living standards in return for the people not questioning the monopoly of power. So the party was able to survive over 180,000 protests in 2010, many of which were of large scale. But this may be changing.

First, income and wealth inequality has become more severe as the country has grown richer. This has raised the awareness among the bottom strata of the society that it is policy made at higher levels, not just corruption and the incompetence of local officials, which bars them from sharing the benefits of growth. Second, the wealthy and the intellectuals are taking more interest in politics and the reform process to protect/fight for their interests, or even to take part in the rent-seeking activity that has emerged as a by-product of economic reform.

The first trend is developing to create a critical mass of social grievances. The second trend is developing into a catalyst for change. The Party's hold on power since 1989 has hinged on its ability to co-opt the educated minority by offering them material benefits and by arguing that democracy would lead to chaos, with the uneducated masses destroying their privileges. That strategy worked well until recently. Disillusion with this deal has driven an increase in political activism. The educated group is realising that upward mobility is capped and that any advancement one manages to gain after hard work can be taken away by the elite group for no reason, because the elites can do and get what they want at will. The misbehaviour of the Party elites is also responsible for their troubles. For example, people were made intensely angry by the government's concealment of air pollution levels, while the leaders in Zhongnanhai[3] installed air purifiers to protect their own health.

With this unfair distribution of power and wealth, education backfires on the government. Since the universities expanded enrolments in the early 2000s, many families have borrowed heavily to pay for their children's tuition. But graduates without political connections have been stranded at the bottom strata of society, living in slums. Meanwhile, the media is full of stories about children of the Party and business elites street racing their Ferraris without fear of arrest. The lack of accountability of government officials, as seen in the continuous flow of financial scandals, food poisoning (notably baby milk powder) incidents, serious man-made accidents etc. only increases social discontent.

Meanwhile, macroeconomic policy still discriminates against the private sector and households. The persistent low deposit interest rates and large interest margins for the banks have deprived households of consumption power and fattened the banks. To fight inflation, the central bank has tightened credit. But state companies have continued to get bank loans, while private firms have been starved of credit and gone belly up. The property sector has suffered from significant distortion, creating a significant division between the "haves" (referring to those who own property) and the "have-nots." This, in turn, has brewed more social grievances.

No wonder domestic capital wants to leave the country. This capital flight incentive may likely reflect the views of many Chinese that fair opportunities to invest at home are scarce and that they are losing confidence in the system. Some may also worry about potential political upheaval, and so are trying to diversify their basket of eggs.

All this is not to say that China will blow up soon. The macroeconomic backdrop is still strong and will help contain such a risk. The point to note is that the rising incentive of domestic capital outflow has structural underpinnings. So it is not unimaginable that depreciation pressure on the RMB could arise from time to time. The potential for capital flight explains why we should not expect full capital account convertibility in China too soon. From a market perspective, the underlying forces are arguing that RMB has entered a normal two-way trading paradigm. Hot money outflow is the first test for its downside risk. Two-way trading is in fact what Beijing is aiming for in its foreign exchange reform and RMB internationalisation initiative.

This brings us to the need for developing tools for hedging RMB foreign exchange risk, which are almost non-existent now. One of the key reasons for limiting RMB demand outside of trade transaction needs, which is then limiting the internationalisation process, is a lack of hedging tools. So using the CNH market (currently only in Hong Kong) to develop a derivative market for such a purpose will go a long way towards helping RMB internationalisation. Finally, capital outflow will increase the circulation of RMB offshore, which will directly broaden the internationalisation process. This should give Hong Kong a golden opportunity to create more RMB investment and hedging products and deepen the CNH market to facilitate RMB internationalisation.

Salvaging the yuan credibility

On the back of these hidden problems, Beijing would need to repair the credibility and public image of the RMB in order to facilitate its internationalisation effort. Otherwise, there will not be a critical mass of foreign demand for and trust in the yuan. Using a rule-based exchange regime by tying the yuan to a basket of currency, for example, to minimise government intervention in the exchange rate may be a way to go. But what is in the benchmark currency basket? Beijing has not made any concrete commitments to move towards such a rule-based FX regime, despite rounds of empty promises in the past.

China has been claiming that it would link the yuan to a basket of currencies since 1994, but nothing concrete has been done. It pledged to do so again in July 2005 when it scrapped the decade-long peg to the USD, but only started to benchmark the yuan's movement against a currency basket in April 2008. But this basket experiment was dropped after 5 months when the collapse of US investment bank Lehman Brothers set off the subprime crisis in September that year, sending shock waves through the global system. Fast forward four years, to June 2012, when China again reiterated its intention to move to a currency basket regime. Given its intention for RMB internationalisation and more financial reforms, it may be more willing to commit to a currency basket this time around than before. Only time will tell if this is not "crying wolf" again.

Then what is this basket? Beijing has not disclosed many details, nor has it said anything about using nominal effective exchange rate or real effective exchange rate for monitoring purposes. NEER is a measure of one currency's value relative to currencies of that country's major trading partners. It summarises and aggregates information contained in a basket of bilateral exchange rates. A rise in NEER means that the home currency is dearer than its trading counterparts', and so the home country's exports are less competitive in the global markets. Contrarily, a drop in the NEER means the home currency is relatively cheaper, and the home country's exports are more competitive.

The REER is effectively NEER adjusted for inflation. In theory, REER is a preferred measure of competitiveness, as it estimates the real value of a currency. In practice, it is a rather cumbersome tool because inflation is a lagging indicator, and it is often driven by non-tradable goods, especially in the case of China. So simply using headline consumer price index (CPI) inflation for making the adjustment on NEER could give a misleading picture of the country's competitiveness

In the case of the RMB, NEER could do a better job in gauging China's competitiveness for the sake of exchange rate policy because China's CPI inflation has been mostly driven by food and commodity prices.

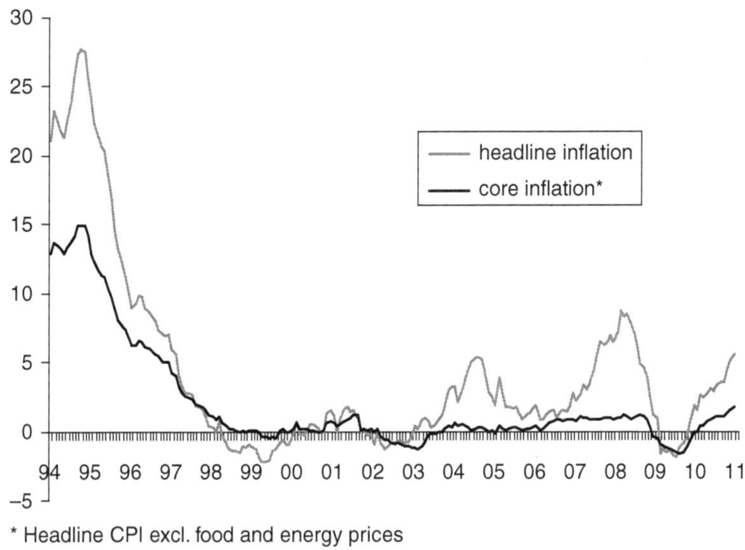

Figure 2.10 Absence of Chinese core inflation
Source: CEIC.

Core (CPI excluding food and energy prices) inflation in China has been absent for more than 10 years (Figure 2.10). Food inflation is largely affected by random factors, notably weather. For commodity price inflation, it affects both China and its trading partners so that the relative impact on competitiveness may be small. So the potential currency basket should preferably be based on NEER.

A model different from the BIS

The Bank for International Settlements (BIS) has long been working with China on constructing a currency basket for the yuan. However, the BIS uses one rule for all countries, with the basket purely based on trade data, and it includes 43 currencies. Such a one-size-fits-all basket may be convenient and useful for research purposes and cross-country comparison, but it is rather impractical for the monetary authorities to monitor such a broad basket on a daily basis.

Further, China's sticky preference for a *de facto* USD-peg policy, which effectively means 100% weight for the USD, will render the BIS theoretical basket not realistic. So given China's policy objectives, its genuine basket could be quite different from the BIS model.

A realistic way to construct RMB-NEER is to pick a basket of currencies, and assign them weights that reflect the Chinese authorities' policy and economic preferences by making the best use of all the information available. What do we know about China's policy objective function in this regard?

PBoC governor Zhou Xiaochuan argued publicly that "shares of trade in goods and services should be the fundamental consideration in selecting basket currencies and assigning weights" and that the currency structure of foreign debt and foreign direct investment should also be considered (Zhou 2005). He also mentioned that there were eleven currencies in the basket, with the USD, euro, JPY and Korean won (KRW) making up the majority; the other seven currencies were the Singapore dollar (SGD), Pound sterling (GBP), Malaysian ringgit (MYR), Russian rouble (RUB), Australian dollar (AUD), Thai baht (THB) and Canadian dollar (CAD). Governor Zhou also mentioned, without elaboration, that the weight of the USD in the basket was lower than 50% (Zhou 2006).

However, Governor Zhou's USD weight is inconsistent with China's *de facto* USD-peg policy most of the time, which amounts to an effective weight of 100% for the USD. The PBoC's public comments on the yuan basket also did not include the Hong Kong dollar (HKD) and the Taiwan dollar (TWD). The reason, presumably, is that Hong Kong merely serves as China's entrepot, and the HKD is linked to the USD.

The case for the TWD is similar, as the majority of merchandised trade between China and Taiwan eventually ends up in the developed markets, and the TWD-USD exchange rate has been very stable since 2002, and most China-Taiwan trade is USD-denominated. So the weights of the HKD and the TWD could all be lumped into the weight of the USD. But given the substantial amount of cross-border trade between China, Hong Kong and Taiwan, the less-than-50-percent weight of the USD stated by PBoC Governor Zhou sounds inconsistent.

Further, China's trade pattern has changed since 2005, as four other economies have become significant trading partners, namely India, Brazil, Indonesia and the Philippines. These economies together account for almost 10% of China's total trade in recent years, compared to about 3% in 2000. So these four currencies should be added to the yuan basket in addition to Governor Zhou's stated eleven currencies.

Using bilateral trade data from China's largest 15 trading partners and incorporating China's policy objectives, we can construct a yuan basket close to Beijing's FX policy objective function. This basket has component weights quite different from the BIS generalised model (Table 2.1),

Table 2.1 Estimated Yuan basket*

	BIS weights	**author's estimates**
USD	21.0	40.3
EUR	18.4	16.0
JPY	16.8	12.3
KRW	8.2	8.3
SGD	3.0	2.9
RUB	1.3	2.7
AUD	1.2	2.5
GBP	3.1	2.5
MYR	2.0	2.4
INR	1.3	2.2
CAD	2.7	1.8
BRL	0.9	1.7
IDR	0.8	1.6
THB	1.8	1.4
PHP	0.8	1.4
TWD	6.6	

*BIS full basket has 43 currencies. Calculations here are based on 2010 data

Source: author, BIS.

and, arguably, is more relevant to China. And it should be updated regularly to take into account China's changing trade pattern.

From the RMB internationalisation perspective, what matters the most is to build RMB credibility on a rule-based system to minimise FX intervention. The purpose is to get buy-ins and gain international confidence in holding the RMB for transaction and reserve purposes.

3
From Money to RMB-nisation

Internationalisation of the renminbi (RMB) did not receive much attention from the financial markets until the late 2000s when China started to promote its currency for international usage ardently.[1] Structural changes in the global economy have emerged to facilitate the rise of the RMB (as discussed in Chapter 1). Despite research on the RMB subject, the motivation for Beijing to push RMB internationalisation (or RMB-nisation, as we shall also call it in this book) has not been well analysed. The financial markets seem to have taken RMB-nisation as given. Academics have mostly put RMB internationalisation in the straitjacket of existing theories and research. But proper understanding of the drivers behind China's decision to internationalise the yuan is key to gauge the success (or failure) of the steps taken and foresee and assess the next steps down the road.

Fundamentally, currency internationalisation is an extension of the functions of money from the domestic economy to the global system through international payments. RMB-nisation certainly fits in with this academic research framework. RMB internationalisation can also be analysed using the demand for money framework, as we shall discuss in Chapter 5. But there are China-specific factors, both from trade and from international finance perspectives, which have prompted Beijing to push its currency up the global league. How about preparing China in the distant future as a net debtor? This may sound crazy today as a motivation for internationalising the yuan. But a globalised RMB, like the US dollar (USD), may well be a catalyst that China needs to jump-start its rebalancing effort, moving its economy from a saving-surplus country (a net creditor) to a major consumption country (a net debtor).

Since China started its RMB-nisation process ardently in the late 2000s, it has generated a lot of hype about a fast internationalisation process providing an exaggerated amount of new growth and business opportunities. These are all unrealistic. A detailed look at Beijing's political agenda suggests that it might not intend to have yuan internationalisation as the top policy priority. It is likely that Beijing is still searching for the roadmap for RMB internationalisation. Rather, it may want to achieve some other objectives by using RMB-nisation as a pushing force. There is also a myth, in my view, that growing foreign trade with the rest of the world would be sufficient for China to deepen and broaden the internationalisation process for the RMB. Dispelling this myth should help sharpen Beijing's internationalisation focus.

Money and currency internationalisation

Money has three functions: As a medium of exchange, a unit of account and as a store of value (for a comprehensive account, see Mankiw 2007). The first two functions of money are always linked to each other, and it is easy to generalise them to the global context through international trade. In this sense, currency internationalisation is just an extension of the functions of money to the global markets. Grassman's law has long established that for trade between developed markets, exporters were inclined to take the domestic currency as the invoicing currency for settling international trade (Grassman 1973). Later research (Page 1977, McKinnon 1979, Carse and Wood 1981, Mundell 1983) has extended the law further in three areas:

1) In bilateral trade between a developed and developing country, the currency of the developed country plays a dominant role as an invoicing currency.
2) In bilateral trade between two developed countries, the choice of the settlement currency depends on the relative size of the economies; the currency of the larger economy is used as the settlement currency.
3) In the trade of raw materials, the USD is always used as the medium of exchange. This is because the homogeneity and large quantity of products transacted warrant an efficient medium for information dissemination. The USD has served this purpose well due to its underlying policy transparency, credibility and deep financial markets.

Once a currency has become an international medium of exchange, it will entrench in the global system and acquire inertia (Swoboda 1969, Tavlas 1991). Empirical research has found that the USD has enjoyed a tremendous amount of inertia that cannot be easily undone (Ogawa and Sasaki 1998). Inertia also means stability of the value of the currency. A stable currency value is what gives it the function of a store of value. From an internationalisation perspective, sound development of a country's financial sector and the freedom of its financial markets are conducive to creating foreign demand for its currency and, hence, conferring on its currency an international store-of-value function (Kenen 1988).

Hence, currency internationalisation is indeed an extension of the functions of money from the domestic economy to the global markets. But there is no rule of thumb for which function(s) should be the dominating factor in determining the sequence of the internationalisation process. Experience from the United States and the United Kingdom show that the medium of exchange and unit of account functions were key to internationalising the USD and the Pound sterling (GBP). But the case for the Japanese yen (JPY) shows that these were only necessary but not sufficient conditions for internationalisation. The JPY has never been an international invoicing currency, but it has been internationalised based mainly on the store-of- value function. This yen experience helps debunk the myth that foreign trade expansion would be sufficient for prompting deeper and broader currency (RMB in our case) internationalisation. We shall discuss this issue later. Let us first look at the motives for China to internationalise the RMB.

Motives for RMB-nisation

Currency internationalisation is a market-driven response to regulatory constraints and evolvement of the international monetary system that make the status of the existing international currencies unstable (see Chapter 1). There is no historical precedent for the Chinese government taking the lead in internationalising its currency (McCauley 2011). Its recent move to do so has been prompted by both international trade and financial management initiatives. Reducing currency risk is the most obvious trade-related motive to internationalise the yuan. Using the USD for trade exposes the Chinese producers, financial institutions and official sector to currency risk.

Chinese exporters typically incur production costs in RMB, but receive payments in USD. Importers buying from overseas pay for their goods in USD, but sell them in the domestic market for RMB. This payable-receivable currency mismatch is a FX risk to both Chinese exporters and importers due to currency fluctuations. Such risk is costly and difficult to hedge under China's underdeveloped capital markets.

Hence, settling foreign trade in RMB would benefit Chinese companies by reducing their exchange-rate risk as well as eliminating the cost of FX transactions.

More RMB-denominated assets would also reduce Chinese financial institutions' exposure to FX risk. This would help reduce the volatility of their capital base,[2] and contribute to strengthening of their competitiveness by improving their funding opportunities through increased accessibility to a larger pool of RMB-denominated assets (Gao and Yu 2009).

China runs a balance of payments (BoP) surplus. It uses this surplus to finance countries with BoP deficits, notably the United States. The Chinese surplus has gone into building up the country's FX reserves which, in turn, have accumulated assets denominated in foreign currencies (mostly USD) through lending to these foreign deficit countries. If these debts to the deficit world were denominated in RMB, then China would eliminate a major source of risk stemming from FX fluctuations, notably depreciation of the foreign currency, on its national balance sheet.

On a global basis, making the RMB an international invoicing currency will help keep trade financing normal under adverse conditions. During crisis periods, there is typically a strong demand for the USD, which is seen as the safe haven currency. Since everyone hoards USD, this excess demand for it creates a liquidity squeeze, and trade financing dries up. The shortage of trade financing was prominently evident in the 2008–9 subprime crisis, and it had a detrimental effect on China's exports, which contracted sharply in 2009.

Chinese financial institutions, whose funding base is in RMB, only have a limited ability to provide USD trade financing. However, if foreign trade could be settled in RMB, the trade financing ability of the Chinese institutions would increase significantly. This would not only allow them to stabilise trade and production domestically, it would also help sustain global, or at least regional, trade financing.

Dollar shortages are usually most acute in the emerging market (EM) economies. If China traded with EM countries in RMB, it could continue to provide financing when dollar liquidity dries up during a crisis. This could, in turn, increase the demand for Chinese products as well as financial services from Chinese banks (Otero-Iglesias 2010), thus helping cushion the damage of the crisis to China.

Domestically, internationalising the RMB will require deepening of the Chinese financial reforms, improving the process of using Chinese financial markets as a platform for lending to and borrowing from the rest of the world and improving the sophistication of Chinese capital markets. All this fits well in China's structural reform programme for upgrading the Chinese economy and creating high value-added service jobs in the financial sector. In particular, such a programme is consistent with the objective of the Twelfth Five-Year Plan, announced by Beijing in March 2011, which is to raise the share of services in GDP, and the goal of the government to make Shanghai an international financial centre by year 2020.

In the long term, it is all about prestige and influence. The use of the RMB as a global currency will strengthen China's influence in the world, a condition that will be commensurate with the rising Chinese economic power in the global economy. An internationalised RMB will also contribute to the increase in China's clout in international institutions, such as the World Trade Organisation, the International Monetary Fund (IMF) and the World Bank, and allow it to play a bigger role in the global financial order.

These motivations have gained increasing credibility following the financial crises (first the US subprime crisis, then the European debt crisis which is still ongoing at the time of writing) set off by the collapse of the US investment bank Lehman Brothers in 2008. Moreover, the US fiscal crisis in 2011 (and it may well re-surface again, depending on how effectively US politicians can resolve the problems) and the ongoing uncertainty surrounding Europe have made Beijing realise that China cannot be too dependent on foreign currencies. Arguably, the subprime crisis has acted as a trigger for Beijing to internationalise the RMB, and the subsequent global development has prompted it to accelerate the RMB-nisation process.

A portfolio perspective

There are two, more intriguing, financial management initiatives behind Beijing's push for RMB internationalisation. The first is the need to diversify in an increasingly positive international investment position. China is the world's third-largest creditor nation after Japan and Germany, although much of its wealth is held in the form of FX reserves as opposed to foreign direct investment like the other two creditor nations.

Diversifying China's massive FX holdings (over US$3.2 trillion as of end-June 2012) away from the USD and the euro appears to be virtually impossible, given the very limited role that other currencies play in the international monetary system. So "RMB-nising" part of the FX reserves may be the easiest way to limit the exchange-rate risk for China as far as it holds part of its wealth in currencies which are bound to depreciate against the RMB in the long term.

Japan indeed followed this line of thought when it softly promoted the internationalisation of the yen in the 1970s. Perhaps the best example of this strategy is the offshore yen-denominated (samurai) bonds that foreign borrowers issued in major financial centres and that were bought by Japanese investors, among others. This way, Japan has increased the share of yen-denominated assets in its wealth pool and reduced its overall FX risk exposure in the country's balance sheet.

The other, far reaching, potential initiative to internationalise the RMB and make it a world's reserve currency, is that Beijing might want to prepare for the time when China becomes a net debtor in the global system, like the United States. This argument may sound remote and crazy at this stage, because Chinese BoP is still accumulating big surpluses. But its reality will come, as China is accumulating an increasing number of contingent liabilities. This trend should become more apparent as its population ages[3] and its productivity stalls with a shrinking workforce and the maturing of the urbanisation process in the coming years. Cheap financing cost is a key consideration in preparation for China's eventual need for net borrowing. The United States is a good illustration of this point. It is able to get cheap financing despite its shaky national finances because the USD is a world reserve currency and almost all US debts are denominated in USD.

These two initiatives could be compatible with each other. China's finances are currently sound, and its external positions robust. But this situation may change in the longer term, notably with its current account turning into a deficit. So it would make a lot of sense for China to start holding part of its foreign assets in RMB for portfolio management purposes in the short term, while preparing to become a debtor nation with RMB liabilities in the long term. To be a debtor in your own currency has tremendous advantages. Just look at the United States, which has become the world's too-big-to-fail nation. Since its foreign debts are denominated in USD, its foreign creditors have no choice but to keep funding the US deficits at very low cost and put blind faith in its sustainability despite its broken finances.

So is China following the US example and preparing to become a net debtor nation in the future? If one looks at the structure of the "dim sum" (offshore RMB) bond market in Hong Kong, the very important role that Chinese firms play in issuing RMB-denominated bonds hints at a tentative yes. Ever since the establishment of the CNH market in Hong

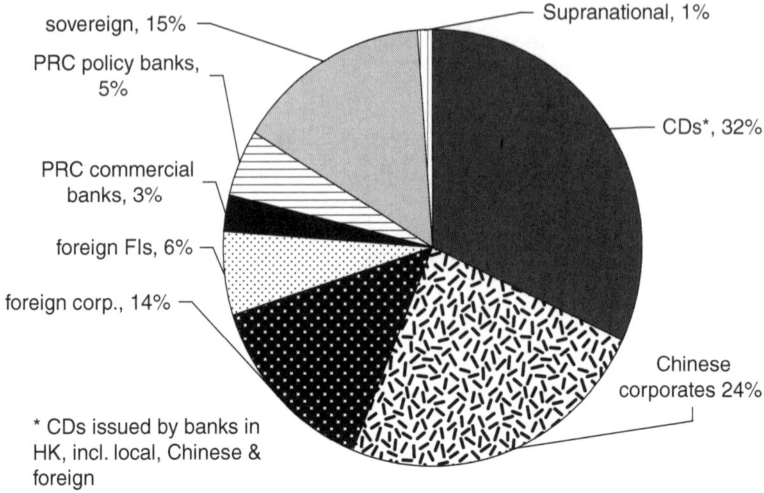

Figure 3.1 Breakdown of CNH bond issuers (2011)
Source: HSBC, Bloomberg, author.

Kong, Chinese borrowers have dominated the issuance of offshore RMB bonds (Figure 3.1). In 2010, about three-quarters of the CNH bonds were issued by Chinese entities. In 2011, about a third of CNH bonds were directly issued by Chinese firms, at least another 25% was estimated to be issued by Chinese banks through CDs. That is, Chinese firms still accounted for almost 60% of all fixed-income instruments issued in the CNH market in that year.

China's borrowing needs will continue to rise, as the country's industrialisation process still has some way to go. As the Chinese economic and financial systems continue to open up, domestic credit demand and funding cost structure will become increasingly sensitive to international market conditions. With most of the developed world stuck in a prolonged post-crisis economic adjustment,[4] which will dictate a long period of cheap funding cost, Chinese entities will likely take advantage of such an environment and diversify their funding sources to escape domestic financial repression by tapping the foreign capital markets. This will, in turn, pave the way for opening up China to become a borrowing nation in the medium term.

The initial agenda

While there are certainly motivations for RMB-nisation, it is unclear if RMB-nisation is Beijing's top policy priority, or if it is only a conduit for the government to push through some other objectives. Many optimistic bankers and financial market players have expected that Beijing would engage in RMB-nisation in full force. Their optimism is understandable because they have business pinned on this process to bring in growth and profits. From an analytical perspective, things may be different. In fact, Beijing may not even have decided on a roadmap for internationalising the RMB at this stage (see Chapter 6).

A series of market opening measures since 2009 which are conducive to RMB internationalisation has invited overly optimistic expectations on the process. In mid-2009, Beijing launched a pilot scheme, since expanded, to allow foreign trade to be settled in RMB. In July 2010, it took another step by allowing offshore banks to transfer RMB among themselves (i.e. establishing an inter-bank RMB market among these offshore banks), opening the way for the creation of RMB-denominated financial products, such as mutual funds. Then in August, in potentially the most crucial change, it allowed offshore banks and central banks to invest in China's inter-bank bond market.

These last two measures were, in fact, a natural development resulting from Beijing's push for the usage of RMB for foreign trade settlement. Arguably, they are unintended consequences of the success of RMB trade settlement, but not necessarily Beijing's intended policy in the beginning. This is because successful cross-border trade settlement in RMB implies a growing accumulation of RMB holdings by China's trading partners around the world. This will increase the demand for parking/investing these RMB funds in liquid and safe assets. As a result, pressure on accessing the RMB bond market has built along with wider adoption of settlement in RMB.

However, even if Beijing is willing to let more foreigners play in the domestic bond market (which is far from certain, as Beijing is still trying to protect the local bond market from foreign influences), there is the other side of the equation (i.e. the willingness of foreigners to take RMB) to consider. Beijing must create the incentives for foreigners to hold and use RMB offshore. That means that China must liberalise further its capital market, sanction more financial product (including derivatives) development and allow foreigners to participate in its onshore asset markets. This is easier said than done.

Also in August 2010, McDonald's, the American hamburger chain, became the first international non-financial company to issue debt denominated in RMB. This has also given the acronym RMB a new twist, in that it may now represent "Ronald McDonald bonds." The issue size of McDonald's RMB bond was tiny, at US$29 million. But it had led many financial market players to believe that Beijing had started an aggressive process for internationalising the RMB, paving the way for its ascent to be an official reserve currency to compete with the USD. That would be an enormous leap for a currency that is not fully convertible.

In my view, the RMB is nowhere near that stage yet. Even on the trade aspect, the RMB-nisation push is still restricted. Despite the hype about Beijing's aggressive push, the amount of RMB trade settlement allowed under the Chinese regulations is subject to a an annual quota of RMB8 billions. In fall 2011, due to excess demand for RMB (much of it was related to speculation of imminent RMB revaluation), the quota was exhausted at a time when market volatility was high. The resultant closure of the quota aggravated the FX volatility in the offshore RMB market and led some companies to reconsider the desirability of using RMB for trade settlement. This only increased scepticism of Beijing's true RMB-nisation intentions right at the beginning.

There may be some other shorter-term goals that Beijing aims at achieving, using RMB internationalisation as a conduit. There may be two other goals – to jump-start the domestic bond market in China by shaking up the local financial market and to rejuvenate Hong Kong's financial sector. While these moves should be seen as positive development in the Greater China area, in the grand scheme of things, they do not necessarily mean that Beijing wants to develop a significant offshore RMB market as quickly as many have assumed to push for aggressive RMB-nisation.

Risks of RMB-nisation

Any swift move on internationalising the RMB would mean a significant shift away from the US dollar as the world's reserve currency. This would have huge implications for financial markets beyond exchange rates. Foreign investors, including central banks, are estimated to have held 50% (or US$3.2 trillion) of the US Treasury bond market. China is the largest foreign sovereign holder, accounting for a quarter of all foreign holdings. The US Treasury market would crash if China and other sovereign holders started to desert it. That would force a sharp rise in US interest rates, strangling America's corporate bond and mortgage markets. All this would crush the US economy and asset market, sending negative shock waves around the world. It would hurt China too, both in terms of the negative impact on its economic growth and valuation of its US dollar assets held in its foreign reserves.

Internationalising the RMB requires the creation of a big offshore RMB market, just like the creation of the offshore-USD (or euro-dollar, as it is known) market in July 1963 in Europe, and subsequently in Asia, following the imposition of the 15% interest-equalisation tax by the United States to stem capital outflow. Contrary to the optimists' view, Beijing may not want to see an offshore RMB market develop too quickly because it may bring an unintended negative impact to the local system.

Offshore currency markets operate essentially like a shadow banking system, which lay at the heart of the US subprime crisis. Banks offering foreign-currency deposits and loans within an offshore currency area (say offshore banks offering RMB deposits and loans in Hong Kong) do not have to observe reserve requirement ratios that operate in the onshore currency area (China, in our case). This gives offshore banks greater latitude to expand their foreign currency (RMB in our context) offerings. But this also means greater risk in the event of a liquidity shock in the offshore market.

Banks participating in an offshore market are also free from the capital adequacy requirements imposed on them in the currency's home market. For example, banks in Hong Kong which offer RMB products outside of China are not subject to the same capital adequacy requirements imposed on banks in China. But these Hong Kong banks are engaging in RMB business, and they are not regulated by the Chinese authorities. Again, this can be a boon to the offshore banks, but it entails greater risk from the home-currency regulator's perspective.

Since the Chinese regulators generally do not impose liquidity requirements on bank assets held offshore (say in Hong Kong), even these assets are denominated in the regulator's home currency (i.e. RMB), these are great risks to the regulators. Such offshore currency markets will act like a shadow banking system, which typically experiences faster expansion during business cycle upswings and sharper contractions during economic recessions than a normal system will have. In case of an offshore crisis, this will transmit the offshore shockwaves back to the home system and amplify its boom-bust cyclical forces which the regulators seek to avoid.

Hence, there are potential unintended negative effects on the world and the Chinese economy that Beijing would not want to experience by pushing for fast growth of the offshore RMB market and aggressive RMB-nisation. Even in the medium term, it is unlikely that China and other central banks can, and will, replace the US dollar in their foreign reserves by other assets and currencies in a significant way.

Internationalisation a slow process

Fundamentally, for the RMB to be truly internationalised (i.e. to become a hard currency accepted anywhere in the world as a medium of exchange and a reserve currency), China has to be a large net importer of goods and a net-exporter of capital to allow its partner nations to accumulate RMB assets in significant size. China will also have to have a strong financial system to withstand significant capital flows, and creditable economic policies to gain international confidence. All this requires significant changes in the Chinese economic structure, which will take decades to achieve.

The ascent of the US dollar and British pound to reserve currency status was associated with at least 20% overseas ownership of their respective domestic bonds, which is representative of a vote of international confidence in their respective economic policies. Currently, international holding of Chinese bonds is negligible. It will take a long time before offshore entities can hold RMB bonds of a similar significant magnitude as the USD and GBP and before China can acquire complete international policy credibility.

How far China wants the RMB internationalisation to go remains uncertain. Beijing has never been clear about this, except a general goal of making China's capital account fully convertible and internationalising the yuan for some unspecified time frame. Japan's experience provides some insight into the uncertainty of this process. Japan backed out of its yen internationalisation effort after a head start in the 1970s for fear of the resultant negative impact on its domestic financial markets. The Japanese government has since taken a passive role in yen internationalisation.

The point is that a weak and underdeveloped domestic financial system is an obstacle to currency internationalisation. And where does China's financial system stand, and how fast is Beijing willing to modernise it? No one knows for sure. In a nutshell, despite all the hype, Beijing's RMB internationalisation effort so far is at an initial stage. Central to the point is that the RMB lacks the foremost prerequisite to become a global currency – free and full convertibility. The move towards this state, in turn, depends on the development of a sound, deep and proper functioning capital market in the country, which may take decades to accomplish.

Central to Beijing's concerns about creating an RMB offshore market as part of RMB-nisation is its quest for control of the economy, the financial system, the currency and interest rates. That is why China's capital account remains largely inconvertible, despite various financial liberalisation measures over the years. Freeing up the capital account would mean allowing non-trade-related fund flows in and out of China freely. This will expose the Chinese economy to sharp currency fluctuations and BoP shocks which Beijing has been trying hard to avoid. So what to make of the seemingly bold moves to internationalise the yuan by allowing foreigners to participate in the Chinese bond market and allowing offshore banks in Hong Kong to transfer RMB freely among them?

Two other goals

My guess is that the market reformers at the People's Bank of China (PBoC) have got the upper hand over their conservative counterparts in the reform debates and got the green light from the senior leadership to experiment with shaking up the domestic financial markets. The way these reformers want to do it is through a shock treatment by liberalising the domestic bond market a little bit under the guise of RMB internationalisation. The Chinese bond market is underdeveloped and as quiet as a morgue! On some days, there are no trades at all. Financial institutions, which are predominately the holders of bonds, tend to hold onto their bonds until maturity. This lack of secondary trading deprives the Chinese bond market of liquidity and a price discovery mechanism.

The reformers at the PBoC want market forces to play a bigger role in allocating capital and resources and setting of risk premium. By allowing some foreigners to play in the domestic bond market, the PBoC hopes to bring in market forces through the back door. However, how effective this move will be is uncertain. Experience is not encouraging, because despite Beijing's moves to list shares of the state companies and bring in foreign investors, the A-share market is still as distorted today as it was 20 years ago.

The other short-term goal Beijing wants to achieve, in my view, in the name of RMB-nisation is to give Hong Kong's financial sector a boost, by giving it an opportunity to expand RMB business and create value-added for the local economy. The measures to encourage greater usage of RMB for international trade settlement will provide a more flexible platform for Hong Kong's financial institutions to offer RMB-denominated investment products. Beijing wants to do

Hong Kong this favour out of self-interest, as it is using Hong Kong as a laboratory for financial reforms. If successful, what Hong Kong has achieved (in this case RMB convertibility) will be rolled out on a nationwide basis in the future.

Most banks in Hong Kong assume that the usage of RMB in Hong Kong's current account and foreign direct investment (FDI) flows would grow significantly in the coming years. So there will logically be an increase in the demand for RMB-denominated investment products to satisfy the desire for holding RMB. With the market participants knowing that there are more RMB-denominated financial products available, the desire to use RMB for trade transactions will rise. This will, presumably, create a virtuous cycle for boosting RMB circulation in Hong Kong, creating more investment products, increasing the incentive for holding and using RMB and so on. The economic value-added coming out of this cycle will be seen in job creation and financial innovation in Hong Kong's financial sector.

However, contrary to most bankers' expectations, Beijing's moves to internationalise the RMB by opening up the onshore bond market for foreign investment and allowing the usage of RMB as the investment currency for FDI going into China[5] do not necessarily boost RMB offshore lending capacity. A further move by Beijing in late 2011 to approve the so-called RQFII (or RMB Qualified Foreign Institutional Investor) scheme in Hong Kong is the most recent example for underscoring this argument. The QFII (Qualified Foreign Institutional investor) scheme is an investment quota scheme only opened to foreigners to invest in China's onshore stock and bond markets by exchanging foreign currencies into RMB. Originally, the RQFII scheme was opened to offshore Chinese corporates in Hong Kong to invest their RMB cash holding back in the onshore capital market.

From an investor's perspective, this scheme swaps his/her RMB cash with an RMB asset. So the net impact on his/her net worth depends on the changes in the RMB asset's value. But from a macro perspective, the RQFII *per se* is a mechanism for draining RMB liquidity back to China. *Ceteris paribus,* RMB liquidity among Hong Kong banks actually falls with the implementation of the RQFII so that their lending capacity is also reduced. The same argument goes for allowing foreign investors to invest in the onshore inter-bank bond market and use RMB as an FDI currency. In both cases, offshore RMB flows back to China via purchases in the bond market and FDI inflows.

From this perspective, it is an illusion that Beijing's RMB-nisation moves will also boost the offshore RMB lending business in Hong Kong.

All this goes back to my view earlier that Beijing does not want to see fast development of a large offshore RMB market in whatever form it may take, for fear of losing control of the currency. It is unlikely that Beijing would accept a situation like the US dollar, which is the world reserve currency, but has 50% of its stock circulating outside of the United States and the US Federal Reserve does not have firm control over it. From this perspective, expectations on rapid RMB internationalisation and development of a significant offshore RMB market are likely to be disappointed.

From money to RMB-nisation

In a nutshell, as China has developed a dominant position in the world manufacturing process, external demand for its products has also risen significantly. This, in turn, has induced external demand for the domestic currency, renminbi. With the accumulation and expansion of external demand, the RMB has naturally and logically become an important currency in the international markets. The theoretical projection for the RMB's future is that, *ceteris paribus*, it will become a global currency with reserve currency status. Conventional wisdom for the sequencing of this development will work in three stages.

First, the RMB will be used more frequently in international trade as a medium of exchange and unit of account. Second, as its importance becomes entrenched in the global system, it will then be taken as the anchor of exchange rate by the authorities abroad. Finally, growing transaction demand for money (RMB) by the international community will create precautionary and speculative demand for the RMB also, and the RMB will function as a store of value on a global scale. It is at this final stage when the yuan will become the world's reserve currency, alongside if not displacing the US dollar.

What all this says is that currency internationalisation starts with expansion of international trade. The USD and GBP behaved according to this sequence. Beijing certainly understands this, and has thus started the yuan internationalisation process by pushing the usage of the RMB as a trade settlement currency. But it is a myth that international trade expansion would be sufficient to deepen and broaden currency internationalisation and make the currency a world reserve currency. The internationalisation experience of the Japanese yen certainly defies this line of argument, and is food for thought for China about its RMB-nisation programme. We shall discuss these issues in the next chapter.

Last but not least, China in some sense has already jumped the gun and made the RMB a reserve currency without following conventional wisdom for the internationalisation sequencing. This is a stunning achievement. But it has been ignored by most people in the international community, including some major monetary authorities. We shall discuss this important, unconventional, development in Chapter 9.

4
Trade Is not Enough

Extension of the functions of money from the domestic economy to the world economy argues that expansion of a country's specialisation and foreign trade will naturally lead to internationalisation of its currency. The economic logic is straightforward and convincing. When a country specialises in trade and develops dominance in the international markets, external demand for its products will expand; hence, there will demand for its currency. The importance of its currency will rise in the global economy, with its functions expanding from the domestic market to the overseas market, from private use to official use, and from the commodity market to the financial market. It will end up as a global reserve currency.

The US dollar (USD) and the Pound sterling (GBP) have gone through these stages in their internationalisation process and acquisition of reserve currency status. China has started its RMB-nisation process recently by promoting the use of the Chinese yuan in foreign trade settlement along the way of its global trade expansion. But arguably, it is a myth that trade specialisation and expansion for a sizable economy like China would naturally lead to internationalisation of the renminbi (RMB). There are lessons to be learned from Japan.

The Japanese yen (JPY) has never been a major trade settlement or invoicing currency, despite the fact that Japan is one of the world's largest trading nations. But still the JPY has moved up to a global reserve currency. The JPY's experience shows that foreign trade is only a necessary but not a sufficient condition for currency internationalisation.

Failing to compete with the USD as the world's medium of exchange, the JPY has competed with the greenback as a store of value in the international financial markets and eventually become a world reserve currency. Beijing to some extent is following the Japanese steps to push

RMB-nisation through the store-of-value function, although at the same time it has not let up its efforts, at least at this stage, on internationalising through trade expansion.

Arguably, the Japanese way of internationalising the yen lacks a robust foundation of transactional demand for yen. Yen internationalisation has mostly been built on a shaky foundation of speculative demand, as its store-of-value function does not stem from the fundamental need for hedging transactional demand risks (i.e. economic shocks). This is food for thought for Beijing in designing its RMB-nisation programme. The real sector (i.e. trade) should be China's primary internationalisation focus, while the development of the financial sector should keep up with the expansion of the real sector.

Internationalisation, the first step

The internationalisation of the RMB, and the corresponding emergence of an offshore RMB (or CNH) market, started in 2004 when banks in Hong Kong were allowed to take deposits in RMB for the first time. In 2007, mainland Chinese banks were authorised to offer RMB deposits in Hong Kong. In 2008, the People's Bank of China (PBoC, China's central bank) signed the first currency swap agreement with the Bank of Korea to facilitate bilateral trade. Since then, more than 20 similar swap agreements have been signed with other jurisdictions, mostly in Asia.

The big push for RMB-nisation came in 2009, when a pilot scheme was introduced in July allowing five Chinese cities, Shanghai, Guangzhou, Shenzhen, Zhuhai and Dongguan, to settle cross-border trade transactions in RMB with Hong Kong, Macau and ASEAN.[1] A total of 324 Chinese firms were initially selected to participate in the pilot project. The domestic participant list was later extended to 67,359 firms in 2010, and the restriction on the number of foreign countries that could settle in RMB with the Chinese firms was also scrapped. Eventually, in early 2012, all restrictions were scrapped; i.e. all mainland Chinese firms were allowed to use RMB as a trade settlement currency anywhere in the world.

On the financial side, in July 2010, restrictions on RMB payments and RMB transfers through banks in Hong Kong were lifted, as long as the RMB funds did not go back to mainland China. At the same time, all corporations were allowed to open RMB accounts in Hong Kong with accredited financial institutions and authorised to conduct payment and transfers offshore. In an effort to further facilitate RMB-trade settlement, China approved onshore trading between the RMB, the Canadian Dollar and the Australian Dollar in late 2011.

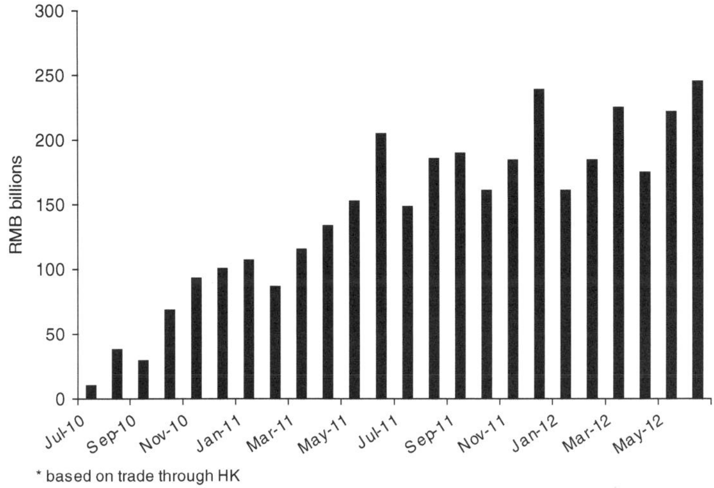

Figure 4.1 RMB trade settlement amount*
Source: CEIC.

These efforts have shown successful results, with merchandise trade settled in RMB soaring dramatically (Figure 4.1). Meanwhile, sizable trade flows have led to the build-up of a sizable pool of RMB deposits in Hong Kong (Figure 4.2). Most of the RMB-trade transactions have been conducted by Chinese importers through Hong Kong. In general, as they have paid RMB to their foreign counterparts, a large pool of RMB deposits has built up abroad.

Since Hong Kong is China's designated offshore RMB market, with a real-time RMB gross settlement clearing system in place for handling RMB transactions, the majority (90%) of China's RMB-trade settlement has been conducted through Hong Kong banks. The dramatic build-up of RMB deposits in the territory has thus come as a natural result of the expansion of RMB-trade settlement. At the time of writing, RMB deposits in Hong Kong account for about 9% of total bank deposits, up from about 1% in 2009.

The development of RMB-trade settlement is the first major step of the internationalisation of the RMB. The head of the Hong Kong Monetary Authority (HKMA) calls this step the "trade bridge" linking the onshore and the offshore RMB markets through current account transactions.[2] Another related development to this trade bridge has been the dramatic growth of the CNH bond market. With significant

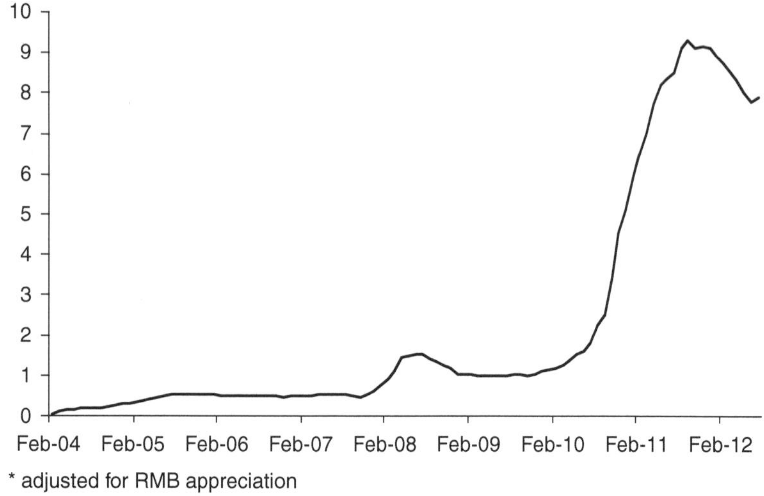

Figure 4.2 RMB deposits* (% of total Hong Kong deposits)
Source: CEIC.

accumulation of RMB in Hong Kong, offshore RMB holders have been looking for yuan-denominated investment vehicles. Indeed, the success of RMB-nisation is contingent upon the growth of an offshore market for RMB securities to satisfy this investment demand.

The development of investment vehicles denominated in RMB began in July 2007 with the first issuance of CNH bonds by mainland Chinese financial institutions in Hong Kong.[3] The initial issuers were carefully selected by Beijing. They included the China Development Bank, the China Export-Import Bank, the Bank of China, the Bank of Communications and the China Construction Bank. All these were either policy banks or commercial banks owned or controlled by the Chinese government. In 2008, McDonald's became the foreign first private sector issuer in the CNH market, followed by HSBC (China) and BEA (China) in 2009. In 2010, other foreign corporations, including ANZ, Caterpillar and Unilever, also issued RMB bonds in Hong Kong to fund their mainland China projects. The growth of the CNH, or "dim sum," bond market in Hong Kong has gone hyperbolic since 2009 (Figure 4.3), though permission for mainland entities to issue bonds in Hong Kong remains heavily regulated by Beijing.

The CNH bond market in HK can be seen as an "investment bridge" linking the onshore and the offshore market through financial account

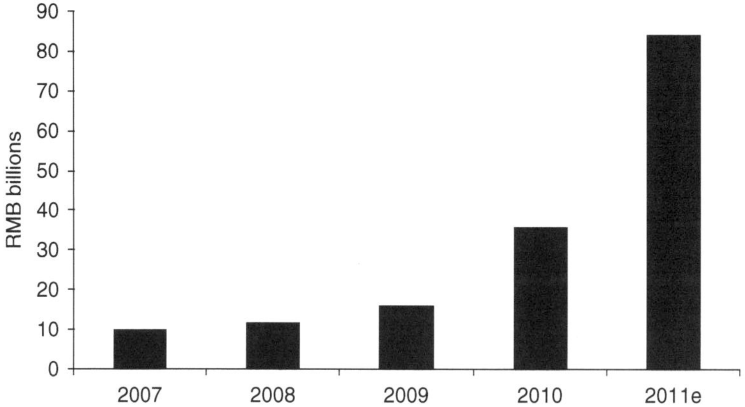

Figure 4.3 Gross issuance of RMB bonds in Hong Kong
Source: Citi, HSBC.

transactions, with companies raising RMB in Hong Kong to fund their activities in mainland China. The dim sum bonds have experienced strong demand since the market's inception, and have led many market players to project unrealistic growth trends into the future.

Euphoria has a limit

The CNH bond market euphoria has spilled over to RMB-denominated portfolio flows, as highlighted by Beijing's approval of the RMB Qualified Foreign Institutional Investor (RQFII) scheme. This is a quota system for allowing RMB in Hong Kong to be invested back into China's equity and bond markets. The initial quota for RQFII was RMB20 billion, granted to 21 mainland Chinese affiliates in Hong Kong in December 2011. Prior to the launching of the RQFII funds, all firms had expected their quota to be taken up by retail investors in no time. But only three funds claimed that they had sold out after launching in February 2012, according to market sources. All the other eighteen were stuck with at least 90% unfilled quota even six months after launching their products!

What is more, Beijing initially designed the RQFII as a retail product, presumably aiming at absorbing the RMB550 billion-strong RMB deposits in Hong Kong back to China. With the failure of the scheme to take off in the retail market, Beijing made an unofficial change in mind, allowing the RQFII quota managers in Hong Kong to sell to institutional clients. However, take-up by institutions was equally poor,[4] partly because of global risk aversion resulting from the European debt crisis and partly because of the market's concern about Chinese credit risk after a series of financial scandals since late 2010 involving Chinese-listed firms in North America and Hong Kong.

The point is that the initial stage of RMB-nisation has generated a lot of blind faith and hype about the ability of the process to create growth and business opportunities. Most people do not care about thinking it through carefully before they make investment and business decisions. Even on the fundamental issue of trade expansion pushing RMB internationalisation, there is a limit it can go. In other words, China cannot rely on internationalising the RMB through trade settlement for too long and hope that trade expansion will make the process successful.

There is no doubt that foreign trade settlement in RMB and, as a result, RMB deposits in Hong Kong will continue to grow. But such growth has a limit that might be reached sooner than many have expected. This is because, hitherto, the sharp growth in the usage of RMB for trade settlement has been a result of Beijing's one-sided offering for its usage, by allowing all mainland Chinese importers and exporters to use RMB for settling foreign trade.

The Chinese firms do have a big incentive to use RMB for settlement, as this is an order from the authorities, and (the real benefit is) it will eliminate their foreign exchange risk (see Chapter 3). But it takes two to tango. Beijing has no control of the usage of RMB by its trading partners. Why would China's trading partners want, and accumulate, RMB from foreign trade when the RMB is not fully convertible, when there are no effective tools for hedging RMB risk, and when there are no investment vehicles for parking or investing the huge RMB-trade proceeds?

Even on the Chinese side, there is still uncertainty about the benefit of eliminating FX risk by using RMB for trade settlement. This is because in a competitive world, if foreign firms were required to assume the FX risk and hedging cost of trading in RMB, they may adjust their prices to the disadvantage of their Chinese counterparts rather than accepting reduced profits themselves. This would, in turn, affect the willingness of the Chinese firms to use RMB as the settlement currency.

The small size, and illiquidity, of the RMB foreign exchange market, which is seen in market segmentation, is certainly an obstacle to foreign preference for accepting the RMB. The onshore deliverable RMB (CNY) market has an estimated average daily turnover of US$25 billion. This includes trade flows, FDI and QFII investment flows. The offshore NDF market, dominated by foreign investors and corporate hedging, has an average daily turnover of about US$5 billion. The nascent CNH (offshore

Hong Kong-based deliverable RMB FX) market also has an estimated daily turnover of US$3 billion, but it has an overlap of eligible participants from the onshore and offshore NDF markets.

These are hardly conditions for developing a full-fledged hedging mechanism for the RMB. From an investment perspective, in 2011 total issuance of CNH bonds amounted to about RMB85 billion (or US$12.5 billion). That was about 15% of all the RMB deposits in Hong Kong; still too small to cater to the huge investment need stemming from the RMB idling in the Hong Kong banking system.

Trade is not enough

Ask the Japanese, and they will tell you trade is not a sufficient condition for currency internationalisation. The JPY has never been a major currency for trade settlement, but it is a global currency with a reserve currency status. Why is that?

From a macro currency perspective, a weak USD which has lost some 45% against the JPY since the 1980s has made it a sticky currency which serves as an international medium of exchange. Note that the incentive for the world (and Japan) to stick with the USD for trade settlement stems from the import side; a falling dollar cheapens import cost. And from a currency internationalisation perspective, imports (not exports) are the key driver for the process. That is because the domestic currency is sent out of the country through imports, while exports absorb the domestic currency back to the country.

Now consider a depreciating USD. It implies that the cost of trade settlement for the Japanese importers using USD is lower (as one yen buys more dollars when the dollar depreciates) than using JPY. So from a cost basis, Japanese importers have a strong preference to settle in USD. The fact that the depreciating dollar has kept its position as the key international trade settlement currency argues that its function as a medium of exchange has overwhelmed its function as a store of value (Ogawa 2001).

Certainly, there are many other issues behind the USD that make it the most favoured and demanded currency in the world for so many decades. In general, these underlying conditions include, but are not limited to, policy, institutions, laws and reforms that aggregate to build the credibility of the USD. The relevance of all this to the JPY's internationalisation is that due to the inertia of the USD as the world's medium of exchange, the yen cannot compete with the dollar on this count. Consequently, the JPY competes with the USD on the store-of-value function front. It does that through exporting capital, including FDI, portfolio investment and international loans.

Being the second-largest creditor (after Germany) to the world, Japan exports a massive amount of capital in JPY. This is effective in internationalising the yen by increasing its offshore circulation. On the other hand, Japan's chronic current account surplus is a handicap to internationalising the JPY, as more yen flows back to Japan than flows out through the current account. Japan has offset this drawback by exporting liquidity through the capital and financial accounts.

Meanwhile, the structure of the Japanese imports has also impaired JPY internationalisation efforts through the medium-of-exchange role. Imports of raw materials, foodstuff and fuels account for over 51% of Japan's overall imports from Southeast Asia (Sato 1999). Since the USD is always used as the medium of exchange in international trade of commodities, the JPY plays little role in settling these import bills. Further, many exports depend on commodity imports. Therefore, Japanese exporters are inclined to settle in USD also to avoid FX risk.

China has a similar situation in this aspect. First and foremost, China's chronic current account surplus is not conducive to internationalising the RMB. On the imports side, commodity imports account for over 40% of its total in recent years; among these, about a quarter were agricultural imports. China's demand for raw materials, fuels, foodstuff and other commodities is expected to rise steadily due to continued industrialisation. However, domestic supply of commodities is projected to shrink due to continued urbanisation and depletion of arable land (Deutsche Bank 2006).

So even increasing Chinese imports may not be as effective as many have thought in increasing the RMB's offshore circulation (i.e. deepening the RMB internationalisation process), as commodity imports are priced in USD. Like Japan, many Chinese exports depend on commodity imports so that the RMB's role as a settlement currency is also constrained.

The invoicing currency puzzle

Even on the export side, the JPY has never taken on any major role as an invoicing currency (Ito, Koibuchi, Sato and Shimizu 2010). The share of USD invoicing in Japan's total foreign trade is particularly high compared to other advanced countries. For example, almost 48% of Japanese exports were billed in USD in 2002–4, compared to 24% in German exports, 26% in UK exports and 33%in French exports.

Meanwhile, over half of Japan's exports to Asia have been invoiced in USD since 1990, and this share has not changed for over two decades.

The small JPY role as an invoicing currency is puzzling from the JPY internationalisation perspective. It was generally assumed that the international use of the yen for invoicing should be growing in Asia with the increase in intra-firm trade between Japanese parent companies and local subsidiaries after years of active foreign direct investment in Asia and other financial investment by Japanese firms (Kawai 1996).

Further, most Asian imports from Japan are high value-added, high-tech goods with strong product differentiation that should give the Japanese exporters a say on using JPY for trade settlement (Fukuda and Ji 1994, Sato 1999, 2003). Yet, even though Japanese firms have built a large regional production and trade network in Asia since 1990, the share of yen invoicing has not increased. Despite China's being Japan's largest trading partner in Asia, the RMB has never been used for trade settlement by the Japanese, until recently when Beijing started pushing RMB-nisation and there was a small amount of RMB-trade settlement between Japan and China. Instead, USD invoicing is far more important and prevalent.

The tendency for most Japanese exporters to invoice in the importer's currency (mostly the USD) when they trade with advanced countries can largely be explained by the pricing-to-market (PTM) behaviour. PTM behaviour means that exporters adjust their prices to conform to the prevailing prices of their export markets. For the importing country, PTM effects can be interpreted as a measure of the stability of domestic prices against foreign prices and exchange-rate movements.

Since most of their exports are destined for local retail subsidiaries, which typically face keen sales and distribution competition in the local markets, Japanese parent firms have a preference to invoice their foreign subsidiaries in the importer's currency (USD most of the time) and assume the FX risk at the headquarters. This is consistent with PTM behaviour (Parsons and Sato 2008). This behaviour has also been extended to the Japanese firms' Asian network.

Although many Japanese firms shifted their production bases to Asia in the 1980s and 1990s, exports from these Asian production subsidiaries are mostly destined for the United States (and Europe). In order to minimise FX risk at their assembly facilities in Asia (which buy from the Japanese headquarters and sell to end markets in the United States), the Japanese parents tend to trade with their Asian subsidiaries in USD. This is PTM extended to the regional level, and it basically explains why the share of yen invoicing has remained small despite the growth of intra-firm sales between Japanese parent and foreign subsidiaries.

Due to the inertia of the USD as the settlement currency in Asia, both Asian and Japanese firms have no choice but to use the dollar as the invoicing currency. Further, hedging cost plays a role in reinforcing the USD inertia. The hedging cost of Asian developing country currencies, including the RMB, is significantly higher than that of the USD and other advanced country currencies due to various restrictions and regulations and the underdeveloped FX markets in the developing world. In this regard, the USD typically has the lowest transaction and hedging costs. The dominant use of the USD as a vehicle currency in the global FX markets has facilitated its usage as an international trade settlement currency, even in trade between countries that does not involve the United States directly (Krugman 1980, 1984).

All these issues are good food for thought for China in its RMB-nisation effort. China's trade structure is similar to that of Japan, which involves importing a lot of commodities. China has a chronic current account surplus, like Japan when it started internationalising the yen in the 1970s. All these factors are not conducive to internationalising the RMB, despite trade specialisation and expansion. On the export side, similar to what Japan did earlier, China is building up its Asian production network as cost rises in the country. It is also increasing foreign investment in Asia and other emerging markets to both secure strategic resources and build international influence. However, the JPY's internationalisation experience shows China that doing all this does not necessarily deepen its currency internationalisation process.

RMB-nisation, the Japanese way?

Failing to internationalise through trade expansion, due to the USD inertia as the world's medium of exchange, Japan pushed through yen internationalisation through the financial accounts. The JPY's role in the global financial markets rose rapidly in the 1970s and 1980s. Yen bonds were issued abroad, medium- and long-term yen loans were made extensively abroad, and foreign investors were allowed into the stock market in Japan. All these helped deepen the yen internationalisation process by exporting capital to the rest of the world, and finally elevate the JPY to a reserve currency status.

Beijing seems to be following in the Japanese footsteps by pushing RMB internationalisation through the financial accounts. This can be seen in a PBoC announcement in February 2012 of a ten-year plan for RMB internationalisation. The plan has three stages and can be summarised as follows:

Stage1: In three years, relax controls on investments directly related to trade; encourage Chinese business to invest abroad.

Stage 2: In three to five years, speed up overseas lending of RMB in support of trade flows and RMB internationalisation.

Stage 3: In five to ten years, allow foreign investors more freedom in investing in Chinese assets, including stocks, bonds and property markets.

At present, only foreign institutional investors are allowed to invest in China's stock and bond markets through small quotas subject to Beijing's approval. Although the Chinese authorities have taken steps since late 2011 to loosen controls on cross-border capital flows by increasing the quotas for foreigners to invest in China's capital markets, these measures are timid. Foreign participation in Chinese stock and bond markets under the new quotas still account for less than 2% of total Chinese market capitalisation.

The general principle behind the PBoC plan is to minimise the potential short-term volatility stemming from liberalising the capital account in the domestic system. In liberalising capital flows, the PBoC plans to loosen controls on capital inflows and long-term capital movement first, and then capital outflows and short-term capital movement. It also aims at liberalising direct investment first and then indirect (portfolio) investments, and allowing foreign institutional investors in first before retail investors.

The rationale for this sequencing is that short-term capital flows tend to be more volatile than long-term flows, and the potential negative impact on the domestic system tends to be bigger for capital outflows than inflows (this latter point is debatable). Direct investment is less likely to cause large, abrupt capital outflows, and non-professional retail investors tend to be less rational (and thus cause more volatility) than professional institutional investors. Thus, they have to be liberalised at a later stage.

The PBoC's plan also suggests liberalising first-grade major markets first before loosening up on second-grade minor markets, and allowing foreign investment into China first before allowing domestic investment abroad. The purpose of doing this is that transaction volumes in the major first-grade markets, such as the Shanghai A-share market, are larger than those in the minor markets. So the first-grade markets are more able to absorb shocks from capital flows. The authorities are obviously concerned about the potential risk of capital outflow (see Chapter 2), and that is why they plan to liberalise non-resident investment in China before domestic residents are allowed to invest abroad.

(Note that this is only a plan from the PBoC. So far, all the internationalisation measures implemented by Beijing have no relevance to this or any other plan. Some of the measures even show policy inconsistency (see Chapter 7). In fact, the central leadership does not have a roadmap for its currency internationalisation efforts, and the authorities have not even had any discussion on the sequencing of RMB internationalisation. See Chapter 6 for more details.)

Caveat of the Japanese approach

However, the way the JPY ascends to a global reserve currency may not be an appropriate way for China to follow because it lacks a robust foundation. Since the yen has never been a major international settlement currency, it lacks the fundamental support of transactional demand. As a result, its role as a store of value also lacks the support of the fundamental need for hedging transactional demand risks (i.e. economic shocks). It can be argued that the internationalisation of the yen was mostly derived from the market's speculative motive on the yen's exchange-rate movement.[5] When the JPY exchange rate was appreciating, the internationalisation process advanced rapidly and smoothly as demand for yen expanded. But during periods of yen depreciation, the incentive for yen demand faded, slowing down its internationalisation process.

Indeed, such speculative motive prompting currency internationalisation is also seen in the RMB. At the onset of Beijing's push for RMB as a trade settlement currency in 2008 and 2009, and when everyone was expecting the RMB exchange rate to appreciate, the share of RMB deposits in Hong Kong's banking system soared. A detailed look at the data (Figure 4.4) shows that the rise in the share of the RMB deposits in Hong Kong's total bank deposits came at the expense of other foreign currency deposits. During that period, the percentage increase in RMB deposit growth was matched almost point for point by the decrease in other foreign currency deposit growth.

Formerly, when some individuals or firms received foreign currencies through foreign trade settlement, they just put these receipts into the banks' foreign currency deposit accounts. But a one-way bet on RMB appreciation prompted these agents to change their foreign currency receipts into RMB deposits. Other people also switched out of their foreign currency deposits and exchanged them into RMB deposits.

Then in late 2011 and 2012, market expectations turned against the RMB, with investors/speculators expecting RMB depreciation. The RMB conversion process was reversed, with people switching out of RMB

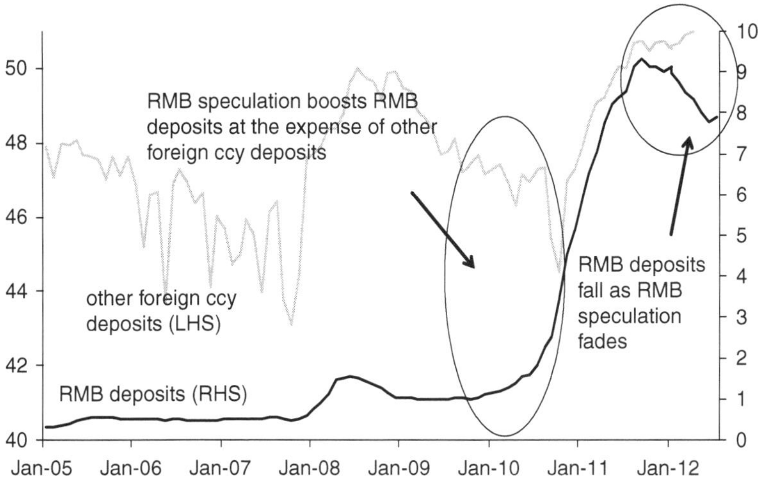

Figure 4.4 Foreign currency deposits (% of total Hong Kong deposits)
Source: CEIC.

and back into other foreign currency deposits. So the share of the RMB deposits dropped, while that of other foreign currencies rose back up (see Figure 4.4). Such volatile behaviour in the RMB deposits in Hong Kong clearly reflected speculators/depositors' portfolio reallocation within their foreign currency holding only. There was no evidence for long-term demand for RMB by switching out of the Hong Kong dollar.

In other words, when market speculation on RMB appreciation was rampant, the offshore RMB pool in Hong Kong expanded swiftly, increasing RMB circulation in the CNH market and thus increasing the degree of RMB internationalisation. But when RMB expectations turned negative, circulation of offshore RMB shrank, hindering the RMB internationalisation process. This is hardly a solid foundation for RMB-nisation.

Regarding the policies for deepening the RMB's internationalisation process, there is a consensus view in China that the capital account needs to be made convertible, but the domestic financial market should be sufficiently developed and strengthened first before opening up the capital account (Lin 2009, Yu 2009, Zhao 2009). However, there is no consensus in the sequencing of the steps for opening up the capital account. We shall examine these factors in subsequent chapters.

In a nutshell, the yen's internationalisation experience has proceeded in an unconventional way in that it has acquired a global reserve currency status without taking up the major role of international medium of exchange. Japan's import structure and chronic current account surplus have impeded yen internationalisation through trade, and prompted the export of yen through capital and financial accounts. In other words, the internationalisation of the JPY was started by taking up the role of a store of value (i.e. reserve currency) but not a medium of exchange (i.e. a trade settlement currency).

All these factors have relevance to China's RMB internationalisation efforts. The lack of fundamental transactional demand support for the JPY means that its internationalisation process is constrained, or even undermined by the market's changing speculative motive. To avoid falling into a similar situation, China should focus its currency internationalisation efforts on strengthening the role of the yuan as a medium of exchange. It is crucial to export RMB through the current account. This means that China's current account will eventually have to turn into deficit so as to induce RMB demand for financial transactions based on the real sector (trade expansion).

Meanwhile, Beijing should encourage imports that are not commodity related. This relates back to the need for China to rebalance its economy by moving away from export-led growth (which reduces offshore RMB circulation) and towards consumption-led growth (which enlarges the offshore RMB pool and increases non-commodity, consumption goods imports). In other words, China's structural reforms to rebalance the economy are necessary steps for deepening RMB-nisation. Finally, financial liberalisation should keep up with the progress in the trade sector so as to create demand for RMB for non-trade purposes. This brings up the subject of the next steps for RMB internationalisation, which we shall discuss in the next chapter.

No Triffin dilemma

Before we move on to discussing the next steps for RMB-nisation, let us address another misunderstanding about China's currency internationalisation process. Some argue that if a country had to run a current account deficit to internationalise its currency, the currency's host country would have to incur a large foreign debt to fund the deficit. Theoretically, a chronic current account deficit and rising foreign debt erode international confidence in that currency, prompting the rest of the world to abandon it eventually. Hence, currency internationalisation becomes self-defeating of its own goal in the end.

Such a view is implied by the so-called Triffin dilemma, proposed by the US economist Robert Triffin in 1961. Triffin's thesis was based on analysing the USD's global role during the gold standard era. It, however, did not state explicitly that a current account deficit was inevitable for the USD to be a global currency. It only argued that if the United States was to export dollars, its foreign debt would grow, leading to an increase in non-resident-holding of the USD. When the growth of the US foreign debt exceeded the growth gold reserves in the United States, foreigners would lose confidence in their dollar assets and start abandoning it. The United States would be forced to sell down its gold reserves to meet foreign redemption, resulting in a balance of payments (BoP) deficit. The USD would then cease to be a global currency (Triffin 1961).

Some economists later used the Triffin dilemma as a theoretical underpinning for arguing that the internationalisation of a currency would inevitably lead to the issuing country running a chronic current account deficit and to a large foreign debt position. When the country's external imbalances get out of hand, international confidence in its currency collapses, pulling it away from being a global currency.

Regardless of Triffin's original meaning, some analysts have suggested that RMB internationalisation will eventually be self-defeating. China's large current account surplus makes it difficult to internationalise the yuan in the beginning. As China's current account turns into a deficit, RMB-nisation will deepen. But as the deficit grows, Chinese foreign debt also grows. The RMB depreciates due to pressure from the negative external balance. The combination of a large current account deficit, a large foreign debt and a falling RMB cannot make the RMB a global currency, because no one will want to hold it. In other words, RMB internationalisation will be restricted by China's current account in the short run, and it will fail in the long run due to the pressures from currency depreciation and a chronic current account deficit.

This view has been proven wrong by both the United States and Japan. It will also be proven wrong by China eventually. Despite the United States' chronic current account deficit and huge foreign debt build-up, the USD remains a safe haven with a global reserve currency status crisis after crisis. One may argue that the USD is unique because of inertia and the fact that the bulk of the United States' foreign debt is denominated in USD. True. This only underscores our earlier argument that internationalising the RMB is a move by China to prepare itself for becoming a debtor nation in the future (see Chapter 3).

For Japan, it is obvious that its chronic current account surplus has not obstructed its yen internationalisation process because it just exports capital to increase the yen's offshore circulation instead of importing goods and services as a way of pushing the JPY overseas. China resembles Japan in this regard. Due to its closed capital account, China has a lot of leeway to facilitate RMB internationalisation by allowing local capital to flow out. As long as capital account controls are progressively lifted, more yuan can flow offshore, offsetting the current account surplus handicap in RMB internationalisation.

RMB outflow channels are numerous, including overseas direct investment (ODI), yuan loans to foreigners, non-residents issuance of RMB bonds, residents buying of offshore assets, foreigner's purchase of the RMB, bilateral currency swap lines between China and foreign governments and so on. Once it has flowed out of China, the overseas yuan pool can grow through a multiplier effect, just like a normal money multiplier on money supply. This offshore RMB multiplier is an additional force boosting RMB-nisation.

However, if capital account liberalisation is delayed, yuan internationalisation can only rely on the trade channel. This will constrain the degree of internationalisation. Opening the capital account is directly related to the next steps for RMB-nisation, which is our topic for the next chapter.

5
The Next Steps for Internationalisation

After a successful first step of launching the renminbi (RMB) internationalisation programme, what are China's next steps for broadening and deepening the process? This question is all the more important in light of some experience that shows that the RMB's being a trade settlement currency might not be a sufficient condition for achieving currency internationalisation (see Chapter 4).

To truly internationalise, the RMB will need to capture a broader base of international demand for it than the hitherto measures have promoted. The success of RMB-nisation depends on the use of the yuan in international financial transactions, not just trade. While Hong Kong, the special administrative region in southern China, will be instrumental in widening the demand for RMB, Beijing will have to create the incentive for that to happen ultimately. It will have to liberalise interest rates and the domestic capital market by sanctioning the development of more RMB products and the derivatives market and make them available to overseas investors. These are daunting tasks that will take a long time to accomplish.

China has been promoting the RMB as an international investment currency since 2010 by creating RMB assets offshore. Hong Kong has been designated as the primary offshore RMB centre right from the beginning. Taipei became the second offshore RMB centre in early 2013, but its market size is only a tenth of Hong Kong's. London and Singapore are trying hard to lobby Beijing to let them develop offshore RMB business also, but the progress has been slow. China is able to command control of the fate of the offshore centres because it has only designated two Chinese banks, the Bank of China (BoC) and the Industrial and Commercial Bank of China (ICBC), as the clearing banks for all offshore RMB transactions (ICBC is designated to clear RMB transactions in Singapore only).

Understanding China's monetary policy objectives will give us a clue as to what kind of RMB asset creation Beijing will favour in the offshore market. This is market intelligence for the investment community.

Meanwhile, the development of the offshore RMB (or CNH) market has the potential of eroding the effectiveness of China's monetary policy. This is because the offshore market provides onshore economic agents an escape route to bypass domestic monetary tightening at times when RMB internationalisation conflicts with China's domestic monetary policy objectives. Given Beijing's liquidity control policy, it will want to limit the number of Chinese issuers in the CNH market, as they are the catalysts for policy conflict. In the coming years, there will likely be a big change in the composition of offshore RMB asset issuers from what we saw in the early days, when three-quarters of RMB bond issuers were Chinese entities which raised funds in Hong Kong and then remitted the proceeds back to the mainland.

Some players and analysts see the next step for RMB-nisation as displacing the US dollar (USD) as the world's reserve currency in the not-too-distant future. That will be a big leap of faith, in my view, due to the inertia of the USD in the global markets and the inherent structural deficiency in the RMB. But that should not bar the yuan from challenging the USD in a regional context. The growth of the offshore yuan market is especially crucial in this context. Structurally, the offshore RMB centres are creating market signals for the Chinese system. It will eventually create pressures for transforming China's financial landscape and monetary policy.

The demand for RMB theory

The demand for money theory sheds some light on the next steps for RMB-nisation. Recall that there are three motives for demand for money: transactional, precautionary and speculative. The first internationalisation phase, by promoting the RMB as a foreign trade settlement currency, is only capturing the transactional demand for money. To fully internationalise the RMB, Beijing will have to capture the precautionary demand for money (RMB as a reserve currency) and the speculative demand for money (RMB as an investment currency in an international portfolio).

These other two RMB demand motives are closely related to the availability of a deep and mature Chinese capital market, with Chinese financial products and hedging tools made available to foreign players. Due to the complications involved, it is impractical for this development to go fast. Without a deep and sophisticated capital market, the RMB cannot challenge the USD's global currency status, thereby causing financial dislocation and political tension along the way, as some have feared. The RMB-nisation measures implemented so far have also shown Beijing's preference for a gradual and cautious process.

Since Beijing started allowing Chinese companies to settle foreign trade in RMB in mid-2009, trade settlement in the Chinese currency has soared. Total foreign trade settled in RMB has risen from under RMB500 million a month in mid-2009 to over RMB200 billion a month currently. The amount will grow as the RMB becomes more commonly used. These RMB funds have been trapped in Hong Kong, where 90% of the RMB trade settlement is done, leading to a significant build-up in RMB deposits. The share of RMB deposits in the Hong Kong banking system has soared from almost nothing in 2004, when the records started, to 9% at the time of writing (Figure 5.1).

However, it can be argued that such dramatic growth rates have come from an almost zero base, and they do not look as dramatic in the big picture. On an annualised basis, the RMB200 billion in foreign trade settled is only about 0.3% of China's total foreign trade. Meanwhile, despite the big jump in RMB deposits in the Hong Kong banking system, its share in the total deposits is still less than 10%. Crucially,

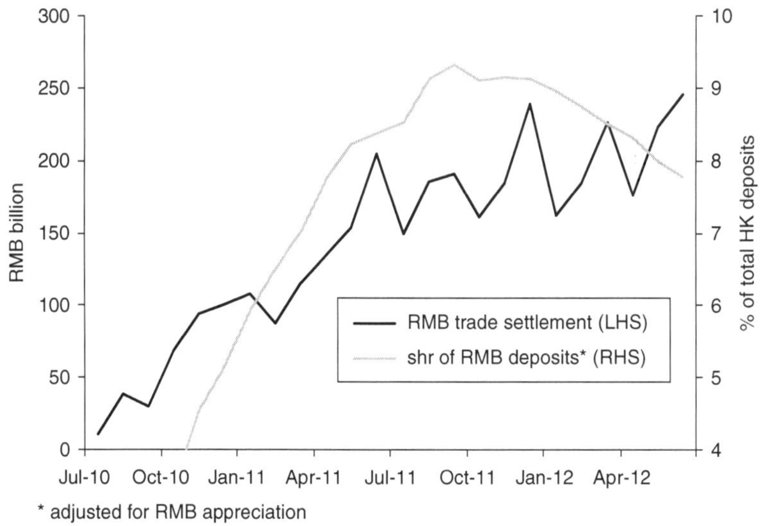

Figure 5.1 Signs of success of RMB trade settlement

Source: CEIC, Reuters.

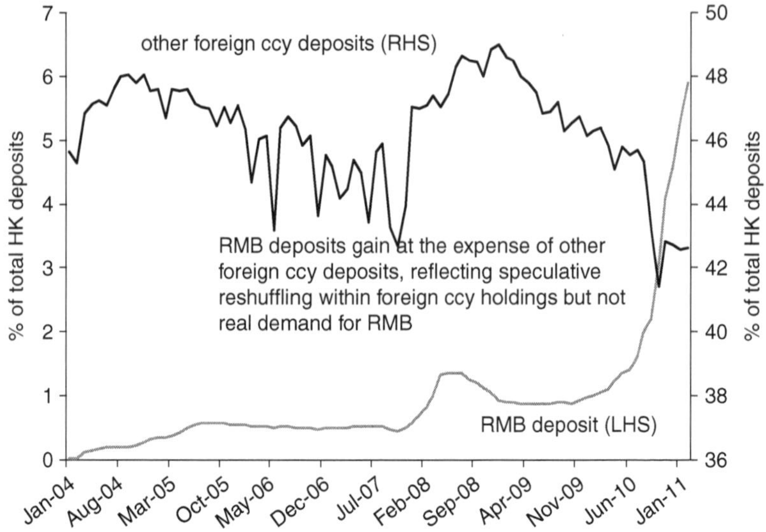

Figure 5.2 Reshuffling of foreign currency deposits
Source: CEIC.

the rise in the share of the RMB deposits in 2009 and 2011 came mainly at the expense of a fall in the share of other foreign currency deposits (Figure 5.2).

All this evidence says that the RMB-nisation process is still at its nascent stage. Fundamentally, as discussed in Chapter 4, as long as China has a current account surplus, it will constrain the currency internationalisation progress, as more RMB flows into China through the current account surplus than flows out. Further, the behaviour of RMB deposit accumulation in the Hong Kong banking system shows that non-trade demand for RMB outside China was mostly speculative (and this is not the same as the speculative demand for money motive), as people bet on RMB appreciation. If the RMB is expected to depreciate, *ceteris paribus*, non-trade demand for RMB will disappear quickly. This has in fact happened.

When the market started to expect RMB depreciation in the second half of 2011, RMB deposits in Hong Kong also started to drop (see Figure 5.1). Granted, as Beijing gradually liberalises capital inflows, more avenues for offshore RMB to flow back to China have also prompted the decline. These avenues include foreign direct investment (FDI) using RMB as the investment currency, increased export trade (by Chinese exporters) settling in RMB, and new and expanded investment quota schemes, like

RQFII, for investing RMB back in China's capital markets. The list will grow over time. But speculation on RMB depreciation has been the major reason for investors to abandon the RMB between late 2011 and 2012.

The fact that the rise in the share of RMB deposits in Hong Kong came at the expense of other foreign currency deposits (see Figure 5.2) in the go-go months between 2009 and 2011 reflected Hong Kong depositors' (speculators') portfolio reallocation within their foreign currency holding only. There was no long-term demand for RMB by switching out of the Hong Kong dollar. Hence, as soon as market expectations turned towards RMB depreciation in late 2011, RMB deposits dropped. The share of other foreign currency deposits rose back up from 44% to over 50% at the expense of RMB deposits.

Such erratic behaviour of the RMB deposit growth is a replica of the Japanese experience when they internationalise the Japanese yen (JPY) (see Chapter 4). It is not a sustainable way to internationalise the RMB. To truly internationalise, Beijing must create an incentive for China's trading partners and foreigners to use and hold RMB other than good and services trade. And this incentive is related to the other two money demand motives: precautionary demand and speculative demand.

In the RMB perspective, the precautionary demand is related to demand for RMB by foreign central banks as one of their reserve currencies, and by the foreign private sector as one form of saving tucked away in foreign currency bank accounts. The speculative demand is related to demand for RMB as an investment vehicle. Both of these motives require more financial liberalisation by China, and more financial products and hedging tools made available to foreign players. But the development of this process is slow due to the deep-rooted structural and institutional reforms needed.

Good reasons to be slow

On a macroeconomic perspective, despite the hype in the markets that RMB internationalisation will go fast, there are good reasons for it to proceed slowly. On a global basis, if the RMB were to replace the USD as the key reserve currency too quickly, that would mean a collapse in the demand for USD. This will indirectly deliver a financial shock to the world economy. This is because the withdrawal of the USD from the global system will deprive it of liquidity, especially in the post-subprime world where growth will remain fragile for some long period of time.

Moreover, the fall of the USD from its supreme global reserve currency status would force a sharp contraction of the US current account deficit, as investors and central banks would be unwilling to lend to support the US deficit. A reversal of the US current account imbalance is needed. But any sudden reversal would be dangerous, as that would create a world recession by killing the largest consumer in the world before Asian, in particular Chinese, consumers can replace the huge US consumption appetite.

Internationalising the RMB also means creating a big offshore RMB market. From a domestic risk-control perspective, Beijing may not want fast development for this because it may bring an unintended negative impact to the local system. Since banks operating in the offshore currency market, and offering onshore currency products, do not have to observe reserve requirements and capital adequacy rules of the onshore currency system, they operate like a shadow banking system, which is what lay at the heart of the US subprime crisis. This gives the offshore banks (in Hong Kong in our context here) greater latitude to expand their foreign currency (RMB in our example) offerings than the onshore banks.

However, this also means greater risk from the Chinese regulator's perspective in the event of a liquidity shock even if it is coming from offshore. The risk becomes more complicated when mainland Chinese banks also operate in Hong Kong and enjoy this bigger business latitude offshore than even their own parents and counterparts in China. Hence, offshore currency markets have the potential to amplify the boom-bust cyclical forces back in the home system.

Indeed, the financial liberalisation measures that Beijing has rolled out so far to facilitate RMB-nisation show that it wants a cautious and slow approach. For example, its moves in 2011 to liberalise the Chinese bond and RMB interbank markets by allowing foreigners to participate, and the launching of the RQFII (RMB Qualified Foreign Institutional Investor) scheme in Hong Kong, are means for draining RMB back to China. This contradicts the essential need to encourage RMB to stay and circulate offshore as the basis for its internationalisation.

To see this, consider the RQFII scheme, which was originally opened to the affiliates of Chinese fund managers in Hong Kong to invest the RMB cash that they raised back into the onshore stock and bond markets. From an investor's perspective, this scheme swaps his/her RMB cash with an RMB asset. So the net impact on his/her net worth depends on the changes in the RMB asset's value. But from a macro perspective, the RQFII *per se* drains RMB liquidity back to China, *ceteris paribus*. The same argument goes for allowing foreign investors to invest in the Chinese onshore bond market, as offshore RMB flows back to China via the bond purchases.

Further, a rule announced in December 2010 deters RMB trading and hedging activity in Hong Kong. Under that rule, a bank offering a one-year forward contract worth US$50 million to buy RMB at a fixed rate, for example, will have to hold ten times the amount of the contract (i.e. US$500 million) of yuan assets in capital to back the deal. This is very costly and restrictive, as yields on RMB assets are very low and are in short supply. While this rule aims at limiting risk taking by banks in RMB positions, it also imposes a big hurdle for developing RMB hedging/ derivative products.

Hong Kong's instrumental role

However, it is a different matter if China allows more financial products to be developed and traded outside China. That will facilitate the RMB to stay and circulate overseas. Eventually, non-trade demand for RMB will rise, setting the stage for full internationalisation. Hong Kong is instrumental for facilitating this process, and as a result it stands to benefit the most. Given China's firm control of the circulation of the RMB overseas,[1] its designation of Hong Kong as the primary offshore RMB centre is, in effect, granting the territory a monopoly to develop offshore RMB business.

Indeed, Hong Kong has been building up its offshore RMB infrastructure by developing a local RMB deliverable (or CNH) market. This market includes offshore RMB bonds (or dim sum bonds) and spot FX trading between RMB/HKD and RMB/USD. The growth of the dim sum bond market has been dramatic (Figure 5.3). As the RMB pool grows in Hong Kong, especially with more and more Chinese importers demanding RMB trade settlement and assuming no significant drainage of RMB back to the mainland, the dim sum bond market will enjoy significant growth in the medium term.

Hong Kong can develop more fully as an international financial centre in the medium term by being the prime offshore RMB centre, just like London has been the key euro-dollar market since 1963 despite competition from other euro-dollar centres. Hong Kong's banking sector will receive new life from the CNH business. But the benefit is not one way. Hong Kong's role as a primary offshore RMB centre, with most if not all of the RMB financial products developed here, is instrumental for Beijing to accomplish its RMB internationalisation goal over the long term.

In particular, Hong Kong is a platform for China to promote the global role of the RMB without risking the potentially harmful effects of capital account liberalisation in the onshore system. No foreign cities will be willing to do this for China. This is one key factor that secures Hong

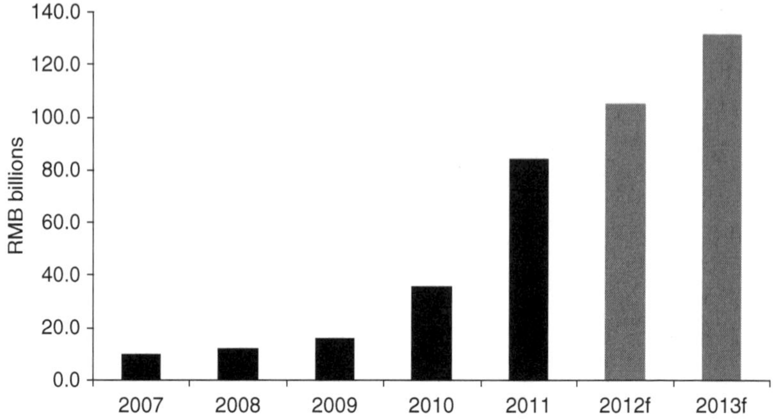

Figure 5.3 Growth of the dim sum bond market in Hong Kong
Source: Citi, HSBC.

Kong's role as the prime offshore RMB centre going forward. But full RMB internationalisation cannot be realised without more active onshore market liberalisation. In the end, it will be difficult to fully develop FX and derivatives markets without substantial capital account opening. So the ball remains in Beijing's court to deepen the RMB-nisation process, though Hong Kong can act as an important facilitator.

Monetary policy clues for RMB-nisation

In the coming years, RMB internationalisation and the related capital account liberalisation will be the most important reform development for China as a gateway for the RMB to achieve reserve currency status. Alongside its push for the RMB to be an international trade currency (which captures the transactional demand for RMB), Beijing has started since 2010 to promote the RMB as an international investment currency (which aims at capturing the precautionary demand and speculative demand for RMB).

Promoting the RMB as an investment currency involves creating RMB assets offshore (mainly in Hong Kong according to Beijing's current plan) so that there will be more vehicles for the offshore RMB to invest in. Understanding China's monetary policy objectives will give us a clue as to what kind of RMB asset creation Beijing will favour in the offshore market. This is crucial market intelligence for the investment and business communities.

Controlling inflation will remain a medium-term macro policy focus for Beijing. Against this backdrop, an important policy concern is whether the recycling of offshore RMB, stemming from asset creation outside the country, back to the mainland will increase onshore RMB liquidity and add to domestic inflationary pressure. The recycling occurs when offshore RMB bond/loan/IPO proceeds are being remitted back to China. When this adds to inflation, the PBoC will be under pressure to "sterilise" this RMB inflow.[2] Thus, the authorities will, in general, discourage those offshore asset creation activities that would lead to excess onshore liquidity inflow adding to inflationary pressure and the cost of sterilisation, especially during times of economic overheating.

There are many ways in which RMB assets can be created offshore. Just to name a few, they can be in the form of

- RMB IPOs raised by, or bonds issued by, or loans extended to, domestic Chinese entities, joint ventures and/or foreign companies for investment back in China
- RMB bonds/loans issued for trade settlement
- RMB instruments issued for investment outside of China.

From a policy perspective, once the RMB funds raised by the Chinese entities offshore are remitted back to China, they will add new liquidity to the onshore system, adding to domestic inflationary pressures. Hence, these types of asset creation in the offshore market will likely be discouraged by the Chinese authorities under an anti-inflation policy backdrop.

However, if the RMB funds are raised by foreign companies offshore and invested in China as FDI, this is liquidity neutral, and should not attract policy resistance from Beijing. This is because in this process, the foreign entities are simply replacing USD FDI, or other foreign currency FDI, by RMB FDI. The same amount of FDI still goes into China, but only in a different currency denomination. If the FDI goes in as USD, that would boost FX reserves and RMB liquidity under Beijing's stable RMB policy. This will prompt Beijing to sterilise the inflow to rein in inflationary pressure. If the FDI goes in as RMB, it would directly add to onshore liquidity and, hence, raise the need for sterilisation. From a policy perspective, the impact on domestic liquidity, inflation and sterilisation cost is the same whether the FDI is denominated in USD or other hard currencies or RMB.

The same logic applies to RMB instruments issued by offshore players for funding trade with China. In this operation, the offshore buyers of Chinese goods will pay RMB to Chinese exporters instead of USD. The total settlement amount is the same, but the foreign buyers simply replace USD payment by RMB, using RMB funds raised offshore. Hence, the liquidity/inflation/monetary policy impact is the same, disregarding the denomination of the settlement currency.

There is another offshore RMB asset class that Beijing should encourage the formation of, especially if it really wants to create a meaningful offshore RMB centre. That is, RMB debt instruments issued for investment outside of China. This asset class has no inflationary impact on China and, thus, does not affect China's monetary policy operations at all. Such debt instruments may also be complemented by FX swapping facilities and are, thus, instrumental for forming a full-fledged offshore RMB centre with derivatives function.

For example, an institution in Hong Kong borrows RMB from another bank, or issues an RMB bond, and uses the proceeds to invest in or trade other, including RMB, securities in the offshore market. The creation of RMB assets under this process does not involve any funds flowing back to China and, hence, has no inflationary and monetary policy implications. Or consider this: A foreign company borrows RMB from a bank, or issues an RMB bond, in the offshore market, and uses a currency swap to convert the RMB proceeds into another currency, such as euro, Pound sterling (GBP) or USD, so that it can swap them back to RMB for repayment upon maturity of the loan or bond. The proceeds are used to invest in offshore projects. Again, this RMB asset (loan or bond) will not lead to any funds flowing back to China and, thus, has no impact on its domestic liquidity and monetary policy.

Indeed, there have been a few of these deals done in Hong Kong, for example by the Asian Development Bank, IBRD and VTB Capital in 2010 and 2011. These bond-cum-FX-swap instruments may become more popular as Beijing's liberalisation stance becomes more relaxed. The likely issuers will be those emerging market countries, such as Russia, Brazil, Indonesia and India, whose funding costs are high due to higher inflation than China. As long as the RMB funding cost in Hong Kong plus currency swap cost are cheaper than their local funding cost, it pays them to issue RMB assets in Hong Kong and supplement them with a swap facility.

Offshore asset creation

RMB trade settlement will remain the single most important source of RMB liquidity in Hong Kong (and other offshore centres as they emerge) in the medium term. The large RMB inflow to Hong Kong through China trade is due to the fact that 90% of the trade settlement involves Chinese importers paying RMB to exporters in Hong Kong.

Meanwhile, on the Chinese export side, China has been moving up the value chain. For example, there has been a steady rise in high value-added exports (relative to China's conventional low value-added exports), such as machinery, equipment and optical items and construction services (Figures 5.4 and 5.5). Improved product value and differentiation will allow Chinese exporters stronger bargaining power to request settlement in RMB. So the need for RMB from overseas buyers (to pay

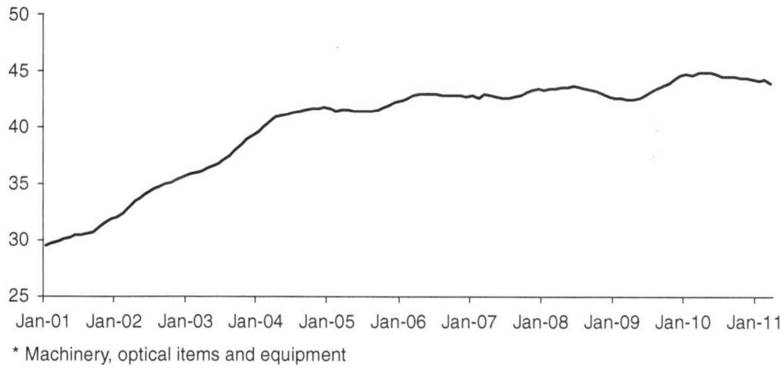

Figure 5.4 China's higher value-added exports* (% of total exports)
Source: CEIC.

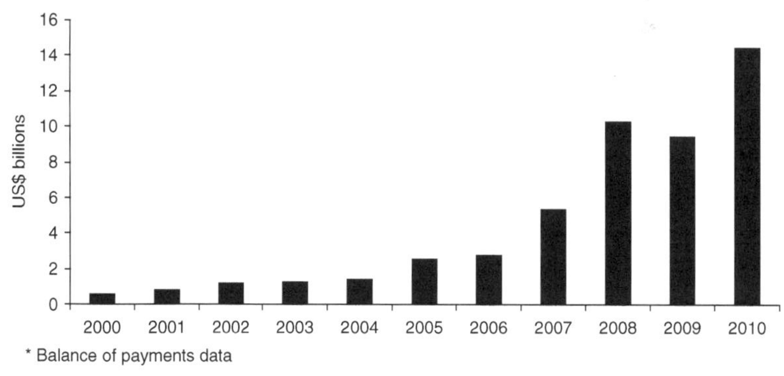

Figure 5.5 China's construction service exports*
Source: CEIC.

the Chinese exporters) will likely grow. This will create demand for RMB funding instruments in the offshore market. In other words, offshore RMB asset creation will continue to expand in the coming years.

Owing to the offshore RMB asset creation preference dictated by Beijing's liquidity control/anti-inflation policy, the composition of RMB asset issuers may change significantly from what we saw in 2010

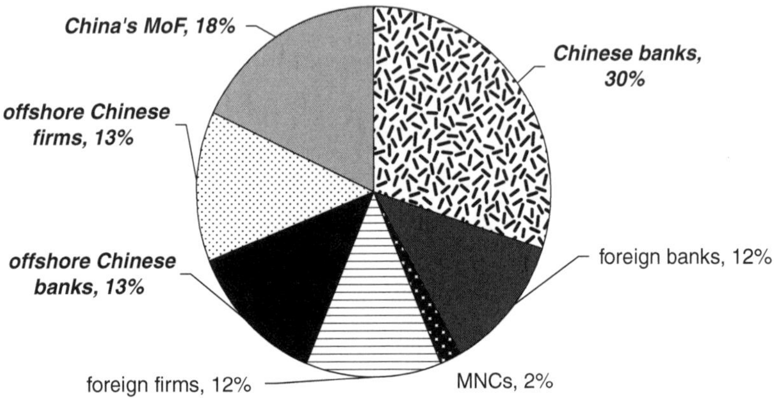

Figure 5.6 CNH bond issuers (% of total, 2010)
Source: HSBC, Bloomberg.

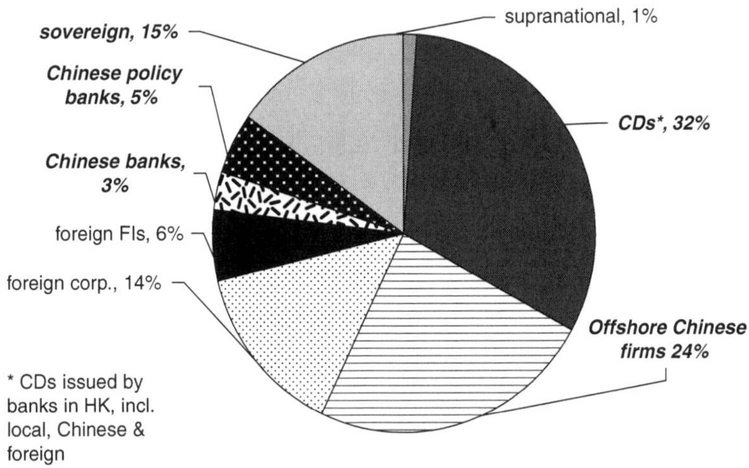

Figure 5.7 CNH bond issuers (% of total, 2011)
Source: HSBC, Bloomberg.

when the CNH market took off. Back then, almost three-quarters of CNH bonds were issued by mainland Chinese entities (Figure 5.6), who then remitted the proceeds back to China (thus adding to the onshore liquidity). But in 2011, the share of the Chinese issuers had dropped to about 60% (Figure 5.7). Going forward, the majority of the CNH issuers will likely shift to foreign entities. They will use the RMB proceeds for Chinese trade settlement and/or investment outside China.

Displacing the USD

Some optimists have made a brave prediction that the next step for the RMB is to displace the USD as the world's major reserve currency in the not-too-distant future.[3] That would be a big leap of faith. RMB challenging the dominance of the USD? Yes. But displacing it? Not for a long time. The fundamental problem for the RMB to overtake the USD as the super currency is two-fold: The inconvertibility of the RMB and the inertia of the USD in the global markets.

The great virtue of the dollar (and also of the JPY, euro and Swiss franc) as a global currency is that they are fully convertible. This means that companies and individuals can do anything with those monies after they receive them as payments – including paying other supplies and buying goods and services around the world, investing virtually anywhere, or converting freely among a range of other currencies. But as Beijing expands apace the opportunities to trade with the yuan, it is moving only slowly to open avenues for companies and individuals to do anything with the yuan other than trade.

Creating an offshore market in Hong Kong helps, as does Beijing's move to allow Hong Kong institutional investors to invest in the onshore bond market. But thanks to onerous exchange controls and red tape, yuan options for all users are still very limited. The flows into and out of the mainland are tightly controlled by quotas and opaque administration and approval processes. Regulations are complicated, and are enforced by a variety of government entities which do not necessarily communicate with each other. Companies in China often complain about a serious lack of coordination between the PBoC, the State Administration of Foreign Exchange (SAFE), the Ministry of Commerce and the Ministry of Finance, which control different aspects of the Chinese financial and economic systems.

There are many other practical problems. For money transfer, for example, Chinese banks typically divide the work internally between one department that handles clearing for yuan between domestic accounts and another department that handles transfers of foreign currencies between domestic and foreign companies. The two operate differently without much coordination. The domestic unit uses China's own national clearing system to transfer money, while the foreign unit works with correspondent banks and the international SWIFT network[4] for interbank communications.

Offshore yuan transactions make life more difficult. Since they involve yuan, the department responsible for foreign transactions assumes that the domestic yuan-transfer unit will do the work. But since they are transfers to overseas accounts, the department that handles domestic transactions assumes that the job comes under the responsibility of the office that handles foreign deals. The resulting responsibility shifting leads to tensions and delays.

Time is a major consideration in today's modern world. Since the world's USD market is broad and deep, global dollar transfers can be cleared within minutes. But yuan clearing takes much longer and involves greater uncertainty, hence risk. For instance, what rules govern anti-money laundering surveillance on yuan transfers? What happens if a transaction fails to clear for some reasons? In the dollar market, there are clear rules in place to handle issues like these, but not for the Chinese yuan. This means higher transaction costs even for Chinese companies to settle in yuan, compared to the conventional cross-border trade in USD. Such inefficiency raises questions of whether even Chinese firms would want to use RMB in foreign trades.

These are short-term problems only, which one may counter. But fixing these problems involves deep-rooted changes in the Chinese legal, financial and economic systems, and in the Chinese mindset. This is easier said than done. The Chinese workforce must be motivated to work; Chinese markets must be made transparent; banks must be commercialised; supervision and regulations must be strengthened; monetary and fiscal policy must be sound and stable; the exchange rate must be flexible enough to accommodate large flows of capital; Chinese interest rates must be freed.... The list goes on. All these are exactly the fundamental changes that China has to make in order to achieve full capital account convertibility, a prerequisite for full RMB-nisation.

But to do so, China would have to abandon control of the financial system and the currency, which have been the two main tools of its development policy and political power. Old habits die hard. Witness Beijing's first reaction to the subprime shock in 2009. It was to further rely on directed lending to boost investment and to reinforce the RMB's peg against the USD in order to sustain exports (Eichengreen 2009). What all this says is that the day for full RMB convertibility, a prerequisite for it to displace the USD, is uncertain. There is too much work involved behind the scene. What is certain is that that day is a very long way off.

The other fundamental problem for the yuan to displace the dollar is the USD's inertia in the global markets. Some 85% of the world's FX trades involve the USD. Oil, copper and almost every other internationally traded commodity is denominated in USD. The vaults of the global central banks and governments are filled with dollar reserves. Over 60% of all global FX reserves are made up of the USD, far more than the 25% for the euro, the 4% for the JPY and the GBP and the 1% for the Swiss franc.

Since the USD market is so large, companies and individuals trade in and out of it at the best possible rates. If one wants to convert Brazilian real into South African rand, the most cost-efficient way is still to trade real for dollars and then dollars for rand, instead of trying to make the exchange directly. How long will it take the RMB to develop such a market to rival the USD? A very long time, for sure.

The dollar has remained the world's dominant reserve currency for some critical reasons that not many other countries can rival so far. The United States' economic vibrancy, transparent government and well-established rule of law have all added up to persuade generations of foreigners to trust the greenback and hold it as a store of value. Old habits die hard; it took decades after the US economy surpassed that of the United Kingdom for the dollar to unseat the GBP as the world's super currency. If the RMB were to displace the USD, it would also mean decades of work even after China had established the necessary qualities of a sound government, rule of law and economic resiliency.

Ironically, rising public debt in the United States has also contributed to strengthening the USD's inertia. The International Monetary Fund (IMF) forecasts that US gross public debt, which is about 90% now, could grow to 110% % of GDP, or nearly US$21 trillion, by 2016. For many countries, such a hefty public debt burden would have scared investors and creditors away, who would abandon their currencies. But the weakness in Japan and the financial turmoil in the euro area (see Chapter 1 for a discussion on the structural changes of these currencies) have increased the emerging markets' demand for "safe-haven"

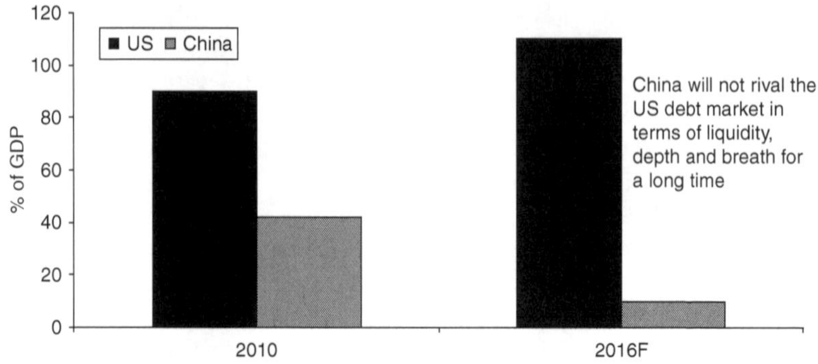

Figure 5.8 Gross public debt-to-GDP ratio
Source: CEIC, IMF.

assets as they continue to build FX reserves. And so far, only the US markets can take on the safe-haven role. Rising US debt has actually cemented the dollar's dominance in the global financial system during financial crises.

When put in this perspective, the gulf between China and the United States in terms of the availability of safe and liquid assets is huge (Figure 5.8). The depth, breadth and liquidity of US financial markets are unrivalled and will serve as a buffer against threats to the USD's dominant status. Before catching up with the United States by building up safe assets, including government debt, the imminent challenge for China is to liberalise its financial markets and increase the availability of high-quality RMB-denominated assets.

There has been some modest development in the breadth, depth and liquidity of China's financial markets over the past decade. But China still comes up short when it comes to the key financial market development in terms of integrity, regulatory and transparency dimensions. Financial system weaknesses will limit the redback's international role. So displacing the USD will certainly not be the yuan's next step of development, as some optimists have speculated.

Cheating on RMB-nisation

Even in the RMB internationalisation process, cheating has emerged due to rent seeking[5] made possible by market segregation and poor regulations. Such cheating suggests that part of the internationalisation process was distorted so that some of the progress was phony. According to bankers in Hong Kong, most of the RMB trade settlements were not real international usage of RMB. Of the RMB 2.04 trillion of RMB trade settlements between 2009 and 2011, only a small portion involved companies outside Hong Kong and China. The bulk of the settlements was phony transactions, driven by mainland Chinese companies transacting with their subsidiaries in Hong Kong arbitraging interest rate differential between the onshore and offshore markets.

In this exercise, a mainland Chinese firm makes an RMB deposit with an onshore bank, earning an interest rate of over 3 percentage points more than it could get in Hong Kong. The firm then gets an RMB-denominated letter of credit (LC) from the bank to pay for a shipment of goods from its Hong Kong subsidiary. The subsidiary then uses the LC as collateral to obtain a USD loan from a bank in Hong Kong at a much lower interest rate than the parent could get in China, usually with a currency swap attached to eliminate the FX risk. This arbitrage activity is meant to skirt Beijing liquidity tightening in the mainland.

According to SWIFT, the global payments system, about 8% of the offshore RMB trade were genuine transactions done outside Hong Kong and China. This arbitrage activity caught the authorities' attention, with the Hong Kong Monetary Authority cracking down on illegitimate RMB payments and threatening banks with hefty penalties if they failed to produce robust evidence to prove the cross-border trade was genuine (Morgan Stanley 2011). Excessive rent-seeking behaviour resulting from systemic and regulatory insufficiency is indeed a large part of China's financial system weaknesses that will impede the progress of RMB internationalisation to the next steps.

Challenging the USD in Asia

But all this does not mean that the RMB will not be able to challenge the USD's dominance, especially in Asia. Beijing has indeed introduced new initiatives to broaden the demand base for RMB offshore, with a potential of eroding the USD's dominance in foreign trade in Asia. Structurally, the growth of offshore RMB centres is creating market signals for the Chinese system. It will eventually create pressures for transforming China's financial landscape and monetary policy.

Beijing implemented a series of new initiatives to keep the process going in the last few months in 2011. They included allowing all Chinese firms to settle foreign trade in RMB with any countries in the world,[6] approving the usage of RMB for FDI in China, allowing more Chinese entities to issue RMB bonds in Hong Kong, directly trading Australian and Canadian dollars (in addition to USD) against the RMB onshore and approving the RQFII scheme, which allows offshore RMB to be invested in China's capital markets through a quota system. The list will grow over time.

All these measures are meant to create a two-way trading mechanism for the RMB between on- and off-shore markets, encourage RMB asset creation offshore and create an incentive for China's trading partners and foreigners to hold and use RMB as an investment and reserve currency, although they are not directly helpful for increasing the RMB's circulation overseas. The point is that successful measures to enlarge the offshore RMB market will sharply increase the potential for the yuan to erode the USD's global dominance.

Of particular importance is the Sino-Japanese collaboration, announced on Christmas day in 2011, of using RMB for trade and non-trade transactions.[7] This is a major step towards expanding the foreign demand base for RMB, as it involves cooperation with Asia's second-largest, and the world's third-largest economy. Japan has also agreed to buy Chinese bonds (up to US$10 billion) in their reserves. When implemented, this decision will for the first time make RMB assets part of the reserves of a G7 economy, and it could be the start of a long-term process for accepting the RMB as a reserve currency.

This Sino-Japanese deal could potentially boost RMB internationalisation significantly through trade invoicing. While China's bilateral trade with Japan is smaller in absolute size than with Europe and the United

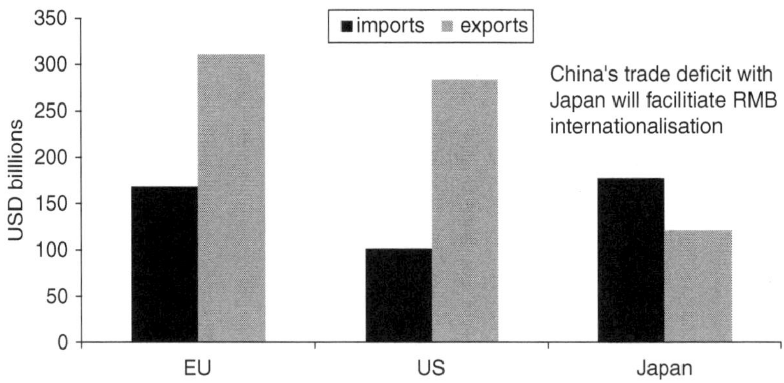

Figure 5.9 China's trade balance with the G3

Source: CEIC.

States (G2), it imports a significantly larger amount from Japan than from the G2 (Figure 5.9). In fact, China runs a trade deficit with Japan, while it runs a trade surplus with the G2. By paying Japanese exporters with RMB,[8] China is indeed trying to replicate its Hong Kong strategy by allowing more RMB to accumulate in Japan. If Sino-Japanese RMB trade settlement expands significantly in addition to Hong Kong, the dominance of the USD in Asia, a least in foreign trade terms, could be eroded.

Changes in China's financial and policy landscape

The rapid development of the offshore RMB market in Hong Kong has created market signals for the Chinese exchange rate and interest rates, while these variables are distorted in the onshore market. An expansion of the offshore RMB market to other centres, such as Tokyo, Singapore, London and Taipei[9] will only strengthen the offshore market's signalling function for the Chinese system, thus making up for its onshore systemic deficiency. Since the RMB traded in Hong Kong is largely market driven, the CNH spot exchange rate and bond yields reflect truer underlying supply-demand forces in the Chinese (and global) system than the onshore markets. The swift growth of the CNH bond market is a reflection of continued opening up of China's capital account, and is thus instrumental for full RMB convertibility eventually.

Continued growth of the CNH bond market will also put more pressure on China to liberalise the domestic bond market. This could, in turn, cost onshore banks their best corporate borrowers. The development could go the Japanese way in 1984, when the rapid development of the euro-dollar and euro-yen markets bid away some of Japan's best corporate borrowers, forcing the Japanese banks to reinvent themselves by lending more to small and medium-sized enterprises (SMEs).

Such development will make a profound change in China's financial landscape where, despite over 30 years of economic reform, SMEs are still starved of credit. A relaxation of the Chinese SMEs' credit constraint will facilitate the growth of the private sector to help productivity growth and economic flexibility in the country's rebalancing effort. These are also the structural underpinning China needs to develop for gaining credibility for the RMB to become a global currency.

From a policy perspective, rapid growth of the RMB offshore market will post regulatory challenges for the Mainland. Despite reforms, Beijing's monetary policy is still quantitative based, with market forces pricing/regulating credit mostly absent. But the growth of offshore RMB markets will erode China's quantitative monetary control. Already, the CNH market in Hong Kong has allowed some Chinese borrowers to skirt onshore liquidity tightening by raising funds offshore and remit them back to China.

This regulatory challenge will only grow with the deepening of RMB internationalisation, putting pressure on Beijing to improve its monetary management in the long term. It needs to shift away from quantitative control for credit and let market forces determine interest rates so as to avoid the conflict between the functioning of the CNH market and onshore monetary policy objectives.

6
China Ready for a Globalised RMB?

Internationalising the renminbi (RMB) is a process of liberalising China's capital account. More precisely, full RMB internationalisation needs full capital account convertibility. Only then will the RMB be trusted and accepted by the world as a global reserve currency. But opening up the capital account involves significant transitional risks which may wreak havoc upon the domestic system. So the relevant questions are whether China is willing to take these risks, and how far has it gone in making the required changes to achieve capital account convertibility and, hence, RMB-nisation.

Judging from China's overall external balance position, China does not face the traditional risks associated with opening up the capital account. However, in terms of domestic preconditions for capital account convertibility, including development in the domestic banking, financial and exchange-rate systems, China falls short of the required progress needed for convertibility in the medium term. To fulfil these preconditions, it will have to push through deep-rooted structural reforms to enhance the role of market mechanism in the Chinese system. This brings up two other questions.

The first one is whether the Chinese authorities are prepared to make those changes that will inevitably weaken the Communist Party's power base. Evidence from the liberalisation process so far and the announced plans by the Chinese authorities show that there was a lack of integrated reform vision for RMB-nisation and that the implementation process risks moral hazard and reform inconsistency.

There is no consensus within the government on how to proceed with capital account liberalisation, let alone the sequencing of removing capital controls and other painful reforms. While yuan internationalisation has been widely discussed in the government, capital account liberalisation and the related interest rate deregulation have been hidden in the shadows.

Hitherto, the steps taken to open the capital account are contingent upon the need for RMB internationalisation. This is, in fact, putting the cart before the horse. Using RMB-nisation to drive capital account liberalisation could lead to missteps in the capital account opening-up process. For example, without China first establishing market-determined interest rates and exchange rates, which are key elements of capital account convertibility, RMB internationalisation could easily go astray.

There is no golden rule for deciding which step, currency internationalisation or capital account convertibility, should come first. Historically, capital account convertibility has preceded the international use of currencies. Some even argue that currency internationalisation simply comes as a by-product of a country's broader economic reforms which underlie capital account liberalisation (Maziad *et al.* 2011).

Arguably, due to China's huge economic imbalances, it should pursue structural reforms to achieve capital account convertibility before pushing for RMB internationalisation. Achieving capital account convertibility essentially means that China needs to deepen domestic capital markets and free up interest rates so that they respond to market signals rather than telephone calls from state planners. But this is a daunting task for the Chinese mandarins.

Without such changes, opening the capital account would be dangerous, as it would create economic shocks through violent capital flows. And without an open capital account, progress on currency internationalisation will be slow. So far, China seems to have put the cart before the horse by pushing ardently for internationalisation but without sufficient capital account liberalisation. To some extent, this strategy has worked, as discussed in Chapter 9. But it is not a sustainable strategy if the fundamentals behind RMB-nisation are not repaired.

Whether the issue is internationalising the RMB or liberalising the capital account, it all boils down to one thing: Let market forces work. This brings up the second, and economically more important, question: Is China ready to allow more significant market forces to work? A case study on Wenzhou suggests no. Leaving the Chinese system in the hands of the market today, given its current state of predatory capitalism on the back of systemic deficiencies and structural distortions, will create chaos and disasters. This reiterates the argument that full capital account convertibility is a slow process, and that fast RMB internationalisation is as much hype as reality. In other words, the RMB is not quite ready to be a global currency yet. That day will come, but it will be a long way down the road.

Not held hostage by foreigners

Capital account liberalisation is a difficult paradox because on the one hand, it often serves as a catalyst for financial market reform and improvement in institutions, especially corporate governance. But on the other hand, it also brings financial volatility from the international environment which often wrecks havoc on the domestic system.

There is no rule of thumb for how to strike a balance between these "collateral benefits" and "collateral damages" of opening up the capital account (Kose *et al.* 2009). The transitional risks cannot be eliminated, but they can be alleviated by having a flexible exchange rate in conjunction with selective and gradual capital account liberalisation measures that are designed to attain certain collateral benefits (Prasad and Rajan 2008).

China's heavily managed exchange rate, which often makes it a *de facto* fixed exchange rate against the USD, has made its situation of capital account opening complicated because it deprives the system of the ability to absorb economic shocks and, hence, makes the economy harder to cope with volatile capital flows. An open capital account with a fixed exchange rate will also erode a country's monetary policy independence, impeding the ability of its central bank to use policy tools such as interest rates for domestic adjustment purposes. Despite its relatively closed capital account, this problem still applies to China because its capital account has become porous due to loopholes and years of economic liberalisation.

The structure of capital flows is a major factor that affects China's ability to prepare for opening up its capital account under a heavily managed exchange-rate regime. The capital structure determines the amount of risk that will hit China when the capital account is opened. On this count, China is safe because not only does it have net capital inflows, but it also has a robust gross capital inflow structure.

Since 2000, FDI has dominated the bulk of China's gross capital inflows. FDI accounts for an average of 63% of China's total external liabilities, while portfolio inflows account for about 10% only. FDI is a preferred kind of capital inflow because it is stable and often brings in technological and managerial transfers. While portfolio inflows tend to bring in the collateral benefits of deepening the domestic equity market, they also inflict high volatility in the domestic system.

The external debt burden is another factor that affects China's readiness to open its capital account under a fixed exchange-rate system. Foreign-currency-denominated foreign debt, especially short-term debt maturing in three years or less, was a major source of vulnerability for the emerging markets (EMs) under open capital accounts in the 1980s

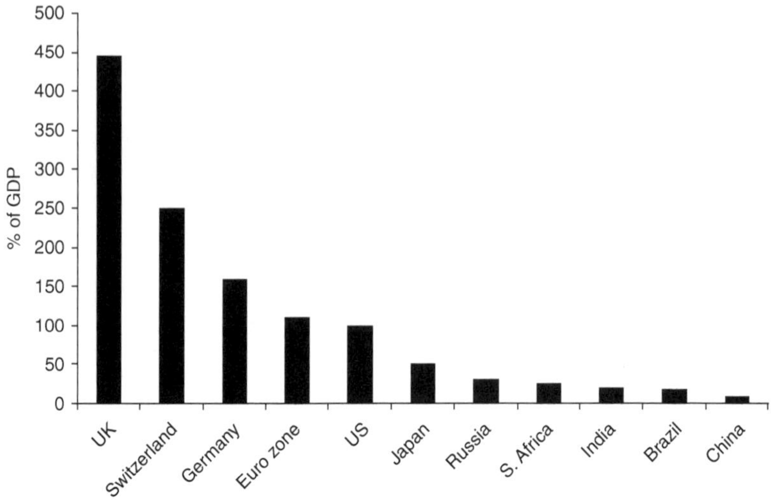

Figure 6.1 Gross external debt comparison (2010)
Source: World Bank.

and 1990s. China scores well in terms of safety on this count. It has the lowest total external debt burden among the major developed markets (DMs) and EMs (Figure 6.1). As a trend, China's gross external debt has fallen from a peak of 18% of GDP in 1993 to 9% in 2010. Overall, China is a net creditor to the world, with net foreign assets amounting to US$1.8 trillion in 2010.

In other words, China has sufficient foreign assets to more than cover not only all its external debt obligations but also its total foreign liabilities. Not all reserve currency economies have such a strong external position. The United States has a huge negative net foreign asset position, amounting to US$2.5 trillion in 2010. The United Kingdom and the Euro area (as a whole) also have negative net asset positions. Other reserve currency countries, namely Japan, Germany (itself as opposed to the whole Euro zone) and Switzerland all have positive net foreign asset positions.

What all this says is that the net foreign asset position of a country is not crucial for reserve currency status. So China's strong and favourable external position is not relevant to the RMB's becoming a reserve currency. It depends on other factors. China's low external debt burden does argue that it would not be held hostage by foreign creditors and investors in case of a financial crisis. It will face very small external risks when the capital account is opened up even before increasing exchange rate flexibility.

Nevertheless, a combination of an open capital account and a fixed exchange rate could complicate domestic macroeconomic policy management by eroding monetary policy independence. This brings in the concern about the first of the three domestic preconditions for moving towards capital account convertibility – a flexible exchange-rate regime with an equilibrium exchange rate.

Wanted: a fair exchange rate

On this front, it is still uncertain how far away the RMB is from its equilibrium value. Perhaps no one knows, as China's economic structure is evolving, data are contaminated and there is no free flow of capital, so that it is not possible to pin down the structural parameters for estimating the fair value for the RMB. But the point remains that a successful transition to an open capital account requires an exchange rate that is close to its underlying equilibrium value. Otherwise, if the capital account is opened when the RMB is significantly under- (over-)valued, it will only lead to violent capital in- (out-)flow, destabilising the domestic system.

As we argued in Chapter 2, the recent evidence of a falling current account surplus in China might not be robust proof for the RMB approaching equilibrium. It could just be a cyclical phenomenon due to a rise in commodity prices between 2006 and 2010 that caused a negative terms-of-trade shock on China. This may be reversed as the commodity cycle turns (when commodity prices fall) so that China's current account surplus may swell again.

China's stubborn trade surplus with Europe and the United States, despite a falling overall surplus, strongly argues that there has been no real change in the trade structure that rebalanced Chinese demand towards domestic consumption. In other words, the RMB's steady appreciation over the years has not shifted China's growth structure to favour imports over exports. So it is doubtful if the yuan's value is approaching equilibrium. Further, years of massive government intervention in the FX market to keep the yuan down strongly suggests that Beijing had done little to make its exchange rate based more on market forces.

China falls short on achieving this precondition for capital account liberalisation that facilitates RMB internationalisation. There are two other preconditions, namely the strength of the domestic banking system and the level of development of the domestic financial markets. Liberalising capital flows poses significant short-term risks if it is not accompanied by domestic financial reforms.

Wanted: a robust banking system

When capital controls are relaxed, typically domestic households and financial institutions will diversify the currency composition of their assets. This will lead to capital outflow from the domestic banking system. If a country's banks are seen as weak, opening the capital account could speed up these outflows, as depositors seek to move funds to the presumed safer foreign countries. This concern is real for China, where bank deposits amounted to almost 200% of GDP in recent years, and over 90% of these deposits are in the hands of the households and non-financial corporations. As argued in Chapter 2, there has been a rising incentive for capital flight (Figure 6.2). If the capital account is opened today, these deposits are likely to migrate out of the domestic banks, triggering systemic risk in the economy.

Such a rising incentive for capital flight speaks volumes about China's own people losing confidence in the domestic banking system. This seems to contradict the evidence that Chinese banks have become stronger after some reforms since the mid-1990s. Back then, the largest banks were technically insolvent,[1] ultimately requiring massive government capital injection and write-off of non-performing loans (NPLs) (Lardy 1998, Ma 2006).

The financial health of the Chinese banks seems to have turned around since the early 2000s. Total NPLs of the major commercial banks have

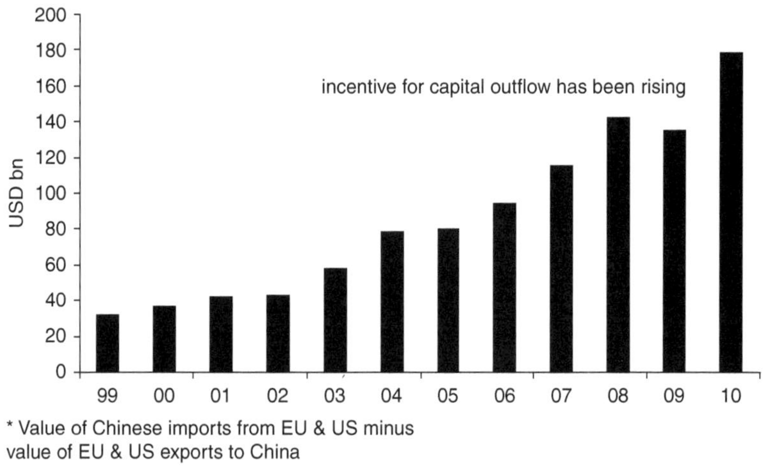

Figure 6.2 Rising incentive of capital flight (approx. by Chinese importers' over-invoicing*)

Source: CEIC.

come down from over 18% of outstanding loans to about 1% in the first half of 2012, according to official data. Though NPLs will be rising again as a result of the 2009 lending binge,[2] they are not likely to go back to the levels seen in the 1990s and early 2000s. In the early 2000s, only eight domestic banks, accounting for a mere 0.6% of total banking assets, met China's minimum 8% capital adequacy requirement. By the end of 2009, all banks in the Chinese system met, and most surpassed, the minimum requirement. Last but not least, the Chinese banking industry recorded an average 16.2% return on equity in 2009 and a 0.9% return on total assets (CBRC 2010). This compared favourably with international banks, such as Standard Chartered and HSBC.[3]

The Chinese authorities have also tightened up their monitoring effort and control over NPLs. The China Banking Regulatory Commission (CBRC) has modelled China's loan classification scheme on international standards and has imposed tough provisioning requirements. By the end of 2009, Chinese banks had an average loan loss provisioning ratio of 155% of total loans, up sharply from 20% in 2003 (CBRC 2010).

Improvement in Chinese banks' profitability over the past decade seems pretty solid, right? Not necessarily. The caveat for this improvement lies in China's interest rate control. The People's Bank of China (PBoC) has controlled the lending and deposit interest structures for many years. Only partial liberalisation has been implemented at a snail pace. Chinese banks were allowed to lend at rates higher than the government benchmark lending rate as early as 1997, when they could charge customers up to 20% more than the benchmark rate. It took seven years for Beijing to scrap this lending rate ceiling, which it did in 2004.

In the same year, China also introduced limited downward flexibility for bank lending rates by allowing banks to lend at a maximum of 10% discount to the benchmark rate. Eight years later, the lending rate discount was increased to 30% of benchmark rate in 2012. But the deposit rate remained under strict control. It was only in mid-2012 when banks were allowed a small leeway to offer deposit interest rates up to 10% more than the official rate.

Such interest rate control has helped inflate banks' earnings because the central bank sets a floor on bank lending rates but a cap on the deposit rates. Thus, the PBoC directly controls the banks' spread between their lending and deposit-taking activities. According to the Chairman of the Bank of China, Xiao Gang, due to interest rate control, the net interest margins[4] that Chinese banks had earned from RMB lending were almost double what they would have earned in a free interest rate environment (Xiao 2010).

Assuming Mr Xiao's estimate was right, this means that banks' net interest income would have fallen by half if interest rates were freed. And since net interest income accounted for 65% of the Chinese banks' profits in 2009, this means that the PBoC's interest rate control could have inflated banks' profits significantly also. Similarly, freeing interest rates would cut the Chinese banks' return on equity and return on assets sharply. In other words, China's controlled interest rate environment has distorted the true profitability picture for the Chinese banks, whose earnings would be sharply less if interest rates were freed. The Chinese banks are much weaker than what their headline earnings numbers show.

This is likely part of the reason why China has shown no interest in liberalising interest rates throughout all these years. The central banks' interest rate control is also a form of financial repression that imposes an implicit tax on the Chinese household (Lardy 2008). Simply, the deposit interest rate cap that banks offer to savers is depriving them of purchasing power just like a tax on income does.

All this also means that Chinese banks are highly dependent on households for staying in business and reaping a profit because 1) their net interest margins are much higher due to the deposit interest rate cap, and 2) households are the dominant source of funding for banks. If the capital account is liberalised under the current distorted system, the banks may likely be forced to raise deposit rates to prevent large deposit outflow from the household sector. This will be hugely negative on bank earnings.

All this brings back the arguments for why interest rate liberalisation is so important as a precondition for capital account convertibility. First, interest rates need to be liberalised to reduce, and eventually eliminate, financial repression before opening the capital account. Otherwise, depositors may likely shift their funds out of the domestic banks, inflicting a liquidity crisis in the system. Second, interest rate liberalisation is essential in the longer term to strengthen China's banking system. A controlled interest rate environment not only stifles competition but also eliminates banks' incentive to price credit risk correctly and operate on a commercial basis. The final result is misallocation of capital under controlled interest rates.

Wanted: deep capital market

A third precondition for capital account liberalisation is well-developed financial markets. The capital market offers an alternative funding avenue for the corporate sector, thus providing competition for domestic banks to speed up their restructuring process and transition to operating on a commercial basis. It also offers an alternative investment avenue for the Chinese savers, thus facilitating the elimination of financial repression.

Development of a deep debt market will make it easier for China to ease restrictions on capital flows. This is because deep markets can easily absorb large capital inflows without creating asset bubbles in the local markets. If the local capital market is underdeveloped when the capital account is opened, domestic firms may borrow funds from abroad to eschew the local distortions and restrictions. This may create the risk of currency and balance-sheet mismatches, just like what Asian banks did before the 1997–8 Asian crisis.

While China has a significant government bond market in terms of absolute size, which is in fact the largest in Asia and the third-largest in the world by market capitalisation,[5] its corporate debt market is not well developed. While the size of the Chinese government bond market is more than a third of China's GDP, the corporate bond market is about 10%, according to Asian Development Bank data[6] (Figure 6.3). The amount of funds raised through the corporate debt market is small, especially when compared with the amount of corporate bank loans.

In terms of issuance, the majority is dominated by a handful of large state-owned institutions, such as the Ministry of Railroads and the major banks. At the end of 2009, non-financial corporate bonds outstanding amounted to less than 3% of GDP. But bank loans were about 100%. Deprived of funding opportunities from the capital market, most non-financial corporates are dependent on bank loans for their financing needs, which is another symptom of financial repression in China. The Chinese bond market is also fragmented, with the inter-bank bond market accounting for some 97% of total issuance and trading, and the stock exchanges accounting for less than 3%[7] (Figure 6.4).

Meanwhile, the FX forward and swap markets have developed relatively fast compared to the bond market, though trading is still strictly controlled. An over-the-counter forward market was started in 1997. But with the RMB exchange rate fixed against the USD, and the vast majority of foreign trade transactions denominated and settled in USD, transaction volume in the forward market is light. Following the de-pegging of the RMB from the USD in mid-2005, China launched an inter-bank FX forward market, and in 2006 formally introduced the FX swap market.

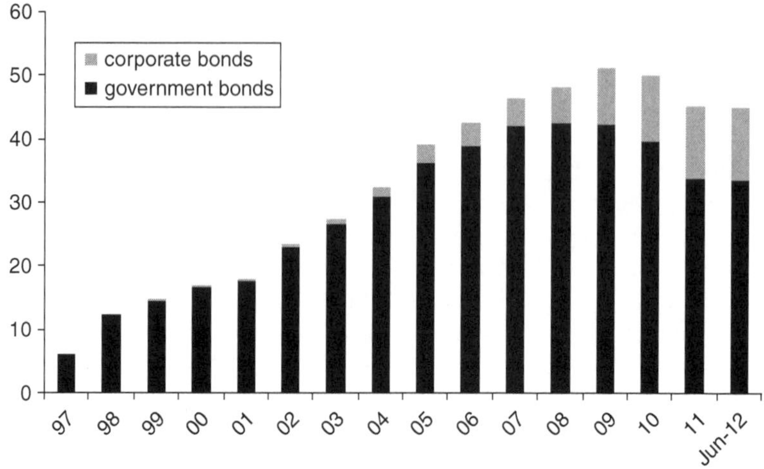

Figure 6.3 Chinese bond market (% of GDP)
Source: ADB, author.

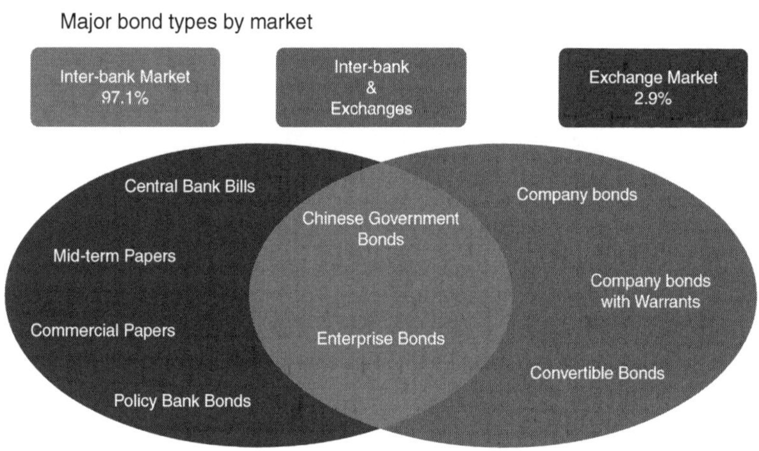

Figure 6.4 China's fragmented bond market
Source: author, official data.

These markets, though small by international standards, have allowed Chinese importers and exporters to hedge their FX risk. This has been especially crucial since 2012, when the PBoC widened the trading band for the RMB against the USD from 0.5% above and below the daily central bank benchmark rate to 1%, thus introducing more volatility to the RMB/USD FX trading.

Lack of vision and a coherent strategy

Technically, China is still some way off from fulfilling the preconditions of capital account convertibility, though it enjoys a strong external position that will help contain the external macroeconomic shocks once when the capital account is opened. Further, it seems that the Chinese authorities do not have a coherent vision for their capital account liberalisation and RMB-nisation strategies. At the time of writing, and after a few years of pushing for RMB internationalisation, there is still no consensus from Beijing for the timing to start the capital account liberalisation process, let alone the sequencing of removing capital controls, interest rate liberalisation and capital market reform.

Measures such as allowing offshore RMB to be invested back in China as FDI, allowing Chinese firms to borrow offshore and expanding QFII and RQFII quotas are hailed by the market as capital account opening steps to foster RMB internationalisation and deepen the CNH (offshore RMB) market. Yes, these are indeed essential steps which are needed. But no, they are not conducive to deepening the internationalisation process and the CNH market unless accompanied by opening the capital account for capital outflows.

FDI in China denominated in RMB has picked up steam since its approval in late 2011 (Figure 6.5). Beijing has also expanded the QFII and RQFII quotas[8] for foreign participation in the domestic A-share market and scrapped all restrictions on Chinese exporters using RMB to settle foreign trade transactions.[9] It has vowed to speed up approvals of QFII and RQFII investors in an attempt to add depth and market discipline to the domestic capital markets. These are necessary but not sufficient steps for deepening RMB internationalisation. For the RMB to be truly internationalised, China needs to be a net importer of goods and services, and a net exporter of capital. This will allow the yuan pool to grow and circulate offshore. It is thus imperative for China to open the capital account for both inflows and outflows.

However, most of the liberalisation efforts since 2009 have been focusing on absorbing offshore RMB back to China. Of course, these measures act to improve two-way trading for the RMB between onshore and offshore markets and to create offshore RMB assets, both of which are crucial for creating non-trade RMB demand offshore. But the RMB pool also needs to grow offshore to generate trading and investment activities for deepening the CNH market and the RMB-nisation process. If not balanced by capital outflow, this asymmetric capital account opening will shrink the offshore RMB pool and, thus, will not be conducive to the growth of the CNH markets.

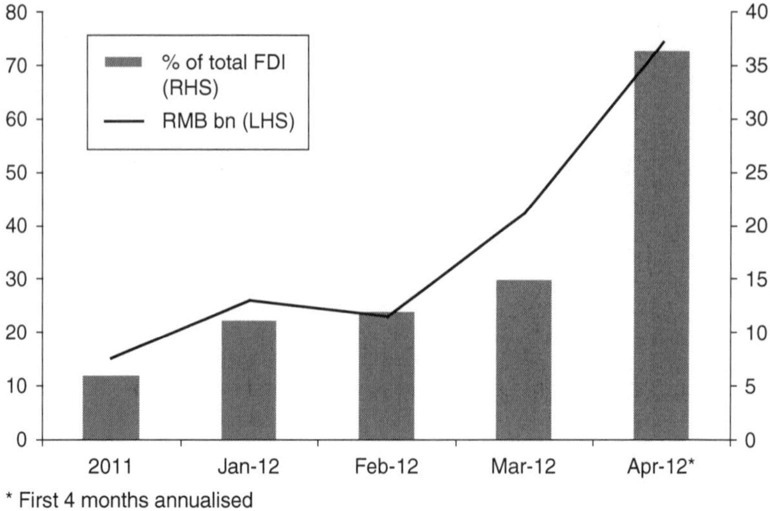

Figure 6.5 RMB FDI in China picking up steam
Source: Reuters, author.

However, full capital account convertibility will bring daunting challenges to China and loosen the authorities' political power base. These challenges have generated hot debates among the Chinese leadership on the roadmap for capital account convertibility. One camp argues for no more delays on liberalisation because the reform conditions are ripe, while another camp calls for slow opening due to the potential risks involved. It seems that Beijing has chosen to take the easy reforms first and leave the difficult ones later. This is reflected by the PBoC's three-stage proposal to capital account liberalisation, which it announced in February 2012.

The first stage would relax controls on direct investment outflows in one to three years. The second phase would relax controls on overseas lending of the RMB to boost internationalisation in three to five years. The longer term (five to ten years) would relax controls on capital inflow first and then outflow, and gradually open the domestic asset and capital markets to foreign participation. The last step of full RMB convertibility would be left to some unspecified time frame in the future.

The first two stages will only involve some cosmetic regulatory changes without changing the root structure of the system. The third phase may involve some structural changes, as it will bring in some global market forces to the domestic market. The most crucial change – full RMB convertibility – that requires major structural changes to the system is left to the indefinite future, according to this proposal. Other important changes, including interest rate liberalisation and reforming corporate governance and the legal and institutional frameworks to support deeper structural reforms have been left unspecified.

Note that this is only a proposal by the PBoC. It is not a policy, and has not been mentioned again, let alone implemented, since its release in February 2012. Rather, the internationalisation and liberalisation efforts have shown confusion and inconsistency, which may also increase the risk of an incoherent reform strategy.

A notable example is Beijing's encouragement of the mainland companies to tap the CNH market for funding. On the one hand, this leads to offshore RMB asset creation which facilitates CNH market development. On the other hand, it raises the question of why Beijing would want to encourage the corporates to borrow offshore while there is surplus saving at home. If the mainland companies cannot get local funding because of the PBoC's policy tightening, allowing them to borrow offshore and bring back the funds is allowing them to skirt onshore liquidity tightening, thus eroding the PBoC's policy tightening effects.

Meanwhile, Chinese borrowers have dominated the CNH market (Figure 6.6). About a third of CNH bonds were directly issued by Chinese firms in Hong Kong in 2011. There was no breakdown for the certificate of deposits (CD) issuers (which accounted for another 32% of total issuance), but the majority of it was expected to have come from Chinese banks in Hong Kong. This means that mainland Chinese entities accounted for at least half of the total CNH issuance for the year. True internationalisation of the RMB would require diversified investor and issuer bases. This underscores the insufficiency of Beijing's fostering RMB-nisation.

Expanding the QFII and RQFII quotas is expected to bring institutional and long-term investors and market discipline to the domestic market. But these expanded quotas account for only about 1.3% for QFII and 0.7% for RQFII of the A-share market capitalisation. This raises doubts about their effectiveness in making any material impact on the Chinese capital market, especially when the underlying system and market structure/distortions have remained unchanged.

Granted, liberalising portfolio and other short-term investments has the potential of causing large and sudden capital flows. Lessons from other EMs, including those in Asia in the late 1990s, show that foreign capital can come pouring in via foreign portfolio investment or local

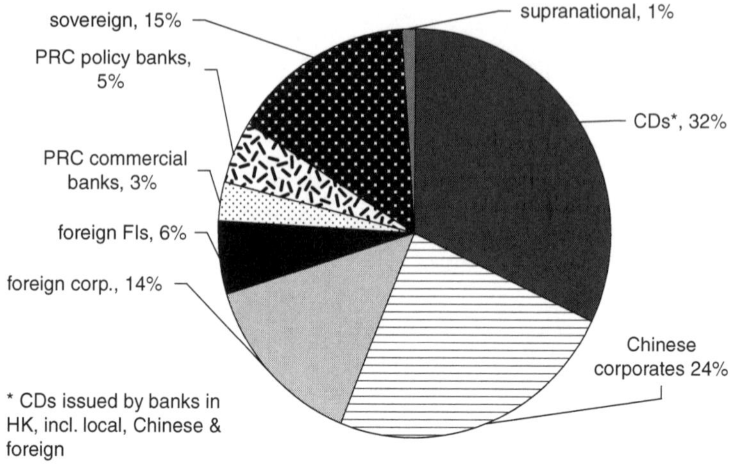

Figure 6.6 Breakdown of CNH bond issuers (2011)
Source: HSBC, Bloomberg.

banks and companies stepping up foreign borrowing. Without a strong banking system and sound regulatory and supervisory frameworks, the influx of foreign capital could result in capital misallocation, fuelling asset price bubbles and economic overheating.

Nevertheless, the steps taken to liberalise China's capital account and internationalise the RMB have insufficient depth and no coherence. The capital account liberalisation measures are piecemeal, driven by the RMB-nisation desire but often without a long-term vision. Conspicuously absent from Beijing's discussion and actions are interest rate deregulation and measures to deepen the domestic bond market. This can be attributed partly to the potential economic risks involved, and perhaps mostly to the threat of the Communist Party's losing control of the economy.

If the capital account is opened in the absence of interest rate liberalisation, a deep capital market and a flexible exchange-rate mechanism, it runs the risk of threatening monetary policy efficacy (Prasad, Rumbaugh and Wang 2005, McCauley 2011). With free capital movement, it will be impossible for the PBoC to continue to control the exchange rate and at the same time have monetary autonomy (i.e. control of domestic interest rates). This is the "Impossible Trinity" theorem,[10] which states that it is impossible to have monetary autonomy, control of the exchange rate and an open capital account all at the same time (Figure 6.7). Beijing can only choose two of the three.

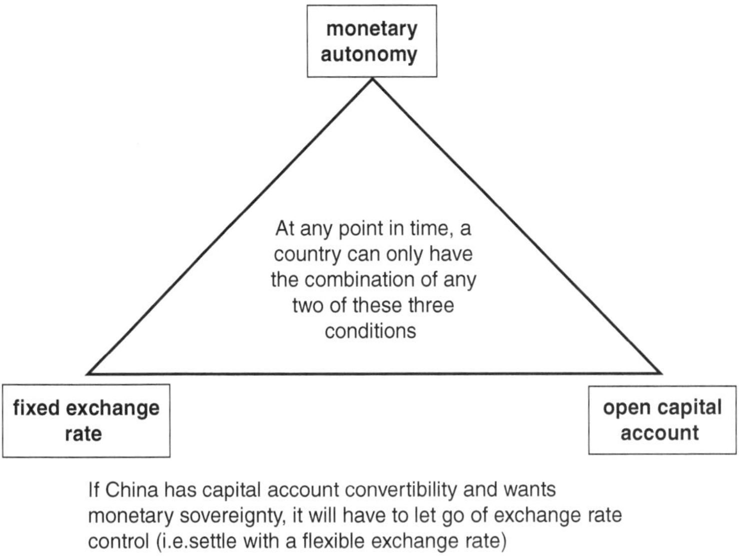

Figure 6.7 The impossible trinity

Source: author.

If it wants monetary autonomy under an open capital account, it will have to let go of controlling the exchange rate. To gradually relinquish exchange-rate control and focus on domestic monetary control, it is necessary to fully deregulate domestic interest rates to ensure an efficient policy transmission mechanism for economic management. Similarly, deepening the domestic bond market can enhance monetary policy impact by absorbing volatile capital flows and minimising their disruption on the conduct of monetary policy.

Can China let market forces work?

RMB-nisation and the capital account liberalisation behind it are all about letting market forces work with minimal government intervention. If the RMB were to become a global reserve currency, the key question, after over 30 years of economic reforms and the ardent push for RMB internationalisation in recent years, is whether China is ready to let the market work so as to gain credibility for and global acceptance of the RMB. In other words, can the Chinese government really let go of control? A look at Wenzhou, a municipality in the coastal province of Zhejiang in Southeast China, gives us a clue to make an assessment.

The quick answer is no! Chaos would erupt, with the domestic economy suffering unpleasant unintended consequences if China were to allow full market forces to work under its current predatory capitalism with significant systemic deficiencies in the institutional, legal, policy, social and regulatory aspects.

Wenzhou is a laboratory for Beijing to experiment with market forces. So it is not subject to most of the policy constraints that the rest of the country faces. It is known for its vibrant private sector, active underground finance (which is also called the curb market or informal lending or shadow banking system) and speculative investment, especially in the property market. This city accounts for only 1% of China's GDP, but reportedly has over 400,000 private, mostly small, firms that rely mostly on the curb market to function. Wenzhou is both a centre for export-oriented manufacturing and a private financial hub, with private firms accounting for 96% of Wenzhou's industrial output and 80% of its employment.

Wenzhou's private small firms are precarious, with an average lifespan of only two years, and only 10% of them are able to access bank loans. But due to its entrepreneurial success, the city is cash rich, with many local entrepreneurs eager to provide private funding outside the banking system. This combination of strong "animal spirit" (credit demand) and cash-rich financiers (credit supply) under financial repression has created a hotbed for underground finance in which market forces work.

Rampant underground finance

While the curb market exists everywhere in China, Wenzhou arguably has the most rampant underground lending. It is a showcase of China's financial fault lines associated with market forces. PBoC survey data show that almost 90% of households and 60% of firms in Wenzhou participate in the curb market, which accounted for a quarter of formal bank lending in the city as of mid-2011. Curb market interest rates are market driven and range between ten times to over a hundred times the official lending rates. Wenzhou's PBoC branch estimated that only about 35% of the curb market lending went to real business in 2011, compared to over 90% in 2004. The rest went to asset punting and black market lending.

Anecdotal evidence shows that during 2008–9, when monetary policy was loose, banks turned a blind eye to risk; they even helped firms "cook" their books to get extra leverage. Many of the loans went into phoney businesses, notably re-lending in the curb market that fuelled

Wenzhou's asset bubble. The party ended in tears when shrinking exports and Beijing's monetary tightening hit Wenzhou hard in 2010. Bank loans dried up; troubled firms had no choice but to turn to money brokers and private lenders, who at times of extreme financial stress charged more than a 100% interest rate in the curb market. Even many credit guarantee companies went under.

These credit guarantee companies provide loan guarantees and advisory services to SMEs and individual customers. China has around 23,000 such firms. They are a product of market demand and play a significant role in facilitating SME financing, lowering banks' lending costs and assisting in bad loan recovery. However, due to a lack of industry standards and poor regulatory supervision, many credit guarantee firms operate in an opaque and unprofessional manner. Most Wenzhou credit guarantee firms also undertook their own lending operations and made risky investments. So when they went bankrupt, they also led to a cascading series of defaults in the city.

While the curb market helps improve capital allocation according to market forces, its rapid development needs proper control. The fact that over 65% of curb market loans have gone into phoney and wasteful investments suggests that underground finance in Wenzhou backfired and posted systemic instability risk to the economy. The risk may come in several ways.

First, banks have direct exposure to the curb market, as part of the curb lending has been funded by bank credit. The PBoC estimates that at least 10% of Wenzhou's underground lending came from direct bank credit. Second, when a business fails because of curb market borrowing, it will not be able to pay its formal creditors and suppliers. Third, due to their opaque operations and exorbitant interest rate charges, the curb market will aggravate counterparty risk during times of uncertainty, exaggerating liquidity crunch and its macroeconomic damages.

When the Wenzhou financial crisis broke in September 2011, the central authorities were alarmed by its potential systemic impact. In response, Beijing launched in March 2012 a pilot reform to legitimise informal lending in Wenzhou, with the aims of restoring order to the teetering informal credit market by increasing transparency and oversight and allowing private capital to participate in the formal financial sector.

In this pilot reform, informal money lenders are encouraged to register as private lending institutions with the blessing of the state. Wenzhou locals are allowed to be licensed as micro-lenders by setting up private lending companies and rural credit cooperatives, and invest in the city's financial institutions; they are also allowed to invest up to US$3 million directly in non-bank entities overseas without the need for a government intermediary and going through the usual cumbersome approval procedure. Beijing has also asked the local authorities to speed up capital market development and encourage the transfer of property rights among private companies.

If implemented properly and nationally, these are significant moves towards resolving financial repression in China. Legitimising underground finance could speed up economic growth by improving capital allocation towards the country's cash-starved private sector entrepreneurs. The move to allow direct overseas investment is also a right step towards opening China's capital account.

Reform vision and incentive problems

Just as Wenzhou is a showcase of China's financial fault lines, its pilot financial reform is a reflection of China's lack of reform coordination and problems of incentive incompatibility and moral hazard. Encouraging the setting up of private lending institutions is right, but there is too much emphasis on establishing a large number of small private institutions. The pilot scheme aims at setting up 100 micro-lenders by the end of 2013, compared to 28 as of June 2012. Indeed, China tried a similar aggressive plan earlier by trying to set up 1,027 village banks nationwide over the 2009–11 period. But only 726 were established. There is always an implementation problem, despite policy directives.

Meanwhile, this "quantity" approach runs against Beijing's aim of building a strong regulatory framework and a sound financial system. Too many micro-institutions will be difficult to supervise and create rent-seeking[11] opportunities, which is the last thing China's financial system wants. They may pose a risk to financial stability, as many of them tend to exceed their mandate through inappropriate activities.

There is also no incentive for the informal lenders to register as formal private lending institutions. Formal lending institutions have too many regulatory constraints, including government lending directives and interest rate control. Indeed, the lack of interest rate liberalisation has significantly eroded the usefulness of this Wenzhou pilot scheme. By remaining informal, private lenders enjoy much more freedom than the formal institutions.[12]

Further, lenders prefer not to register their loans in order to avoid paying taxes. Borrowers, especially entrepreneurs, prefer to keep their financing secret to prevent their private capital from being tripped up in legal recourse in case of financial problems/disputes. All this has given rise to incentive incompatibility problems between the government and Wenzhou's financial sector.

The moral of the Wenzhou story is that China is not ready to let market forces work due to significant incentive problems and systemic deficiencies. The whole macro backdrop for RMB-nisation is made complicated by the lack of reform vision and a coherent liberalisation strategy. Strong vested interest and rent-seeking activities have aggravated the daunting challenges and policy dilemmas that China is facing. Contrary to the market hype about big steps in RMB internationalisation creating enormous profitable opportunities, China's capital account convertibility and RMB internationalisation will and can only proceed slowly.

7
Creeping Reforms Raise Systemic Risk

Structural reforms are the essential elements behind full renminbi (RMB) convertibility and, hence, internationalisation. So far, China has been pursuing gradualism in its economic reform and financial liberalisation programmes. This approach has resulted in a creeping reform pace, but it has also avoided major risk blowouts. However, there are reasons to believe that China's reform process has come to a crossroads, as its economy has become more market orientated and complex. This economic evolution has contributed to China's confusing and inconsistent reform moves in recent years. This, in turn, underscores our argument that the Chinese leadership lacks a coherent reform vision (see Chapter 6), which will adversely affect the RMB-nisation process going forward.

Trying to understand China's reform moves is like trying to understand the fickle mind of a cat. It moves back and forth, is illusive and often contradictory. On some occasions, China has demonstrated a strong resolve to make tough choices during tough times by choosing a mix of Keynesian and Austrian post-crisis solutions. This has arguably increased both domestic and foreign confidence in building a sustainable Chinese economy to commensurate with a globalised RMB and a reserve currency status. A wave of financial reforms since late 2011 has also led many to argue that RMB internationalisation would be speeding up and the RMB would become a reserve currency in the not-too-distant future.

These are more hype than realistic expectations, in my view, because China does not have enough structural reforms to back up a globalised RMB yet. In fact, China's structural reforms have shown a confusing stop-go pattern since the late 1990s. The 2008–9 subprime crisis has disrupted the structural changes that the leadership has pushed through, and there are no signs that they have been restored. The ongoing European crisis has added uncertainty, which may delay China's economic restructuring further. Beijing also seems to be reluctant to push for faster and deeper structural rebalancing behind the RMB-nisation process because it involves uprooting the old economic management model and weakening the Communist Party's power base. All these issues contradict the strong reform resolve that the leadership exhibited earlier. They also do not bode well for the optimistic view that the RMB would become a global reserve currency soon.

Financially, what ails China is not the cost or availability of capital, but the allocation of it. Cutting interest rates, as many had called for during the 2011–12 economic slowdown, will only compound the problem of cheap money fuelling asset bubbles and delaying structural rebalancing. The good news is that Beijing seems to be recognising the problem and trying to rectify it by implementing some reforms that amount to interest rate and financial liberalisation. This is structurally positive for China's efforts to build a global currency.

The bad news is that these are measures implemented only at the margin of the system, and they are plagued by moral hazard. This calls into question the resolve of the Chinese authorities to pursue deeper reforms than what have been done hitherto in order to deepen RMB-nisation. Half-hearted reforms will only keep China's medium-term reform and growth outlook uncertain. This is also not conducive to internationalising the yuan.

Since allowing greater cross-border RMB flows and capital account liberalisation are mutually substitutable, these two steps of reform must be done at the same time and prior to RMB internationalisation. Without an open capital account, RMB-nisation can still proceed, but only with great limitations. These are the cruel realities that the redback is facing on its way to becoming a global currency. The road is tougher, more complicated and longer than many have thought.

Reform resolve, how strong?

In the first half of the 1990s, China's economy went through a huge investment bubble. The macro data were impressive: Average GDP growth between 1992 and 1995 was a stunning 13%, driven by sustained money and credit growth averaging annual expansion rates of 40% and a dramatic rise in investment-to-GDP ratio, with inflation soaring to 26% a year. Even more extraordinary was the micro backdrop. The banking system back then was less than ten years old, and the only borrowers in the system were state-owned enterprises (SOEs) with a similarly short history of budgetary independence. The inexperienced central bank was essentially passive for much of the period with no monetary tools at its disposal. The result was a frenzy of ill-advised capacity investment in almost every sector of the economy, with a sharp expansion in various unregulated and levered derivative instruments also.

When the authorities, under the premiership of Zhu Rongji,[1] finally put an abrupt end to the party by introducing monetary discipline and curtailing lending in 1995 and 1996, the hangover was predictably severe. Reported capacity utilisation in some industries dropped to as low as 30%; net profit for the entire state industrial sector was barely positive in 1996 and 1997, with tens of thousands of companies reporting heavy losses, and corporate investment demand fell precipitously as a share of output. Official data were spotty in the 1990s, but market estimates suggest that underlying non-performing loans (NPLs) were over 50% of total bank assets at the peak, making China essentially a record holder in Asia, rivalled only by Indonesia at the height of the 1997–8 Asian crisis.

Faced with this situation, guess what the Chinese government had done? Keep in mind that the bursting of the China bubble was a very different phenomenon from the crisis in Asia at the time. China was a closed economy with little overseas financial exposure, and as a result there was no retreat of foreign creditors and no threat of a currency collapse. So China could have gone for using heavy fiscal expansionary measures to avoid a sharp economic downturn, while buying time for a very "soft" and gradual deleveraging of the corporate sector with no aggressive capacity shakeouts and job losses.

However, then Premier Zhu Rongji chose a tough route to tackle the problems. The government did go the Keynesian way by expanding fiscal spending considerably to prevent GDP growth from contracting, with a spate of new budgetary outlays and investment projects. But it also followed the Austrian discipline by taking the painful decision to close down inefficient state factories and shops and lay off tens of millions of state workers. This marked China's decade-long SOE restructuring and resulted in a sharp improvement in economic efficiency in subsequent years.

In the process, tens of thousands of SOEs were partially or fully shut, with over thirty million workers laid off with a minimal monthly severance stipend. Enterprise plant and equipment facilities were either discarded outright or consolidated into viable firms for phased-in disposal.

As a result, the share of loss-making state-controlled enterprises in the industrial sector has fallen persistently and dramatically (Figure 7.1), while profits of the state-controlled firms have risen sharply (Figure 7.2) since the late 1990s.

All this has shown that uniquely among its Asian counterparts, China chose a combination of Keynesian (fiscal expansion) and Austrian (strict monetary discipline and economic reform) policy as its post-crisis solutions. The beauty of this approach lies not in the nature of growth when times are good, but rather in the policy choices when things are

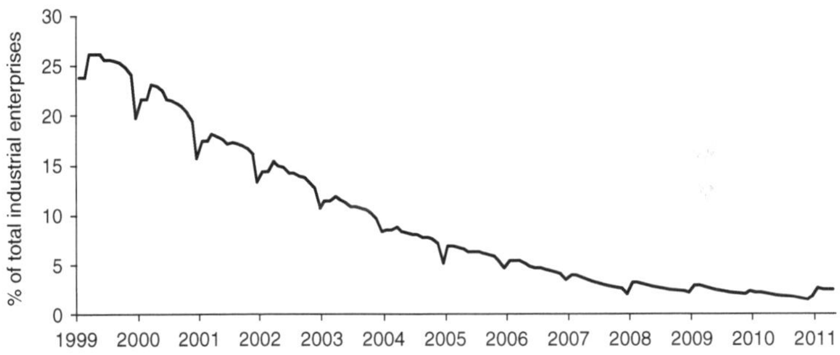

Figure 7.1 Share of loss-making government-controlled enterprises*
Source: CEIC, author.

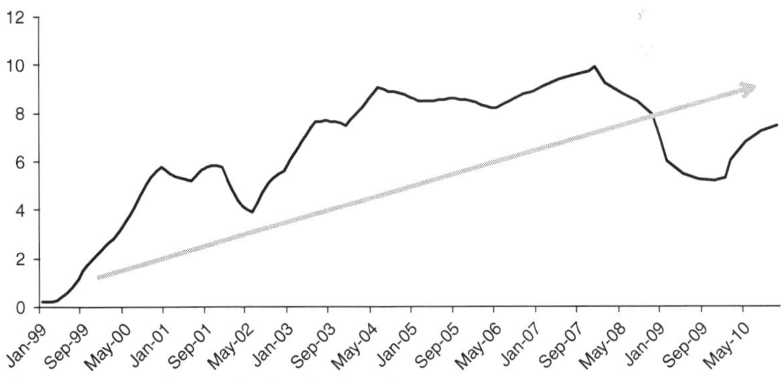

Figure 7.2 Profit-to-cost ratio (state-controlled firms*)
Source: CEIC, author.

bad. That is why China was able to achieve a rapid reduction in excess capacity and a rapid return to growth after the 1997–8 Asian crisis.

This is impressive, and should lay the foundation for the eventual ascent of China to being a global power with the RMB as a reserve currency. Well, not so fast. China had not had any major structural reforms for more than a decade after Zhu Rongji's SOE restructuring effort. The next reform wave came only in the years between 2004 and 2006, and it was focused on the financial sector, with the real side of the economy left untouched.

In this reform effort, the banks' lending rate ceiling was scrapped, and they were allowed to lend at interest rates up to 10% less than the People's Bank of China's (PBoC's) benchmark rate. This was the first interest rate liberalisation in China's modern economic history. There were also other capital market reforms implemented, but they were timid experimental moves (Lo 2012). The reform agenda has then gone quiet again, as policymakers have focused on short-term survival policies to deal with the global and regional financial crises, including the US subprime crisis in 2008–9 and the European sovereign debt crisis in 2010, which is still ongoing at the time of writing.

So does China have a reform resolve? Yes. But how strong is it? We do not know because the signals are mixed. What seems to be clear is that the Chinese leadership that took over the helm since the turn of the millennium seems to be less determined to make painful changes than their predecessors. They seem to be more keen on implementing financial reforms than making changes in the structure of the real economy, as if the two types of reforms are mutually exclusive. This, of course, is incorrect, as financial reforms without underlying structural economic changes will go disarray. But Beijing has made some surprising financial reform moves recently, which have raised hope for more reforms to come.

New financial reform initiatives

A slew of financial liberalisation measures in 2011 and 2012 generated market excitement that the authorities might be in for some serious changes. Some market players even argued that these reforms would lead to fast capital account convertibility (with some expecting capital controls to be lifted by 2015) and give RMB internationalisation another big push.

Even the government seemed to be giving out such a signal. The National Development and Reform Council (NDRC) announced in early 2012 the medium-term targets for making Shanghai a centre for RMB products, credit pricing, trading and settlement by 2015. These targets have crystallised Beijing's plan of making Shanghai an international financial centre by 2020, and they have also prompted speculation that China's capital account would become fully convertible in just a few short years.

Following the encouragement of mainland corporates to borrow in the CNH market and the allowance of using RMB as a FDI currency to invest in China in the second half 2011, Beijing surprised the market by announcing in March 2012 a pilot scheme to allow residents in Wenzhou city[2] to invest directly abroad and in local (Wenzhou) financial institutions. Then in April, it expanded the RQFII and QFII quotas by RMB50 billion and US$50 billion (adding to the original quotas of RMB 20 billion and US$30 billion), respectively. It also widened the USD/RMB trading band to ±1% from the daily central rate set by the PBoC from ±0.5%.

In another surprise move in mid-2012, the PBoC started allowing onshore banks to offer saving deposit rates up to 10% higher than the official benchmark rate (no deviation from the benchmark rate was allowed before) and offer lending rates up to 30% less than the official benchmark rate (while the previous discount was only 10%). The CSRC also launched a high-yield bond market by adopting a registration, but not approval, system which greatly simplified the issuance procedure. Despite all this effort, China's bond market development remains nascent, with corporate bond financing accounting for about 17% of all new bank loans.[3]

Of particular importance in these reforms are the Wenzhou experiment, the widening of the RMB trading band and the relaxation of the interest rate control. The latter is the first interest rate liberalisation effort since 2004. Financial markets in Hong Kong have jumped for joy, seeing these moves as big leap towards RMB internationalisation. In fact, they are only incremental changes and small steps towards capital account liberalisation. But they do carry some long-term important implications for China's financial sector.

Big implications

While the steps are small, they show Beijing's willingness (though not necessarily with a strong resolve, see below) to address some of the structural flaws in the system. In particular, the changes in the domestic interest rate structure, the gradual opening up of the domestic bond market, the emergence of the trust companies and the banks' wealth management products (WMPs) all represent steps, albeit small, towards financial liberalisation.

Regulatory reforms have facilitated the growth of the domestic bond market, which saw bond issuance up 60% year-on-year by volume in the first half of 2012 when all other forms of financing were sluggish. China has three bond regulators,[4] who have long and cumbersome approval procedures for bond issuance.[5] But this has started to change since 2012, when the PBoC started simplifying and speeding up the approval procedure. This has put pressure on the other two regulators to follow suit.[6]

Meanwhile the emergence of trust companies has created competition with banks for deposits, and has prompted many banks to develop WMPs to attract/retain deposits by paying higher yields than saving deposits. Though WMPs account for only about 12% of total bank deposits, and the total assets of the trust companies are only about 4% of total banking assets,[7] they are already creating competitive pressure by challenging the banks' dominance. All these suggest that China's financial landscape might be in for some structural changes.

On the interest rate liberalisation front, the cost to the banks was significant. On the surface, the two interest rate cuts in June and July 2012 only cut banks' margin by 6 basis points[8] (Table 7.1). However, since banks were eager to lend amid slowing credit demand, they were motivated to offer loans at the floor rate (30% below the official benchmark rate). Banks were also in competition with trust and mutual fund products for funds, so they were motivated to offer deposits at the ceiling rate (10% above the official benchmark rate) to attract funds. Lending at the floor rate while paying depositors at the ceiling rate means that the banks' margin had effectively been squeezed by a total 150 basis points (Table 7.1), not 6 basis points (Figure 7.3).

In fact, banks' average margin have been cut to 294 basis points (or 2.94 percentage points) from 332 basis points since the first interest rate liberalisation in 2004 if they had lent at the floor rate at all times. The point is that significant margin squeeze should prompt the Chinese banks to improve efficiency. Greater interest rate flexibility, by China's standard, should also help improve capital allocation. But the fact that interest rates are still being controlled means these "liberalisation" moves are marginal.

The creation of a high-yield (junk) bond market and the advent of the trust companies and WMPs (which are not subject to loan quota restrictions) offer non-bank funding avenues for the unprivileged non-state firms and help improve capital allocation. Meanwhile, junk bond yields are market driven. The Chinese trusts extend loans or make equity investment and package them into fixed-income products, while the

Table 7.1 Structural change of bank margins

Interest rate (%pa)	Before 1st rate cut on 8 Jun, 12	Btwn the 1st & 2nd rate cut (5jul)	After 5 July, 12
Benchmark 1-year lending rate	6.56	6.31	6.00
Benchmark 1-Year deposite rate	3.50	3.25	3.00
Benchmark spread	**3.06**	**3.06**	**3.00**
Change in spread		0.00	*–0.06*
Cumulative change			*–0.06*
Lending rate floor	5.9	5.05	4.20
Deposit rate ceiling	3.5	3.58	3.30
Lending floor deposit ceiling spread	**2.4**	**1.47**	**0.90**
Change in spread		***–0.93***	***–0.57***
Cumulative change			*–1.50*

Source: CEIC,author.

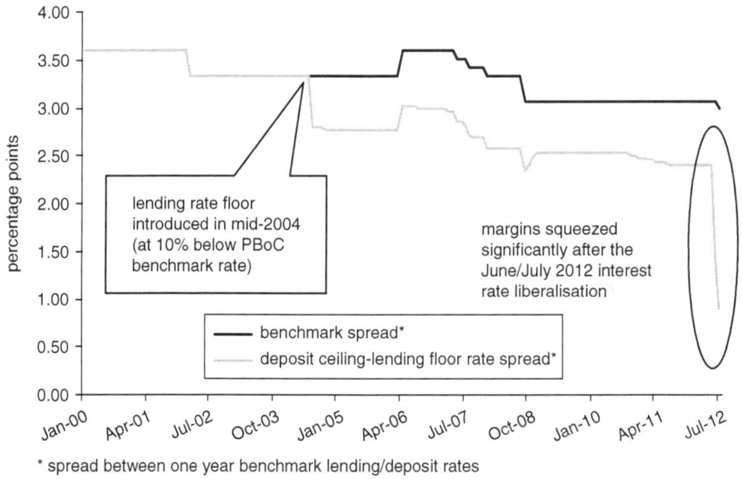

Figure 7.3 Chinese bank margins
Source: CEIC.

WMPs sold by banks are loans repackaged as short-term investment products. Both the trust products and WMPs eschew the official deposit rate cap and offer higher yields to savers. All these moves are indirect ways to liberalise interest rates and help ease financial repression.

One needs to be realistic with these changes though. While they do carry a positive signal that Beijing is getting on with financial reforms after a long rest, they are only experimental moves, but not big steps to accelerate capital account and currency convertibility, as some in the market have speculated. Unless there is a strong conviction to push through more and deeper structural reforms, full capital account convertibility, a prerequisite for full RMB internationalisation, is not likely in just a few years. But quicker and deeper reforms, especially those in the real economy, may prove to be a tall order because of the clash between the macro reform drive and the micro distortions that act to erode the macro incentive.

On the macro front, as discussed above, China has exhibited some strong resolve to make tough choices during tough times. It has also made some impressive progress in restructuring the economy towards the right direction (see the next section). However, on a micro basis, the Chinese system is still plagued by serious incentive distortion and excessive rent-seeking[9] problems. They act to erode the structural improvement from the macro front. Correcting these micro problems is more difficult than rectifying the macro woes because the former are deep rooted in the nerve centre of the Chinese political economy and vested interest bases (see Chapter 10).

The lack of bank lending to the non-state firms (Figure 7.4) and the creeping pace of interest rate liberalisation reflect the deep-rooted distortions in the system and the huge growth obstacles facing the private

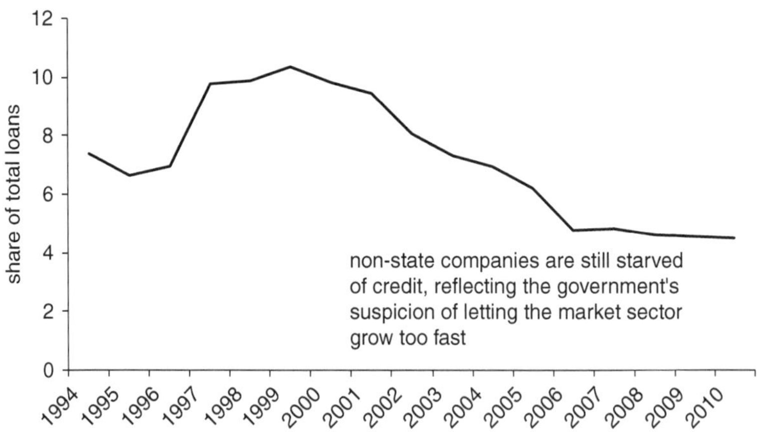

Figure 7.4 Bank lending to non-state companies
Source: CEIC.

sector in China. One of the NDRC's targets is to raise the share of direct financing through the capital market to 22% of total financing in the economy by 2015. This may help relax the private sector firms' budget constraint and contribute to long-term growth sustainability by allowing them to tap the capital market for funding. However, it remains uncertain how fast and how deep Beijing will allow the capital market to develop to compete with the banks.

More crucially, the NDRC had no plans for interest rate liberalisation in its 2015 targets, despite its stated goal of making Shanghai a financial centre for setting credit pricing benchmarks. Interest rate control is distorting capital allocation incentives and spurring the development of a shadow banking system, which lay at the heart of the US subprime crisis and is creating potential systemic risk in China (see Chapter 6).

This distortion creates macro policy problems because the lending frenzy through the shadow banks frustrates the PBoC's monetary control by offsetting its tightening policy. Do not bet on fast interest rate liberalisation, however, because this involves other deep reform elements, including liberalising the banks from government control and allowing rapid growth of the capital (including derivatives) market with transparency, which Beijing may not be ready to do swiftly yet.

Structural shift disrupted

On the real side of the economy, there were also some trends developed between 2005 and 2008 showing that China might be moving away from export- and investment-led growth to consumption-led growth. This structural rebalancing is essential for full capital account and RMB convertibility by helping to rectify the distortions in, and thus minimise the shocks to, the underlying economy when the capital account is fully opened up. During this period, export and investment growth were falling while domestic consumption (as approximated by retail sales) was rising. But these trends were disrupted by the US subprime crisis and have not resumed their pre-crisis development trend since then (Figure 7.5).

The ongoing (at the time of writing) European crisis may further disrupt China's rebalancing effort. The risk is that those initial signs of structural shifts before the subprime crisis may not have been entrenched, since Chinese consumption as a share of GDP has not turned up (Figure 7.6). This implies that more needs to be done to reboot structural shifts going forward.

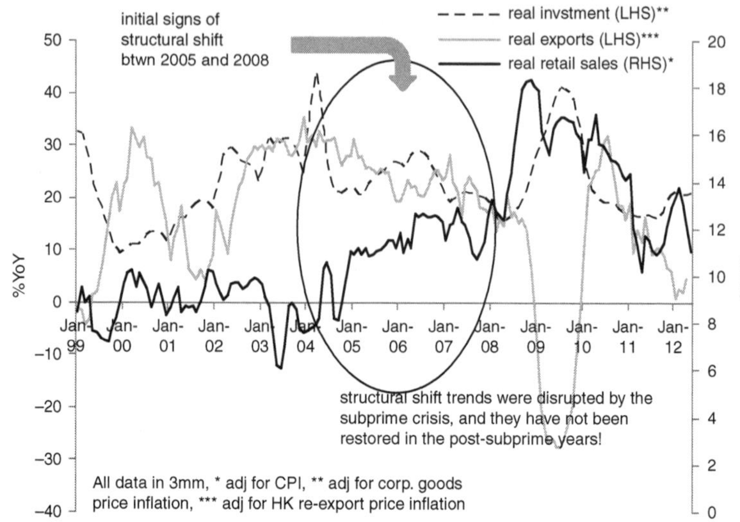

Figure 7.5 Signs of structural shift disrupted
Source: CEIC, author.

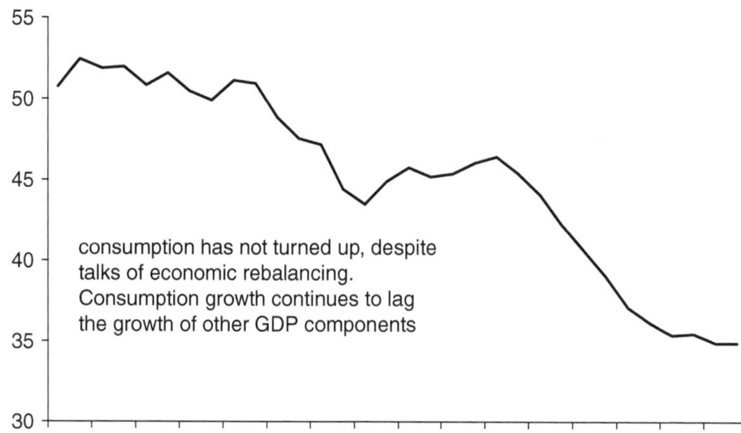

Figure 7.6 Chinese consumption as % of GDP
Source: CEIC, author.

Meanwhile, high on Beijing's radar screen in the structural transition process is the risk of capital flight. If it becomes a serious issue, capital controls would remain, and the capital account and RMB convertibility efforts would be delayed. Indeed, this risk is real. The worsening of

China's over-invoicing problem may be indicative of an ever-increasing incentive for capital to leave the country if the floodgates were opened (see Chapter 2).

Perhaps because of this risk, Beijing has been slow in liberalising capital outflow. But such a policy is myopic. Provided there is a mechanism to allow orderly outflow, liberalising capital outflow would not only reduce China's reserve accumulation, which has become a macroeconomic policy problem, but would also generate more "collateral benefits." These benefits will include providing Chinese households with opportunities to diversify their saving portfolios internationally and stimulating domestic reforms by creating competition for domestic banks that currently have an excessive reliance on domestic households for funding and on government monopoly for profitability.

China's initiatives to encourage corporate capital outflow so far have been limited to large state-owned firms and focused on a narrow set of sectors, notably natural resources. For the RMB to take on a more international role, FDI outflows should involve more participation from the private sector. This underscores our argument in Chapter 6 that China needs to balance its RMB-nisation effort by allowing capital to flow out as well as allowing it to flow back in.

However, in the absence of a deep domestic financial market and the support of relevant supplementary market liberalisation policies, the benefits of capital account opening for capital outflow will be limited. For instance, Chinese households are only allowed to send an equivalent of US$50,000 a year out of the country. This is a large amount for an economy with a per capita income of less than US$5,000 a year. But the absence a well-developed securities market makes it difficult for most households to take advantage of the opportunity to pursue international diversification of their saving portfolios. The incentive will, thus, be to send capital out of the country illegally, underscoring the risk of capital flight that acts to delay RMB convertibility.

In this context, liberalising capital inflows may help reduce the risk of capital flight by allowing foreign investors to play a role in developing deeper and fairer domestic financial and asset markets to regain public confidence. This along with the entry of foreign banks into the domestic system will increase competition in the banking sector which will, in turn, benefit private savers and borrowers.

Moral hazard and systemic risk

In the development of the domestic bond market, including the junk bond market, the government has implicitly guaranteed all local bonds, including LGFV (local government financial vehicles) borrowing, by directing banks to bail out companies on the brink of default. That is why there has not been any domestic bond default so far. This has encouraged a belief that debt defaults are impossible, just like the belief earlier that IPO prices would always rise after listing. While this implicit government guarantee makes the newly created junk bonds, WMPs and trust products attractive to investors and thus facilitates their launching, it also creates moral hazard among investors/savers, bond issuers and product distributors.

The ultimate goal of financial liberalisation is to have market-driven interest rates to allow efficient capital allocation in the economic system. But to achieve this, Beijing will have to uproot China's economic management model. China's financial and monetary policy development has been based on a closed financial system. This has allowed Beijing to ignore market discipline and keep interest rates low and stable without having to worry about arbitrage and volatility of fund flows; to manipulate economic growth using policy discretion without having to worry about damaging bank asset quality; and to bail out banks and state companies without concern about the negative consequences of capital flight and exchange-rate volatility. These benefits are only possible with a closed capital account, which shields the domestic system from foreign influences and market discipline and locks up local funds at home.

Opening the capital account and removing capital controls will change the game. Beijing would have to remove many of the domestic financial restrictions that have given it the power to "manage" the economy at will. It would have to integrate the domestic capital market into the world markets. But this would lead to the end of its state-directed banking practices. The "Impossible Trinity" (see Chapter 6) would come into play and force Beijing to choose between controlling the exchange rate and the domestic interest rate.

In a nutshell, Beijing would have to conduct economic management under free capital flows, a new task that it has not been exposed to before. Most important, and perhaps worst of all, these changes would have to come more or less at the same time, raising the risk of policy misstep.

The potential impact of deeper financial reforms on the Chinese banking system represents another risk. Given financial repression, especially on the deposit side, freeing interest rates will lead to a sharp rise in deposit rates relative to lending rates, thus hurting banks' net margins. Opening up the capital markets will bid deposits away from the banks, leading to potential systemic instability. Finally, opening up the capital account will just give the Chinese savers one more avenue by which to leave the domestic banking system.

So there are reasons to expect Beijing to go slowly on financial liberalisation that encompasses open capital account and free RMB convertibility. Whether the reform glass is half full or half empty, time will tell. Indeed, China's future reform process is at a crossroads, which argues that Beijing's past practice of small steps and gradualism may need to change to adapt to the changing domestic and external structural dynamics.

Reform at a crossroads

All this means that Beijing's incremental and experimental (arguably piecemeal) reform approaches may become increasingly untenable. In some cases, they could even create risks of their own. The increasing complexity of the economy means that those critical reforms relating to broad macroeconomic issues, like exchange-rate flexibility and capital account liberalisation, cannot be isolated to specific geographical areas.

As the economy becomes more sophisticated, some of its factors of production become more mobile, and more able to take advantage of economic distortions in the system. If China continues with a slow approach to change, the reform process will carry the risk of being overwhelmed by the rent-seeking activities of these mobile factors. In others words, from now on China may need to take bigger strikes to push for bigger reform steps. But this requires a strong resolve.

Crucially, China will face many challenges if it is to move beyond middle-level income status into the club of high per capita income countries. Evidence shows that no country in the modern world has managed to grow persistently without relying on private enterprise and decentralised private markets. Examples include the Soviet Union before its collapse, China before market reforms began in 1978 and Cuba since Fidel Castro's revolution in the late 1950s. China's private sector has led its dominance in textiles, electronics and other consumer and producer goods. It has followed the model of the "Asian Tigers" – Hong Kong, South Korea, Taiwan and Singapore – and relied heavily on exports produced by cheap labour. In the process, China has accumulated huge foreign reserves, as Taiwan, Japan and other rapidly growing Asian economies did in their development years.

Developing countries, such as China, need not get everything right to grow rapidly through exports to the developed world. They only need some strong sectors that use world markets to fuel overall growth. Japan's rapid growth from the 1960s to the 1980s was led by a highly efficient manufacturing sector. Yet at the same time, Japan also had a large and inefficient service sector and an agricultural sector that was riddled with subsidies and inefficient incentives.

That situation is similar to China today, which still has inefficient SOEs with excessive employment and low productivity despite the restructuring in the 1990s. Its agriculture sector still has serious incentive distortion problems due to price controls and government intervention. No doubt, the importance of the SOE sector has fallen over time, but even local Chinese economists estimate that it still controls directly or indirectly about half of the non-agricultural economy.

A notable example is the state-controlled finance sector that makes cheap loans to large and often inefficient SOEs. While most of the downstream price controls have been lifted, the economy still suffers from strict control in many important areas, such as energy prices, credit and migration, which creates structural barriers to efficient growth.

However, this is not to say that a bold move such as leaping from a controlled system to a democratic economy is the way to deliver sustainable growth for China. For example, India experienced rapid growth after it began to shed a socialist orientation in 1991 and encouraged private initiatives in investment. However, economic progress has also been remarkable under autocratic rule, such as Chile under Augusto Pinochet, Singapore under Lee Kuan Yew and Taiwan under Chang Kai Shek.

The point is that there is no correlation between democracy, which is closely related with person freedom, and rapid economic growth. So it is unfair to argue that China's growth will be doomed if it does not move towards a democratic system as part of a drastic reform programme. In fact, an argument can be made that China does not need to move towards a democratic system (Bell and Li 2012).

Access to global markets will allow poor countries to grow rapidly, but only up to a certain extent. While much has been made of the fact that China's aggregate GDP surpassed that of Japan in 2010, what all that means is that China's per capita GDP is only about 10% of Japan's, since China's population is ten times more than that of Japan. Despite its great economic advances, China still has a long way to go to catch up with a rich country. One may argue that China is quite different today after over 30 years of reforms. Even its locally owned government enterprises are more efficient than the national SOEs. This is mainly because local government enterprises have to compete against each other, while national SOEs often receive monopoly positions granted by the government.

However, competition among government enterprises is only a partial substitute for competition among privately owned enterprises because the latter has a much stronger element of market discipline than the former. So if China wants to really open up and internationalise its currency along the way of its economic evolution, it will have to take economic reform to a higher level by reducing the influence of the SOEs, especially the national ones, and allowing a bigger role for market discipline in allocating resources. This is not to say that the market does not fail; it does at times. But experience has shown that no country can sustain strong growth without giving market forces a dominant hand in the economy.

Developing countries improve their technological base by importing technologies and knowledge developed in advanced economies. That is why China has encouraged FDI, in part to get access to the technologies of the advanced countries, including Japan, Europe and United States. Allowing the usage of RMB as a FDI currency dose not really help attract further FDI and foreign technologies to China. Using technologies developed by others is still important in China's future reform programmes, but it must also develop more of its own technologies to advance further, in order to acquire the quality of growth that would underpin a globalised RMB going forward.

Beijing will need a strong resolve to implement deep-rooted reforms in the coming decades to achieve all this. With some enlightened leadership, along with greater faith in competition and market forces, China stands a fair chance to achieve its ambition of truly globalising the RMB and making it a reserve currency. However, to some senior leaders in the government, they need a leap of faith in the market. This is where the risk of derailing reforms and the RMB-nisation effort comes in, because that leap of faith is directly related to the resolve of making fundamental changes to the old system that will involve relinquishing control. This is also where political reform has come into play (see Chapter 10).

RMB-nisation without open capital account

Is capital account liberalisation really that crucial for RMB internationalisation? That is a question often asked by the financial market players who are keen on capturing investment and business opportunities stemming from the RMB internationalisation process. Many wonder whether, if China keeps the capital account closed or limits it to just a very small opening, RMB-nisation can proceed and still deliver the expected economic and financial benefits? The quick answer is yes, but only to a limited extent.

Since RMB trade settlement can still take place with capital controls, internationalisation of the currency can continue as far as trade settlement (Chinese importers settling foreign trades in RMB) pushes it. But that means that the use of RMB for non-trade purposes and, hence, the internationalisation process, will be severely limited without an open capital account (see Chapter 5). To put it differently, if foreigners can only receive RMB through the trade channel, the amount of RMB liquidity made available in the offshore market will only be a small fraction of the potential RMB demand. As a result of the limited liquidity flow from the trade channel to the offshore market, the use of RMB as a source of financing will also be constrained.

In the end, RMB as a reserve currency will be virtually impossible because illiquidity in the offshore RMB market cannot accommodate the large size of transactions conducted by the sovereign reserve managers. This will reduce the incentive for central banks to hold RMB in their reserves and for sovereign fund managers to hold yuan assets in their investment portfolios. In other words, capital controls are a key barrier for RMB internationalisation, but the offshore market is a great facilitator. The development of an offshore market and open capital account are two key elements for internationalising the RMB.

Essentially, a well-developed offshore market with centres across different time zones is needed for a major global currency, because such a currency needs the facility of 24-hour trading around the world to cater to non-residents' transactions. Regarding the RMB, non-residents will only be willing to use and hold it if they have the convenience and ability to trade RMB and RMB-denominated products in the offshore market across different time zones. Meanwhile, full capital account convertibility will allow non-residents to obtain and trade RMB from non-trade channels. This is another key incentive for foreigners to hold RMB and RMB-denominated assets and use the yuan as a funding currency.

As Beijing's designated offshore RMB market, Hong Kong, has been instrumental for the RMB-nisation process. But there is also confusion about Beijing's true intention in China's financial liberalisation plan by playing Shanghai and Hong Kong off against each other. This has created jitters among some Hong Kong bankers, who wonder if the territory's interests will eventually be compromised by Shanghai displacing Hong Kong, despite Beijing's RMB-nisation rhetoric for promoting Hong Kong in the short term. In the following chapter, we shall explore these issues in the context of the potential rise of other offshore RMB centres, namely London, Singapore and Taipei.

8
RMB-nisation Needs Offshore Market

Some argue that the removal of capital controls and the opening up of the domestic capital market would be sufficient to internationalise the renminbi (RMB). The development of an offshore RMB market would play no role in the process. They cite the experience of some countries which opened their capital accounts and domestic capital market to foreign participation without developing an offshore currency market at all. This is a misunderstanding. There is little evidence to support the case of currency internationalisation without an offshore market. The experience that these observers cite refers to the countries' financial liberalisation process, but not currency internationalisation.

For our discussion, we define an offshore market as an aggregate of different offshore centres for trading an asset or a financial instrument (RMB, in our case) across different countries and time zones.[1] These offshore centres, in turn, tend to exist in jurisdictions with political stability, legal and institutional transparency, professional operations, sound financial infrastructure, availability of talent, free capital and information flows, low taxes and a simple regulatory framework.

Hong Kong is, arguably, best suited to be the prime offshore RMB centre (known as the CNH market in the financial community), at least before China achieves full capital account convertibility, despite raising competition from other centres such as Singapore, Taipei and London. International trade (through Chinese import payments) will remain the key source of offshore RMB accumulation before China fully opens up its capital account. Hong Kong has a natural advantage on amassing RMB more efficiently than other centres. It also has a first-mover advantage on developing RMB trading infrastructure, and enjoys political support from Beijing.

Nevertheless, there are still doubts about Hong Kong's role in Beijing's grand plans for financial reform. The central government has stated that it wanted to make Shanghai an international financial centre by 2015 (by implication displacing Hong Kong's role). This has also spurred speculation on full capital account and RMB convertibility in just a few years. Not so fast. This is because the deep-rooted reforms that are needed to achieve these goals will involve making changes to the nerve centre of the Chinese political system and the vested interests. There can be division of labour between Hong Kong and Shanghai in China's road to full RMB internationalisation. The two cities do not have to resort to cut-throat competition.

There is also a debate on the need for developing offshore RMB business in the onshore market in China. The market's views are split, and Beijing does not have a policy stance on this issue. The general sense is that developing offshore RMB business in China is not urgent, or even not necessary, for internationalising the RMB. The domestic offshore business can wait until the offshore market is fully developed. The United States is an example, with its offshore US dollar (USD) business being developed onshore almost 20 years after the birth of the Eurodollar market.

Finally, although China is developing an offshore (CNH) RMB market, it has designed tedious regulations to segregate it from the onshore (CNY) market. This creates market inefficiency, and underscores our argument earlier that China needs to work more on developing a coherent reform vision for its RMB-nisation strategy. As long as market segregation remains, CNH/CNY market convergence is unlikely.

Offshore centres are needed

There has been a debate over the need for developing an offshore market as part of the RMB-nisation effort. Some have argued that to achieve currency internationalisation, removing capital controls and opening the domestic capital market would be enough. There is no need for developing an offshore currency market. This is wrong. If a particular currency is to become a global currency, it needs an offshore market as a catalyst and a facilitator.

International experience shows that offshore currency market and offshore currency business in the domestic market were developed alongside the currency internationalisation process of several major currencies. For example, the USD internationalisation was accompanied by the development of both the Eurodollar market (with London as the prime offshore centre) and a domestic market for offshore USD business in the United States (through the International Banking Facilities, or IBF). The internationalisation of the Japanese yen (JPY) was also accompanied by the development of the Euroyen market (with key centres in London and Singapore) and the domestic Japan Offshore Market (JOM). Last but not least, the development of the offshore market for the Euro (with major trading centres in London, New York, Singapore, Tokyo and Hong Kong) has been crucial for its internationalisation.

To see the importance of the offshore currency market, consider the following facts: In 2010, of the total USD FX trading volume (including spot, forwards, swaps, options and other derivative instruments), 80% were transacted outside the United States. For the Euro and JPY, about 77% and 72%, respectively, were traded outside the home markets. By comparison, over 80% of the RMB spot and forward FX transactions took place onshore in China, and FX derivatives hardly exist in any meaningful sense. This situation is not compatible with an internationalised RMB.

Some may counter that there were countries that did not rely on offshore markets at all, but just liberalised their capital accounts and opened their domestic capital markets to foreign participation. But note that this is so either because these countries were not aiming at promoting the international usage of their currencies (for example, Singapore) or because the currencies of these countries (for example, Brazil, South Korea and Mexico) did not have the potential to become a global currency due to their economic insignificance in the global context.

Under such circumstances, opening up their capital accounts has to do with their goal of financial liberalisation, but not currency internationalisation. Even with full capital account convertibility, these countries use other major currencies, such as the USD, euro and JPY, for international trade settlement, foreign investment and pricing of commodities instead of their home currencies.

So international evidence does not support the view that currency internationalisation does not need the development of an offshore market. A more accurate interpretation of these small countries' experience should be that an offshore market is not needed for their move towards capital account convertibility, which is not related to any currency internationalisation motives in their context. Indeed, an offshore market is essential for a global currency for the simple fact that it needs to be traded 24 hours a day.

For a currency to be accepted internationally for global trade and investment, the trading/investment counterparts will want to be assured of a convenient, safe, credible and low-cost market for transactions. Crucially, it needs to be traded across all time zones, i.e. 24 hours a day in the context of any particular centre. Since an internationalised currency is used for global trade settlement, international commodity pricing, financing and investment, and FX reserves around the world, most of these transactions will be done between non-residents of third countries/parties unrelated to the domestic economy. It is obvious that these trades can only be transacted effectively in an offshore market with centres spanning across different time zones.

A specific use of international currencies is called the "third-party usage," which trades in the offshore market. The USD is a good example. Between 50% and 75% of global USD FX transactions are classified as third-party usage that arises and trades outside of the United States. Regarding China, third-party RMB usage may arise when someone borrows RMB outside China, then swaps it into another currency for usage in a third country outside the one where the borrowing originates. Or it may arise when someone buys/borrows RMB in the offshore market to invest in RMB-denominated products in the offshore market. Finally, it may also arise when someone obtains RMB to pay for goods and services outside of China. These transactions cannot be effectively done without an offshore RMB market.

An offshore market is also essential for domestic monetary management reasons, although it may also erode the effectiveness of quantitative-based monetary policy, like in China (see Chapter 5). The usage of a global currency, such as the USD, in international markets is primarily unrelated to the domestic economy of the issuing country. For example, offshore USD deposits amount to almost half of the United States' broad money supply (M2). If there were no offshore market and all these deposits had to be held onshore, the massive number of cross-border transactions for trade financing, investment, third-party usage and hedging by non-residents in other countries would lead to huge cross-border capital flows, creating massive FX and interest rate volatility and administrative and macroeconomic policy burdens.

The relevance of all this to China is clear. The development of an RMB offshore market will allow the overseas supply and demand forces to be cleared offshore, thus minimising the unnecessary volatility in the domestic system. To catch up with the modern world, China also has to abandon its quantitative-based monetary management and allow market forces to determine the price of credit. This will help avoid the potential conflict between the functioning of the offshore RMB market and domestic monetary policy objectives (see Chapter 5). The conflict arises because the offshore market is market driven, but the onshore system is controlled. Making the functions of both onshore and offshore markets based on market forces will naturally resolve a lot of the policy conflicts.

The offshore RMB market

China has been trying to nurture the development of an offshore RMB market, albeit in timid steps. It has designated Hong Kong to be "the" offshore RMB centre as a start, though there is also limited RMB trading in London, Singapore and Tokyo. Since 2011, Beijing has entered into discussions with Singapore, Taipei and London to develop more offshore centres. This is a right move. To truly internationalise, the RMB will need to capture a broader base of international demand than the trade liberalisation measures have promoted (see Chapter 5). Creating more offshore centres is conducive to generating more offshore RMB demand.

As a region, Asia has an edge over the developed markets in developing offshore RMB centres. This is because China runs a large trade deficit with Asia (Figure 8.1). So when China settles foreign trades with its Asian counterparts in RMB, more yuan are paid and accumulated

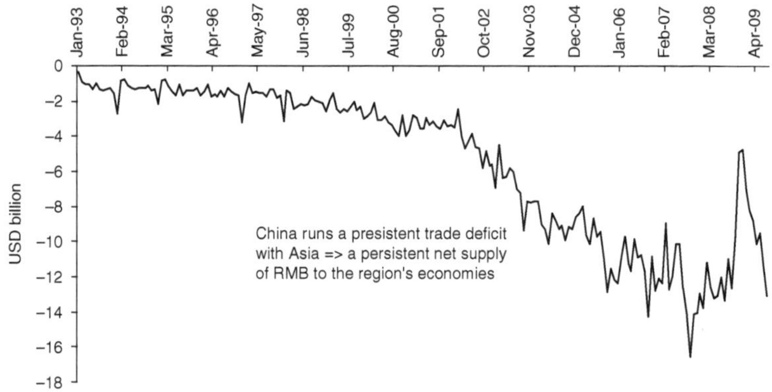

Figure 8.1 China's trade balance with Asia
Source: CEIC.

in the Asian system than are received and absorbed back to China (as Chinese imports from Asia are larger than exports to the region). In contrast, since China runs a large trade surplus with the developed markets, notably Europe and the United States, more RMB are received and flow back to China than are paid and left in the developed world when China settles foreign trades in RMB.

Among all the potential offshore centres, Hong Kong is best suited to be the leading hub. It will likely remain the prime offshore RMB centre in the years to come, despite the emergence of other centres. To put Hong Kong's competitive position in perspective, look at London, which is bidding to be another offshore RMB centre. London was established as the first euro (offshore) dollar market in July 1963, when the investment community tried to avoid the 15% interest-equalisation tax imposed by the United States on the outflow of onshore dollars. Despite the emergence of other euro dollar centres in Europe, North America and Asia, London has remained the prime euro dollar market in the world.

Hong Kong enjoys three significant advantages over other offshore centres: 1) it has a natural advantage of accumulating a critical mass of RMB; 2) it has a first-mover advantage on building up RMB trading infrastructure and 3) it has Beijing's political support. These factors will create inertia for offshore RMB trading in Hong Kong and strengthen its CNH development.

Critical mass of offshore RMB

Before China achieves full capital account convertibility, international trade settlement will remain the key way for accumulating RMB offshore. The pool of offshore RMB comes from foreigners accepting yuan from Chinese importers as the trade settlement currency. This is what happens in Hong Kong, which executes over 80% of all offshore RMB trade settlement for China. Since Beijing started promoting the RMB as a trade settlement currency in mid-2009, RMB trade settlement has soared (Figure 8.2) from an average of RMB40 million a month in 2009 to over RMB150 billion in 2012. Ninety percent of this RMB trade settlement came from Chinese importers demanding payments in RMB.

All these RMB inflows have manifested itself in soaring RMB deposits in the Hong Kong banking system, from RMB895 million in 2004, when the record started, to over RMB550 billion in mid-2012, or 8% of total deposits in Hong Kong. But it is noteworthy that almost all of this increase in RMB deposits came at the expense of other foreign currency deposits,[2] as Hong

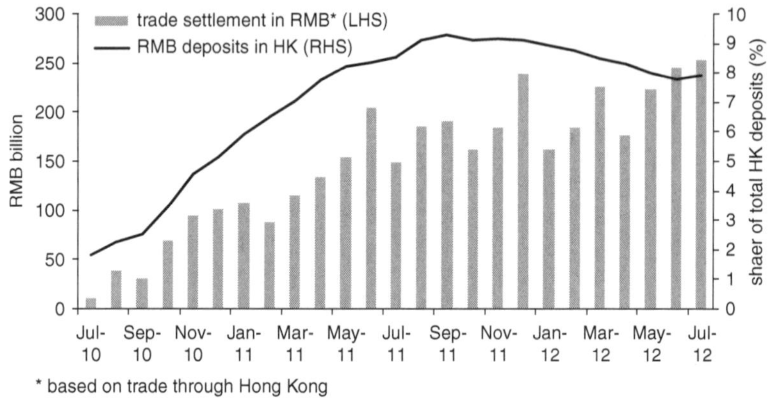

Figure 8.2 RMB accumulation in Hong Kong
Source: CEIC.

Kong depositors bet on RMB appreciation and so switched out of other foreign currency deposits into RMB (see Chapter 4).

Hong Kong has a natural tendency of accepting RMB from Chinese importers because it is part of China; it is a financial reform laboratory for China; and it is the biggest exporter to China compared with Singapore and London. This is equivalent to saying that China imports the largest amount of goods and services from Hong Kong among the three economies. Thus when the Chinese importers pay in RMB, Hong Kong accumulates the largest amount of RMB in its system.

Indeed, Hong Kong's exports to China account for an average of 16% of all Chinese imports since 2005. However, the same cannot be said of the other two potential offshore centres. First, their exports to China are small. Singapore's and the United Kingdom's exports to China only account for an average of 3.0% and 0.6%, respectively, of China's total imports since 2005 (Figure 8.3). Second, why would Singaporean and British (and other trading partners') exporters want to settle in RMB when it is not fully convertible; when there are no effective tools for hedging RMB risk; and when there are no investment vehicles for parking or investing the huge RMB trade proceeds?

Since Singapore is the trading hub for the Association of Southeast Asian Nations (ASEAN), we should also take into account its accumulation of RMB through ASEAN's exports to China. Indeed, ASEAN's exports to China account for an average of 11.0% of all China's imports since 2005, but it is still much less significant than Hong Kong's. Further, Hong Kong accumulates all the RMB in one single market, but Singapore

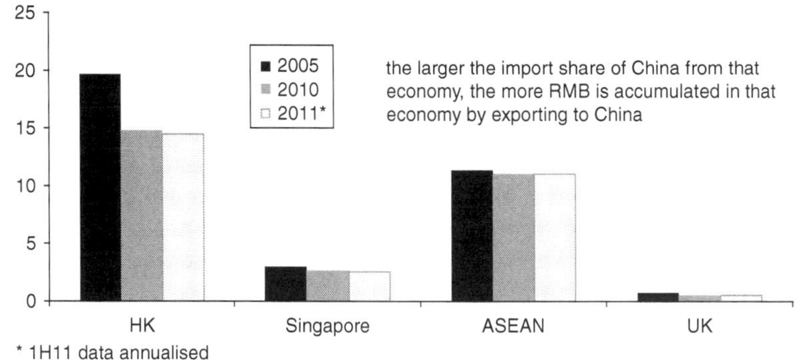

Figure 8.3 Chinese imports from Hong Kong, ASEAN and the United Kingdom (as % of China's total imports)

Source: CEIC, author.

has to accumulate through nine other ASEAN neighbours. So arguably, Singapore suffers from market fragmentation and has a less efficient cost structure for developing an offshore RMB centre than Hong Kong.

Singapore also compares unfavourably with Hong Kong on other fronts. The number of Chinese tourists visiting Singapore, another way for it to accumulate RMB through tourism export, is only 12% of those visiting Hong Kong. The currency swap agreement between the People's Bank of China (PBoC) and the Monetary Authority of Singapore (MAS) is far smaller than that of the PBoC with the HKMA. Note that currency swaps with the Chinese government could help the foreign central bank acquire a large amount of RMB liquidity in a short period of time, and would help build confidence and credibility for banks that are willing to engage in offshore RMB transactions. Further, local Singaporean interest in holding RMB has been eroded by the faster Singapore dollar appreciation, which amounted to 6%–7% a year against the USD in recent years compared to 3%–4% a year of the RMB.

In a nutshell, Hong Kong has almost all the advantages of being an offshore RMB centre that Singapore has, except for the lower land prices in Singapore. The two countries are even in the same time zone, but Hong Kong's geographical position is more central than Singapore's (basically within four hours flight of anywhere within the Asian region). All this is not to downgrade the potential importance of Singapore. Indeed, when the RMB becomes fully convertible, due to the over-the-counter (OTC) nature of FX trading and Singapore's leading position as a FX hub,[3] it is conceivable that Singapore could gain market share in RMB trading over time.

What about London and other centres?

From the international trade perspective, it is obvious that London has limited RMB accumulation capacity. This will remain its largest handicap for the City to become a sizable offshore RMB centre in the medium term. Only when China eventually opens up its capital account fully will London (and other offshore centres) be able to accumulate RMB in significant amounts from non-trade avenues. But London is not waiting. In April 2012, UK Chancellor of the Exchequer George Osborne and the City of London jointly announced a plan, known as the Hong Kong-London Forum, to establish London as the RMB business centre in the West. This initiative has also received a blessing from Beijing, though the Chinese government has not actively followed up with the idea since then.

Active members in the Forum include Chinese and European banks (the Bank of China, HSBC, Standard Chartered Bank, Deutsche Bank and Barclays Capital), with the UK authorities (the Bank of England and UK Financial Services Bureau) as observers. The Forum proposes specific actions to provide technical, infrastructure and regulatory support for developing RMB offshore business in London. However, in the short term, the effectiveness of this plan to boost London's offshore RMB role is constrained by the limited RMB pool in the UK (see above Figure 8.3) and the lack of a clearing bank, which are both at the mercy of China's policy.

In terms of financial market capability, London enjoys certain advantages over other developed markets and European centres in developing an offshore RMB centre. Many European companies have already chosen the City as the centre for their financial operations. So the generic financial infrastructure has been set up in London so that a move onto the RMB-specific trading platform will not be too difficult. The prevalence of European operations also means an established market with critical size for London to market and distribute RMB products and services.

London is the largest FX trading centre in the world. This makes it indispensable to the development of RMB products. With a trading day which overlaps that of China and the rest of the world, London's time zone has a clear advantage of global trading. The City also has a large institutional investor base with a focus on Asia. These investors naturally have a keen interest in RMB products. In early 2012, RMB FX trading in London already accounted for a quarter of total offshore RMB FX trading volume. In the longer term, as investor demand grows,

London's edge of well-established infrastructure will enable it to expand its offshore RMB trading.

Hong Kong's comparative advantages in direct access to liquidity in China, having Beijing's political support and having its influence on China's strategic decision (on RMB-nisation policy) make it an ideal partner for London to co-develop offshore RMB business. This is indeed the motivation behind the Hong Kong-London Forum. The combination of Hong Kong's first-mover advantage and direct China linkages with London's vibrant market dynamics and Western reach creates value in offshore-offshore collaboration between the two centres.

The future of the offshore RMB market may take the form of a hub-and-spoke model,[4] where Hong Kong (or Hong Kong-London) will be the prime offshore RMB centre (the hub), with other centres linking to the hub like the spokes of a chariot wheel. The Forum will act as a platform for fostering individual countries' effort to engage China in the RMB-nisation process (for example, foreign central banks diversifying their FX reserves into RMB, and foreign investors accessing onshore Chinese capital markets).

New York has yet to express any keen interest in developing into an offshore RMB centre. This is partly due to the lack of recognition of the long-term potential of the RMB as a reserve currency, and largely due to the lack of political support stemming from fears about the RMB becoming a significant challenger to the USD's global currency status. Sino-US political tensions over issues in Asia and the Middle East certainly do not help the RMB development. The US regulatory regime is also more complicated and demanding than that of the United Kingdom and other jurisdictions, which makes it difficult for the Chinese banks and funds to operate in the United States. Thus, among the various offshore RMB centres, New York's growth will likely lag behind that of Hong Kong, Singapore and London.

Another, but often ignored, potential offshore RMB market is Taipei. Taipei's market size is small for the time being, and its main problem for developing offshore RMB business is political. But in terms of economics, its conditions for development are favourable. Taiwan's growing economic ties with China and improving political climate mean that Taipei could be instrumental for RMB internationalisation, and a mini-offshore RMB centre could take off soon.

Cross-straits political tension has obstructed the development of offshore RMB business in Taiwan. Until recently, nearly all trades between Taiwan and Mainland China have been invoiced and settled in USD. But following the improvement in the cross-straits relationship recently, the authorities on both sides of the Taiwan Strait have started to allow some trade settlement in RMB through offshore banking accounts. This is still in an experimental stage, so the scale is very small. Further development will depend on the continued improvement in cross-straits politics.

In terms of economics, Taiwan is well-positioned to help deepen China's RMB-nisation process by accumulating a significant amount of offshore RMB and building up two-way RMB flows. First, Taiwan-China trade has grown dramatically over the years, rising from about US$10 billion in 2000 to almost US$130 billion in 2011. More crucially, China runs a chronic trade deficit with Taiwan (Figure 8.4), which is crucial for

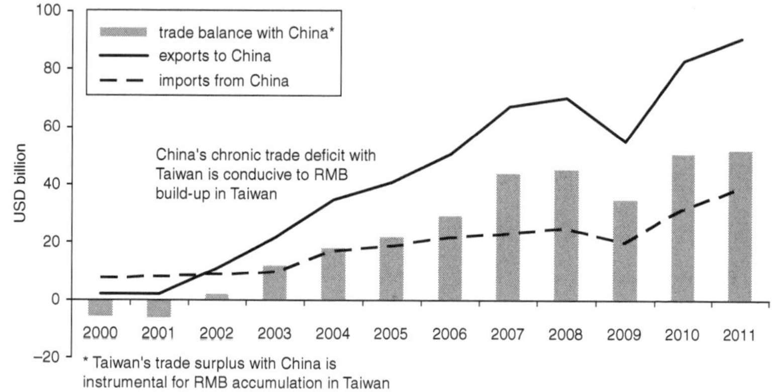

Figure 8.4 Taiwan-China trade balance
Source: CEIC, author.

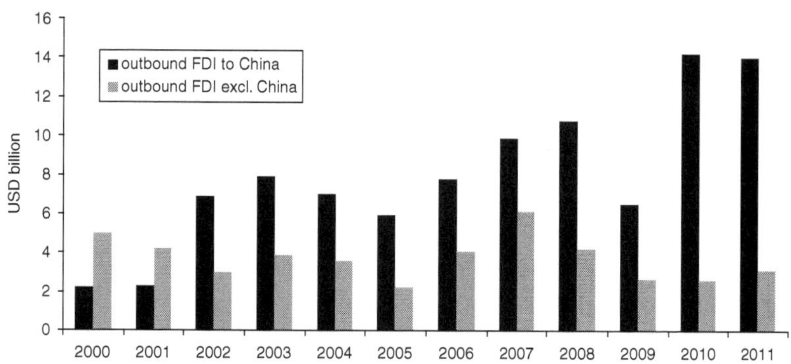

Figure 8.5 Taiwan's outbound FDI
Source: CEIC.

generating RMB outflow to Taiwan. China is also the prime FDI destination for Taiwanese investors (Figure 8.5), indicating that demand for offshore RMB funding in Taiwan will grow. Meanwhile, Chinese tourist arrivals in Taiwan have also risen significantly to a record of 1.8 million in 2011 from 330,000 in 2008.[5]

At the time of writing, Taipei and Beijing are working on an agreement on cross-straits TWD/RMB currency clearance. Growing economic ties between the mainland and Taiwan mean rising demand for cross-straits remittance services. Operation of the currency clearance agreement will facilitate an increasing amount of RMB trade settlement and investment with China and, thus, foster the development of Taipei into an offshore RMB centre. Following this, wealth management product denominated in RMB may develop in Taiwan, and RMB funding facilities may be made easily available to Taiwanese firms.

Granted, Taipei will not likely be able to gain in scale or scope of the CNH market in Hong Kong, or even Singapore and London. But its close economic ties with China should make it a mini-offshore market. In a hub-and-spoke framework, Taipei may well be a satellite centre linking to the Hong Kong hub like a spoke of a chariot wheel for helping to deepen RMB internationalisation.

What makes Hong Kong the offshore hub?

Chinese exporters' demand for RMB settlement is not conducive to the growth of offshore RMB centres. This is because such demand absorbs RMB back to China, but does not increase its supply overseas. However, if more foreign buyers of Chinese goods and services cave in to Chinese demand and pay in RMB, this will increase the demand for offshore RMB funding and is, hence, positive for offshore RMB asset creation. This is instrumental for deepening RMB-nisation.

The question is whether Chinese exporters have the power to demand payment in RMB. Chinese exports have been climbing the value chain to secure new foreign demand. There has been steady growth in China's exports of "high" value-added goods and services (as compared with China's conventional low value-added exports), such as machinery and equipment and construction services (Figures 8.6 and 8.7). This change in China's export structure should give Chinese exporters bigger bargaining power in demanding payment in RMB. So the need of foreign buyers for RMB to pay Chinese exports will grow steadily. This will, in turn, create demand for RMB funding instruments and prompt RMB asset creation in the offshore market.

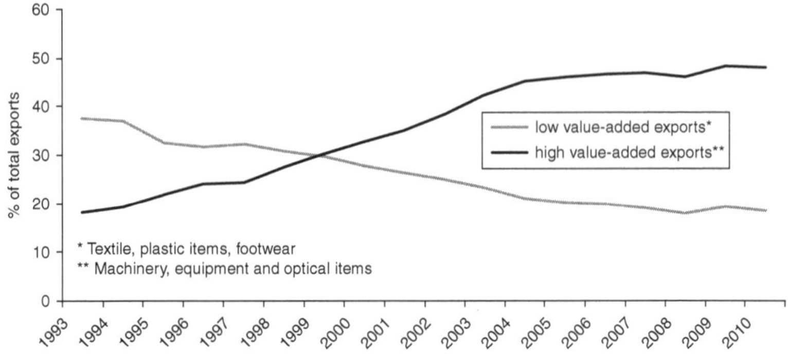

Figure 8.6 Chinese exports climbing the value chain
Source: CEIC, author.

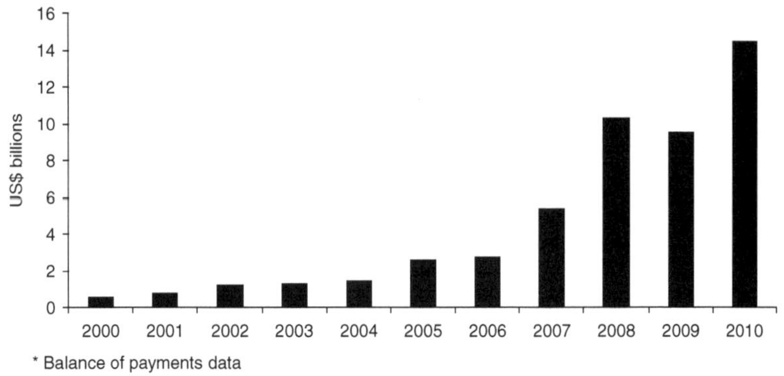

Figure 8.7 China's construction service export on the rise*
Source: CEIC.

All this brings us back to the basic point that there needs to be more RMB investment and hedging vehicles and a trading infrastructure developed offshore to create the incentive for non-trade demand for RMB. Hong Kong is the only CNH centre so far that has developed a complete RMB trading infrastructure to support the development of offshore RMB products and a two-way trading mechanism.

While trade flows have increased RMB accumulation in Hong Kong, China has also put in programmes to allow offshore RMB to flow back to China. These include opening up of the onshore interbank bond market for foreign participation, launching of the RQFII[6] and RMB-denominated IPO listing in Hong Kong[7] and so on. While all these programmes are

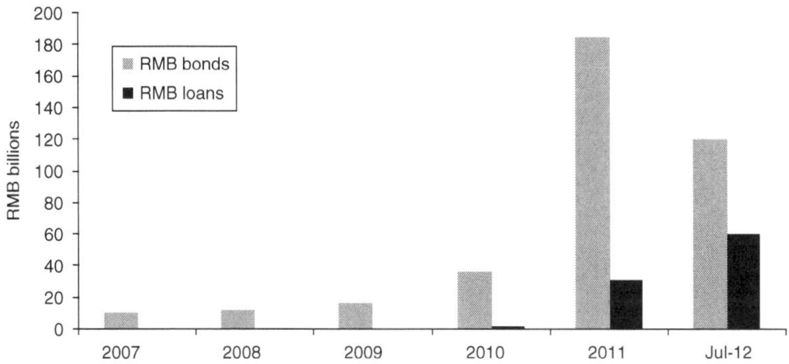

Figure 8.8 Gross issuance of RMB bonds and loans in Hong Kong
Source: Reuters, Bloomberg.

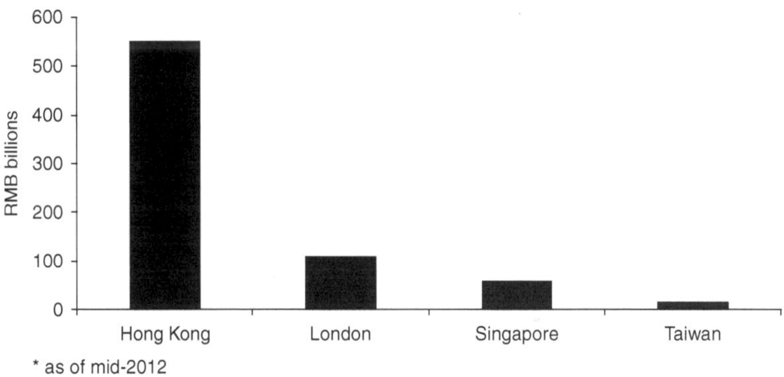

Figure 8.9 Offshore RMB deposits*
Source: Reuters.

meant to establish a two-way trading mechanism between Hong Kong and the mainland, they also act to reduce the RMB pool overseas. From a policy perspective, these can also be seen as tools for Beijing to control the growth of the offshore RMB market. This underscores our argument that RMB internationalisation and its corresponding offshore market development are slow processes.

With the blessing of Beijing, Hong Kong has also developed an offshore-RMB (or dim sum) bond market and an RMB loan market, both of which have grown dramatically since Beijing's RMB-nisation push (Figure 8.8). Meanwhile, the CNH foreign exchange market has also gained significant momentum, with its liquidity growing from about US$600 million a day in early 2011 to over US$2 billion in 2012. This market is rivalling the liquidity of the NDF market, though it is still about a tenth of the onshore CNY daily trading volume. The CNH FX market is expected to be larger, and more important, than the NDF market soon.

Given the political, economic and technical advantages that Hong Kong has, it is no wonder that it has accumulated the largest pool of offshore RMB (Figure 8.9), which is a basic factor for determining the relative importance of an offshore centre compared to its competitors. In a nutshell, with a natural advantage of accumulating a critical mass of RMB offshore more efficiently than other potential centres and a leading edge on developing CNH products and trading infrastructure, Hong Kong will stand up to the rising competition and remain a prime CNH centre going forward, just like London is a leader in the Eurodollar market.

Offshore RMB business in China

A contentious issue is whether China should also develop offshore RMB business in the country to serve non-residents based in China. There is no consensus market view, and Beijing has no policy stance on this issue. Proponents of setting up domestic offshore RMB business argue that China should follow the United States' IBF or Japan's JOM models to segregate the onshore and offshore RMB business in the country. The purpose of these is to prevent undesired fund flows between the two markets (for arbitrage purposes, for example) and bureaucracies, and a confusion of duties between bank departments handling on- and off-shore funds (see Chapter 5).

Operationally, setting up offshore RMB business in China should be straightforward. Based on the current bank infrastructure for managing offshore FX transactions, China can simply apply the same risk management framework to manage the two types (onshore and offshore) of RMB transactions. Based on the needs of the real economy, offshore RMB business in the country, say based in Shanghai, can serve the overseas business needs of non-residents.

Due to the high costs of overseas branch offices or technical difficulties in managing overseas offices, many non-resident companies would prefer to open offshore accounts in China to conduct cross-border RMB businesses. If there are no onshore facilities for handling these offshore

RMB business needs, this demand will naturally leak to the offshore RMB centres, such as Hong Kong, Singapore and London.

Opponents of the idea argue that, though some countries tried to develop offshore currency centres in the domestic market, they could not compete with the major offshore centres in London, New York, Hong Kong and Singapore. So the domestic offshore centres did not serve any real purposes. Regarding China, when given a choice between holding RMB assets in an offshore account in China or in a genuine offshore centre like Hong Kong, non-residents would most likely choose the genuine centre due to its transparency, professionalism and rule of law.

According to this view, offshore RMB business in China is unlikely to gain a critical mass. As long as the RMB remains not fully convertible, strict segregation between the onshore and offshore RMB markets is needed. This means developing two sets of tax and regulatory policies for the two markets in China. This will only create an extra administrative burden and red tape with little efficiency gains, given the limited potential of the domestic offshore business.

The key issues are the demand conditions for domestic offshore RMB business and risk management of the on- and off-shore business in the domestic economy. Obviously, if there is insufficient demand to create a critical mass for the offshore business and if risks are difficult to manage, it is not worthwhile to develop. Investment banks, such as Deutsche Group, have done extensive surveys and had discussions with investors, commercial banks and mainland business experts, and found no conviction by the market on the development of offshore RMB business inside China.

Technically, China's opaque and shifting regulatory system also does not help develop domestic offshore RMB business, as it will only complicate the inherent distortion in the system. There will also be serious administrative and implementation problems due to the sheer size of China's banking system. For example, allowing a few small banks with existing offshore FX operations to include the RMB may have little systemic impact. But if all domestic banks are allowed into doing offshore RMB business in the country, this will likely create administrative chaos, moral hazard[8] and rent seeking,[9] given the serious bureaucratic and incentive problems of the system.

Beijing does not yet have a policy stance on the development of domestic offshore RMB business. It does not have to hurry, in my view. The decision can wait until the offshore RMB market becomes mature.

By then, there should be enough information and data to assess if the offshore RMB business is worthwhile to be developed onshore, say in Shanghai. The risk/reward assessment by then will spur policy debate and, eventually, prompt a consensus for developing offshore RMB business in the country.

This was what happened in the United States. Its IBF only came into existence some 20 years after the advent of the Eurodollar market. When the US government saw the Eurodollar market's negative impact on the US banking industry, it finally reached a policy consensus on developing the offshore USD business onshore; hence, the birth of the IBF to counter the effects of the Eurodollar market on the US banking sector. For China, instead of developing an offshore RMB business onshore to compete with the offshore market, it should focus on expanding the scope of investable RMB products both onshore and offshore to deepen the RMB-nisation process.

Market convergence reveals reform vision problem

Convergence by market forces

There are a number of players involved in making the onshore RMB/USD exchange rate (i.e. USD/CNY in market jargon) converge with the offshore rate (USD/CNH). They include onshore and offshore corporates, policymakers and financial institutions. However, there are tedious Chinese regulations designed to keep the offshore market segregated from the onshore market so that full convergence by market forces is not possible. This policy choice makes the overall RMB FX market inefficient and fragmented at this stage. But this also means that improvement can easily be made when RMB internationalisation deepens over time.

Under the current market set-up, onshore corporates have two choices when making overseas transactions in USD. Either they must trade at the onshore USD/CNY rate if they want to bring the trade-related transaction proceeds onshore, or they can trade in the offshore market at the USD/CNH rate, but then they cannot bring the proceeds back to China under the current regulations.

Let us consider the case when offshore RMB is weaker than the onshore rate (i.e. a USD buys more RMB offshore than onshore). Under this condition, the onshore exporters (who receive USD) will have a strong incentive to buy RMB and sell USD offshore because RMB here is cheaper than in the onshore market. The greater the disparity between off- and on-shore rates, the greater the incentive for the onshore exporters to sell USD and buy RMB offshore. This forms part of the market mechanism for convergence; buying will push up the offshore RMB rate towards the onshore rate. Meanwhile, there is no incentive for the onshore importers (who pay in USD) to sell RMB for USD offshore because they can pay for their imports at a more favourable (cheaper USD) onshore rate.

On the other hand, if the RMB is stronger offshore than onshore (i.e. USD/CNH is stronger than USD/CNY), there is a strong incentive for the onshore importers to go offshore and sell RMB and buy USD to pay their import bills. This selling by the importers will push down the offshore RMB rate towards the onshore rate. Note that the onshore exporters with USD are absent in this case, as they would not want to sell USD for RMB at an unfavourable (cheaper USD) offshore rate. They would rather trade it for RMB onshore where the USD is stronger. This will put upward pressure on the onshore RMB, thus helping the convergence between USD/CNH and USD/CNY rates.

Similarly, offshore exporters receiving RMB also play a role in fostering the convergence mechanism. If the RMB is weaker offshore, offshore exporters could arbitrage the two exchange rates by first converting its RMB export proceeds into USD in the onshore market, where the RMB is stronger, and then convert the USD back into RMB in the offshore market at the weaker USD/CNH rate.

This simultaneous selling RMB onshore and buying back RMB offshore generates an arbitrage profit for the offshore exporters. The resulting supply and demand dynamics also help the two exchange rates converge. But there is a limit on this activity, as the PBoC has imposed a quarterly quota of RMB8 billion on all RMB trade settlement transactions. This means that in aggregate, total RMB trading activity (including arbitrage) cannot exceed RMB8 billion a quarter, disregarding how the arbitrage amount is distributed among the offshore exporters.

On the other hand, if offshore RMB is stronger than onshore, there is no arbitrage activity by the offshore exporters. But offshore importers (who pay in RMB) will have the incentive to sell USD for more RMB in the onshore market, where the USD is stronger (RMB is weaker), and use the RMB proceeds to pay for their imports. This activity helps divert the selling pressure on the USD in the offshore market to the onshore market, thus helping convergence of the on- and off-shore exchange rates.

There is also an informal arbitrage, which arguably is an inefficient activity that the offshore firms can do in Hong Kong. It involves the transference of RMB between corporate and individual retail accounts. If the offshore RMB exchange rate is stronger than the onshore rate, the offshore corporates may be able to use individual retail accounts to buy RMB at the onshore rate, as permitted by Chinese regulations. Then it can transfer the RMB to the corporate account and sell it for USD in the CNH market at a higher RMB exchange rate to reap an arbitrage profit. Again this simultaneous buying and selling of the RMB versus the USD helps the on- and off-shore market rates to converge.

But such an arbitrage is inefficient, as each individual account can only buy up to RMB20,000 a day. So a corporate will need to use numerous individual accounts for multiple transactions over a period of time to make the arbitrage worthwhile. Further, transaction spreads are wide, as the transactions are retail trades. This means that there must be a wide divergence between the on- and off-shore rates for such arbitrage to take place. The wide divergence also means that there must be market inefficiency.

Convergence by brute force

The convergence process can also be forced by government intervention, which bureaucrats argue is needed for safeguarding the convergence process for the on- and off-shore FX markets. This works through a RMB400 billion swap line between the PBoC in China and the HKMA in Hong Kong. But the HKMA can only use it for keeping the offshore RMB exchange rate from surging above the onshore rate (i.e. by selling RMB and buying USD in the CNH market).

This policy reflects the mainland authorities' ignorance about the market mechanism, and a lack of reform vision, as it is based on the naïve assumption that offshore RMB will always be stronger than onshore RMB (i.e. the government itself has bought into the one-way bet for RMB appreciation, when the market can in practice go either way). Hence, there is no corresponding reverse swap line set up, with which the HKMA could buy RMB and sell USD in the CNH market to keep the offshore rate from falling significantly below the onshore rate.

Convergence by inefficient arbitrage

Onshore and offshore banks play a combined role in pulling the on- and off-shore RMB exchange rates closer through arbitrage. But the banks are not allowed to engage in direct arbitrage activity. Instead they are allowed indirect arbitrage via the NDF market. For onshore banks, they are barred from participating in the CNH market at all. But they are permitted to trade FX in the onshore CNY and NDF markets. Thus, onshore banks can only exploit arbitrage opportunities between the CNY forward rates and NDF forward rates.

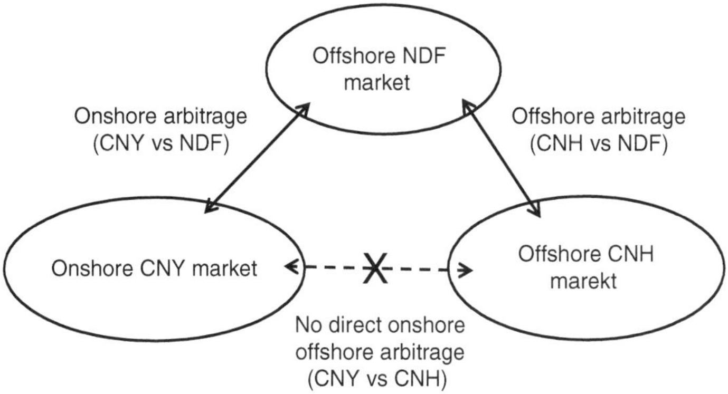

Figure 8.10 Inefficient arbitrage between CNY and CNH markets
Source: author.

Meanwhile, offshore banks are barred from all onshore activity. So they cannot trade onshore CNY at all. They can instead trade in the offshore CNH and NDF markets. Thus, offshore banks can arbitrage between the CNH forward rates and NDF forward rates. Hence, the NDF market is the only common place where on- and off-shore banks can trade and arbitrage. There is no direct arbitrage between the CNY and CNH markets at all (Figure 8.10). This indirect arbitrage through the NDF market, which suffers from market liquidity and depth problems, is obviously inefficient in bringing the on- and off-shore RMB exchange rates together.

Corporate activity, political intervention and bank arbitrage do help convergence between the onshore and offshore RMB exchange rates. But the policy in place, which the mainland authorities called safeguards for convergence, shows a lack of coherent reform strategy and a lack of understanding of how the market works. Intense investor activity can induce opposing forces that pull and push the CNH and CNY rates away from each other. If investor demand for CNH rises sharply relative to the supply of RMB in the offshore market, then the offshore RMB exchange rate will move significantly higher than the onshore rate, and vice versa.

The Chinese authorities should have the vision for two-way RMB trading as a natural practice in the RMB internationalisation process, and implement policies to facilitate a fair and smooth trading environment. Instead, they have bought into the one-way bet on RMB appreciation themselves, which they seek to prevent, and put in a one-sided policy for curbing CNH strength only, but not for arresting its weakness. This is clearly seen in the PBoC's swap agreement with the HKMA (see above). The bottom line is that China needs to work more on developing a long-term reform vision to take RMB-nisation to higher levels. Market segregation and inefficiency will remain in the medium term, and they are not good for deepening RMB internationalisation.

9
RMB – The Third Major Reserve Currency

Conventional wisdom has it that a currency will achieve a global reserve currency status after it is fully internationalised. That is, a global reserve currency status only comes after the currency can be freely used for all international transactions. China has proven this wrong. The yuan is not yet fully convertible. But by definition, it has become a reserve currency, as it is already held by some central banks as a reserve asset.

Granted, the renminbi's (RMB's) weight in the world's official reserves is negligible today, as it is held by a limited number of small central banks only. But a trend is growing that the global central banks are diversifying out of the US dollar (USD), and the RMB is being studied for its role as an alternative asset held in the official reserves. If Beijing continues its efforts on pursuing structural reforms to liberalise its capital account and internationalise the RMB, the red-back could become the third major reserve currency after the USD and euro within a few years (Smith 2012). This may sound shocking, but it is not. The current third-largest reserve currency (actually there are two: the Japanese yen [JPY] and the Pound sterling [GBP]) accounts for only 4% of global central bank reserve allocation.

Academic studies on reserve currency history and development focus on the use of currencies for foreign trade transactions (Eichengreen 2010). From a macroeconomic perspective, the allocation of currencies in the official reserves is linked to the choice of currencies for settling international trade. But from a portfolio investment perspective, the choice of currencies for reserve management purpose may be different from the choice of currencies for foreign trade settlement. The foreign demand for RMB has recently been benefiting from the portfolio choice of some, albeit small, central bank reserve managers in addition to their countries' international trade needs.

This is not to argue that the RMB will displace the USD's super reserve currency status (which accounts for over 60% of global central bank reserves) anytime soon. Indeed, the USD's inertia is so strong that no other currencies could challenge its super status for a long time, in my view. What the challengers, including the RMB, could do is only to erode the USD's dominance. The dollar is down after the subprime crisis, but it is not out yet.

Regarding the RMB, one way to help gain reserve currency status is to be included in the International Monetary Fund's (IMF's) Special Drawing Rights[1] (SDR), which may encourage the world's central banks to add RMB assets to their reserve portfolios. There is a window of opportunity for getting into the SDR. The IMF is due to re-weigh the SDR component currencies in 2015, and the RMB stands a chance to be included, even though technically it still falls quite some way short of meeting the SDR criteria.

A trend of more central banks accumulating RMB may already be in the making without anyone noticing it. This is because a currency bloc based on the Chinese yuan is emerging in Asia. The gravitational force of economics is pulling an increasing number of countries towards China. Eventually, the major developed economies will not be able to ignore the RMB in their reserve management. The uncertainty is with the timing for when this inclusion of RMB in the major countries' official reserves is going to happen.

Rocking the "reserve boat"

Some central banks in the world are changing their investment rules to include the RMB in their foreign reserves. The most notable example is the Central Bank of Nigeria, which announced in September 2011 an explicit target of holding up to 10% of its FX reserves in RMB (China Daily 2011). Of particular importance also is the Sino-Japanese collaboration, announced in December 2011, of using the RMB for trade and non-trade transactions.[2] In this announcement, Japan also said it would buy up to US$10 billion in Chinese bonds for its reserves (*Wall Street Journal* 2011). Granted, this amount is less than 1% of the Japanese FX reserves, but it carries a significant signal for the other global authorities and the world investment community. When implemented, this will for the first time make RMB assets part of the reserves of a G7[3] economy, and it could be the start of a long-term process for accepting the RMB as a reserve currency.

Adding the yuan to a country's reserves is becoming a trend, partly because global reserve managers want to diversify out of the USD, which could remain in prolonged weakness in the post-crisis world (see Chapter 1), and partly because it would be ridiculous to not have the currency of the world's second-largest economy in a country's FX reserves. The primary objective of a FX reserve manager is capital preservation, but his/her performance is also judged by the returns on the portfolio. Hence, the currency composition of a reserve portfolio should maximise the holding of currencies and assets that are safe and likely to boost the asset value of the portfolio, and minimise those assets that may erode the returns and the asset value of the portfolio.

As a result, the reserve manager's choice of currencies in his/her portfolio may not necessarily be the same as the policymaker's choice of currencies that are needed primarily for international trade settlement. For example, on a macro basis, the effect of externality, or peer pressure, may reinforce the use of the dollar for international trade transactions: When everyone is using it, I should also use it. So a policymaker has an incentive to hold more USD in the FX reserves to satisfy the foreign trade needs.

But reserve managers may view this differently because there is a potential risk of overexposure to the USD that could wreak havoc on his/her portfolio's net asset value and returns. This risk is increasing in the post-subprime-crisis world, as the USD is going to be a weak currency (both in the form of falling value and falling global influence). The reserve manager would want to diversify out of the USD into other currencies. The RMB stands out as a prime candidate, as it is backed by China's rising economic clout and has not been affected by the global financial crisis since 2008.

After all, China's rising economic impact on the global economy and financial system will prompt economic agents around the world to increase the usage of the yuan in international trade and non-trade transactions. Remember, one of the key incentives for China to internationalise the RMB is to use it as an alternative funding and trade financing currency, especially during crisis periods when USD financing typically dries up (see Chapter 3). This is a strong reason for central bank reserve managers to hold RMB both as a lender of last resort to supply RMB and as a reflection of the change in the relative importance of the world's economic powers.

The rising importance of the RMB's global role underpins the bilateral currency swap lines that China has signed with over 20 other central banks around the world since 2010. These bilateral swap lines are also evidence for the RMB's ascent to reserve currency status before it becomes fully internationalised; evidence that proves conventional wisdom wrong (that a currency will only achieve reserve currency status after it becomes fully internationalised). Although these currency swap lines have typically been presented as international trade tools, they also play a role in official reserve management, as they serve as a conduit for the corresponding foreign central banks to access China's onshore bond market to source reserve assets. So the swap lines, in fact, help promote the yuan's reserve currency status.

The giant and the dwarfs

The diversification of central bank reserves out of the dollar is a recent phenomenon that has mainly come after the US subprime crisis. Arguably, the crisis is a watershed for the US economic supremacy, as it led to the downgrade of the US sovereign credit rating from the highest AAA rating to AA+ by Standard & Poors in mid-2011. This has led the world to reassess the relative credit risk of holding US government and agency bonds and to a corresponding reassessment of the performance risk of holding USD assets.

The fall of the United States' economic dominance has also given China an opportunity to assert influence on the global stage (Lo 2012). The enthusiasm for RMB exposure can be seen as a recognition of China's emerging economic powerhouse status. This is not to argue that the RMB will replace the USD as the world's supreme currency anytime soon. Indeed, it will not, due to the USD's inertia and China's inherent structural and systemic deficiencies, which could take years to correct (see Chapter 6).

Despite its erosion in recent years, the share of the USD in the world's official reserves remains the largest, accounting for over 60% of global central banks' reserves, according to the IMF. The dollar has enjoyed such strong dominance for such a long time (see below) that it has crowded out other reserve currencies. But this may pave the way for its own decline because this prolonged dominance has created inertia for using the USD, which may also have lowered the entrance barrier for a strong new reserve currency contestant (such as the Chinese yuan).

It is not that difficult to become the world's third major reserve currency, in terms of the share in the world official reserves allocation. According to the IMF's calculation, the euro is the second-largest reserve currency after the USD, accounting for about a quarter of all central banks' reserves. It is followed by the JPY and GBP, both of which have a 4% weight in global reserve allocation, and the Swiss franc (CHF), which accounts for about 1% of world reserves. What we have here is a situation of a giant (USD) and four dwarfs (the euro, JPY, GBP and CHF), with their heights represented by their allocation weights in the global reserves. *Ceteris paribus*, it will not be difficult for the RMB to climb and overtake the JPY and GBP to become the third major reserve currency in the world. Why?

Take a look at Japan. Despite its heavy weight in global GDP, the adverse conditions of Japan's high debt (Figure 9.1), low yield (Figure 9.2) and structural economic deficiency (see Chapter 1) have argued for a structural underweight investment position in Japanese government bonds (JGBs) in central bank reserve portfolios. Successive Japanese governments have

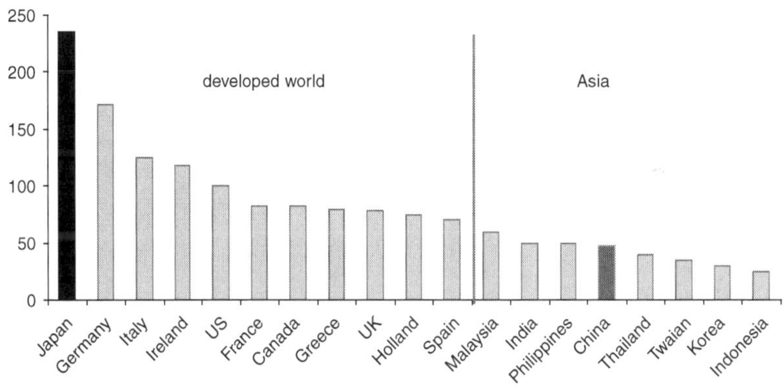

Figure 9.1 Public debt to GDP ratio (2010)
Source: CEIC, author.

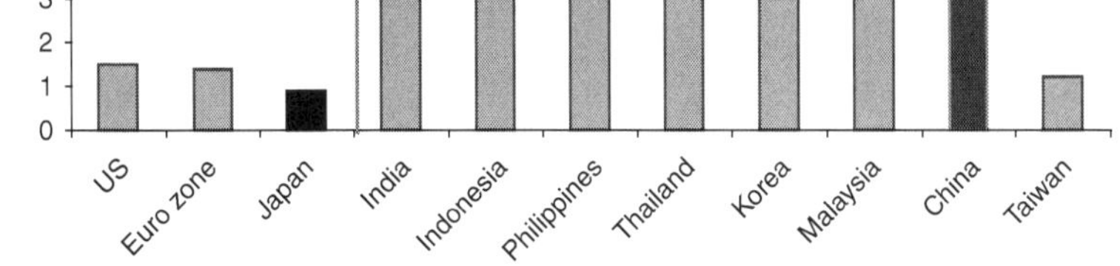

Figure 9.2 Average ten-year government bond yield (%, 2011)
Source: CEIC, author.

also shown little intention on internationalising the JPY after a head start in the early 1970s; Tokyo has not had any appetite in promoting the yen as a reserve currency. All this, in turn, contributes to the yen's low share of official reserve allocation.

In contrast, the Chinese government is keen on internationalising the RMB and seeing it become a world reserve currency.[4] China also has a light government debt burden (see Figure 9.1) and is, in fact, a net creditor to the world. This makes Chinese sovereign bonds an attractive asset class for inclusion in central bank reserve portfolios.

As for the CHF, its attractiveness as a reserve currency is hindered by Switzerland's tiny government bond market. The Swiss National Bank (SNB) has also become increasingly interventionist, mainly to curb the strength of the CHF in recent years during the European sovereign debt crisis. The major defect of the Swiss markets is that they are too small to handle significant market volatility that a global reserve currency is supposed to withstand. Last but not least, both the CHF and the GBP are tied to the fortunes (or misfortune, in the current European crisis context) of the Euro zone economy and, thus, to the value of the euro.

But the euro has an uncertain future (see Chapter 1)! Its 25% global reserve allocation is arguably small relative to the global weight of its economy, which is roughly the same as the US economy. It is also interesting (or rather puzzling) to note that the current global reserve allocation to the euro is not much higher than the combined 18% weight that the pre-euro currencies had in central bank reserves in 1999.

So despite all the structural changes that many Europeans have argued that were good for the European Monetary Union, the euro has remained "un-loved," and has not made much headway in gaining a larger allocation in the world's official reserves. In fact, the euro has had an underweight allocation in global FX reserve portfolios by birth! Given its uncertain future, the euro's underweight inertia may be stuck for a long period of time.

The global financial crisis has shown the world, in particular China, that living in a USD-dominated world was not necessarily in the best interest of the trade-oriented economies when USD financing dried up, like in 2008 and 2009. This may have prompted Beijing to start promoting the RMB as a foreign trade settlement currency in June 2009. The purpose was to reduce reliance on the dollar. The crisis has also prompted central bank reserve managers to reassess their inherent strategy of having a large exposure to USD assets.

Hence, the world's central banks have slowed down significantly their accumulation of US debt securities since mid-2011, when Standard &

Poors downgraded the US sovereign credit rating from AAA. Before this, global central banks' holding of US agency debts had already started falling in 2008 after Washington nationalised the US mortgage agencies Fannie Mae and Freddy Mac. The trend of central banks diversifying out of the USD looks set to continue due to a revamp by the reserve managers of their traditional USD-dominated management strategy.

Meanwhile, China's initiative to actively internationalise the yuan is rising to meet this diversification need. Granted, more reforms are needed to fully integrate the RMB in the global system and the official reserves. The trends from China are pointing in the right direction, though the process towards full RMB convertibility is by no means smooth sailing (see Chapters 6 and 7). Some small central banks are buying into the Chinese internationalisation story and leading the way in accumulating the RMB in their reserves. This, in turn, shows that full capital account convertibility is not necessarily a prerequisite for RMB to become a reserve currency.

Externality from the small central banks

There may be a virtuous effect on the promoting of the RMB's reserve currency status from the small central banks which are accumulating it in their reserves. Their action may prompt other central banks to follow suit; this is called an externality or a copy-cat behaviour. This effect may become stronger as and when China liberalises its domestic interest rates further to allow market forces to determine the price of Chinese credit. Interest rate liberalisation will mean higher Chinese yields, as the credit pricing constraint is freed from financial repression. The Chinese government bond yield is already more attractive than the G3 currencies (see Figure 9.2 above). From an investment perspective, higher returns will certainly enhance the appeal of RMB-denominated assets both to central bank reserve managers and global investors.

It is an economic fact that China's capital account will need to be opened fully for the RMB to be fully internationalised, or convertible. The structural reforms for achieving this end goal are indeed daunting and, hence, will not (and cannot) proceed as quickly as many have expected. RMB-nisation without a fully open capital account is possible, but only to a limited extent (see Chapter 7). How big the share of RMB can grow in the global reserves is also contingent upon the extent of China's capital account liberalisation and RMB internationalisation.

Given the current trends, it may not be difficult for the red-back to gain a share of over 4% of global reserve allocation, and displace the

JPY and GBP as the third major reserve currency. But it will definitely be a much bigger hurdle for it to grow by another four percentage points from thereon. The ball is in Beijing's court, as the weight of the RMB in global reserve allocation depends on how far and how fast it is willing to allow deep structural reforms to go. For the foreseeable future, the USD will remain the giant in global reserve allocation, while the RMB will join the exiting small group of dwarfs and become the second-tallest dwarf after the euro.

The United States may be down, but not out

We are not talking about the RMB replacing the USD, or even seriously eroding the USD's share in global reserve allocation in the medium term. In fact, most of the decline in the USD's reserve allocation from over 70% since the early 2000s was due to the rise in the share of the euro from 18% to 25% between 2000 and 2003. Since then, the allocation weights of both the USD and the euro have stabilised at around 63% and 25%, respectively. What makes the USD's share so stubborn has to do with the economic fundamentals and credibility that have been built up behind the dollar and that give it the inertia of global reserve currency.

Fundamentally, the United States still has an unmatched research and higher education establishment to support its economic power that stands behind its currency. While it is almost certain that we are moving into a multi-polar world and a multi-currency reserve system in the years ahead, and that the United States' power will certainly be constrained or even eroded, it will remain the most flexible and credible among the large economies in the world. If there is a rising sense of China overtaking the United States as the next economic powerhouse, this may even be good for the United States, as it should give US politicians the push to tackle their fiscal and financial challenges, and Americans the drive to fix their balance sheet (to save more) in order to prevent their country from slipping from the world stage.

The notion of America's "decline" eroding the USD's supremacy is not as simple as what meets the eye. The debate about the United States' decline involves issues of absolute versus relative decline and concepts like "resilience" and "passivity." Some facts are discernible and measureable, like GDP, military power and demographics. Others are not quite readily measurable. Hard data do not produce evidence that the United States is going into a decline and its currency is about to be deserted. For example, in absolute terms, US GDP increased by 21% in constant dollars between 2000 and 2010, despite the shattering setbacks of the bursting of the dot-com bubble in 2001 and the eruption of the subprime crisis in 2008–9. In 2010, US military spending (US$697 billion) was 55% higher than in 2000, and its population was 310 million, an increase of 10% since 2000.

The notion that demography is destiny may be a stretch, but demographics are important when, as in the United States, population increase (due to higher birth and immigration rates than other countries, including China) cushions the impact of an ageing population. The US population in fact grew by 0.16 percentage points more than China's between 2000 and 2010. What matters more than absolute numbers is the population's composition of prime working-age people versus dependents. Compared to most developed economies and China, the US demographic composition is relatively favourable, with the United Nations projecting that the US working-age population will grow by 30% by 2050, while that of China's will fall by 3%.

Nevertheless, there were also some important declines relative to the rest of the world. In 2000, US GDP was 61% of the combined GDPs of the developed world. But that share fell to 42% in 2010. In 2000, US GDP was slightly more than eight times that of China, but it dropped to slightly less than three times in 2010. In other words, the United States increased its GDP, population and military spending from 2000 to 2010 in absolute terms. But in relative terms, they have declined.

Some US data show significant increases, some show declines and some are mixed. What the numbers do not tell is as important as what they convey. Omissions include the societal and systemic factors that stimulate or impede creativity, innovation, entrepreneurship and new ventures. The numbers also ignore the effects of culture, property rights, law and political freedom in the short- and long terms. Nor do they foretell how China's so-called "social capitalism" will fare in long-term competition with the flexible US prototype.

The point is that, for comparing and forecasting the resilience of countries and regions, the hard data often ignore more than they convey. And what the data have ignored are often the very important traits that stand behind a currency (the USD in this case) and give it the long-term credibility to be the world's reserve currency.

The US dollar inertia

All this goes into explaining the inertia that the USD has enjoyed, despite rising competition from the other currencies in the global reserve allocation. Indeed, lacking the structural and technical underpinnings to replace the US dollar is not a problem limited to China. It is also a common problem facing all other reserve currencies. The strength of the dollar in the wake of the subprime crisis, even though it was of the United States' own making, underscores its safe-haven role. In other words, even the self-inflicted subprime crisis has failed to shake the world's confidence in the dollar, with the US Treasury market remaining the destination of choice for risk aversion.

The depth and liquidity of the US Treasury market means that it is the only large financial market to function smoothly during a financial crisis. The euro has serious problems behind it that are creating increasing doubts about its long-term survival. So it is still no challenger to the dollar as the world's most important reserve currency. The yen is hamstrung by Japan's debt-deflation quagmire and the lack of structural reforms, which have persisted for over 20 years now. The Swiss bond market is too small to accommodate central bank reserve flows, let alone the cross-border private sector and speculative flows.

In addition, the dollar is still supported by the strong US political relations with most of the world's largest foreign reserve-holding countries. Japan, South Korea, Saudi Arabia, Kuwait, Qatar and the United Arab Emirates are all sheltered under the US military umbrella. It is in their interest to ensure the USD does not face any undue pressure. Finally, the United States has the policy flexibility to deal with economic stress. The Fed can set monetary policy independently, while the dollar can adjust freely to domestic economic needs. In contrast, individual Euro zone members are constrained by the straitjacket of European Central Bank policy, which distorts idiosyncratic economic adjustment needs.

What about the SDR? Former PBoC governor Zhou Xiaochuan's suggestion, in March 2010 at a G20 meeting in London, to replace the USD by the SDR as the world reserve currency is a solid idea. But it is not practical even in the medium term. Technically, it would be very complicated to implement the idea of a super-sovereign reserve currency (whether it is in SDR or some other currencies or a currency basket) because of the inertia in the USD's global status. Most international trade and financial flows and, hence, the international unit of accounts are based in dollars. The global payments and settlement systems are thus dominated by the green-back also. It will take a very long time to evolve into some alternative forms to replace the dollar's international reserve currency and medium-of-exchange status.

Fundamentally, the SDR is not a medium of exchange in the real world. There are no SDR assets at all. The SDR is only a unit of account in the IMF. When the IMF allocates SDR, the recipient countries exchange them for local currencies at the local central banks. That money is then used to buy goods and services, invest and trade with other countries. No one is using, or will likely use, SDR in international trade.

Crucially, who decides the issuance and the pricing of the SDR – the IMF? Asia and many other EM economies will almost certainly object to that, given the track record of the IMF's economic prescriptions which have put their economies into hardship. China does not want to empower the IMF either. That is why at the April 2009 G20 summit in London, when Russia proposed an IMF/G20 Working Group to assess the idea of a global reserve currency, there were no words from China at all.

There is no credible successor to the USD in the medium term. No other economies and financial markets are large and deep enough to replace the United States as a safe haven during crisis periods. The euro, or even the RMB, may become an alternative down the road, but that is a long way away. The SDR is a very long-term idea, even if it will work. Some basic steps are needed first to make it a real currency before one can even think about its role as a reserve currency.

The SDR, a fast track

However, the SDR may be a fast track for the RMB to elevate its reserve currency status. Currently, the SDR only includes four reserve currencies, namely the USD, euro, JPY and GBP. The IMF is due to reassess the weightings of these currencies in 2015, with the possibility of adding new currencies, such as the RMB. There has been some speculation that the IMF might just do that in its re-weighting exercise.

The direct global effect of including the Chinese yuan in the SDR will not be big, as the SDR accounts for only 5% of world official reserve asset holdings. But the implication could be big, as even the prospect of the RMB becoming a SDR component currency might create a virtuous cycle where anticipation of deeper RMB internationalisation (stemming from being a SDR component) would prompt more central banks to hold the yuan, which would then actually deepen its internationalisation and prompt more central banks to hold more of it. The cycle could snowball and push the up weighting of the RMB in global reserve allocation to challenge the JPY, GBP and CHF, which currently have not more than 4% of reserve allocation.

France has been an ardent supporter of the RMB, with former president Nicholas Sarkozy making explicit proposals in G20 meetings in

2011 to include the RMB in the SDR as an important step towards reforming the international monetary system. However, China itself has been more cautious about including the RMB in the SDR basket. The PBoC has instead suggested the IMF to study the possibility of including the BRICS currencies (Brazil, Russia, India, China and South Africa – the world's largest fast-growing emerging economies) in the SDR. It has also argued that China was in no hurry to have its currency in the SDR, as the SDR has so far been only a symbolic currency basket (Reuters 2011).

That may just be an excuse that China uses to cover the RMB's shortcomings. Technically, the yuan cannot be a SDR component by the IMF's Balance of Payments (BoP) definition of a freely useable currency. The SDR basket consists of the four currencies that are issued by IMF members (or monetary unions that include IMF members) that are the largest exporters in the world, and have been determined by the IMF as freely useable. The latter condition was added as a formal criterion in 2000 and is open to interpretation, as is the number of component currencies. However, the notion that a freely usable currency ought to qualify for the SDR basket has been intensely debated.

First, it does not strictly mean full currency convertibility. Second, the RMB has already met some of the conditions for a freely useable currency; notably it has been fully convertible on a current account basis since 1999, and is being increasingly used in international trade settlement (Figure 9.3) and in the denomination of offshore deposit accounts since 2009 (Figure 9.4). According to official data, RMB trade

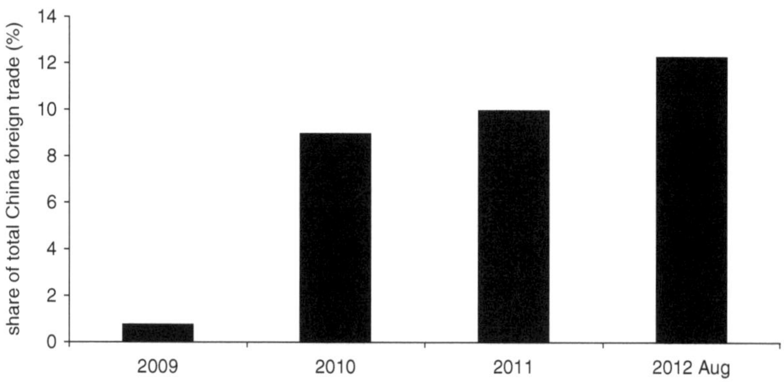

Figure 9.3 RMB trade settlement
Source: CEIC, author.

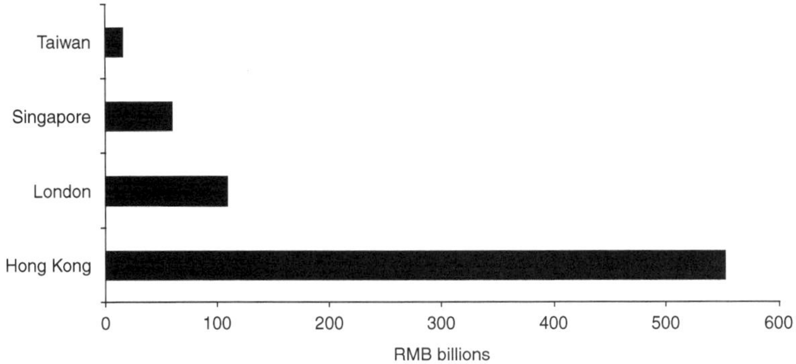

Figure 9.4 Accumulation of RMB offshore (June 2012)
Source: Reuters.

settlement accounted for over 12% of all China's foreign trade in August 2012, up from less than 1% in 2009. Meanwhile, offshore RMB deposits have grown from virtually zero in 2004 to about 8% of total bank deposits in Hong Kong, while they have also been accumulated in other centres, such as London, Singapore and Taipei, though at smaller amounts.

The IMF has kept its stance on SDR component currencies flexible, knowing that the decision of including a currency, such as the RMB, in the SDR basket is ultimately political. In November 2011, it proposed four indicators for assessing a currency's potential for inclusion in the SDR, including trading volume of that currency in spot FX markets, trading volume of its derivative instruments in the FX and over-the-counter (OTC) markets, market-based interest rate pricing mechanism and currency composition of official FX reserve holdings. However, it has not specified any benchmarks for these indicators, thus leaving the final decision of inclusion with the politicians.

China has likely fulfilled the first condition, and is working on the second one. Interest rate liberalisation is the biggest obstacle, given China's slow pace (and unwillingness) in this development. It is moving ahead nevertheless, with the most recent, albeit very small, interest rate liberalisation move implemented in July 2012 (see Chapter 5). If our discussion above turns out right that the RMB climbs to the third major reserve currency, the fourth criterion would be met in a few years. In a nutshell, the IMF has left itself considerable room to manoeuvre according to the change in political winds. As some analysts have argued, the IMF needs China a lot more than China needs the IMF (Prasad and Ye 2012).

The rise of an RMB bloc

Due to the momentum of RMB accumulation in official reserves by some small central banks recently and the rapid growth rate of FX reserves in non-China Asia, the actions of reserve managers will be crucial in affecting the development of the RMB as a reserve currency. The support for including the yuan in official reserves is especially strong in Africa and Latin America, notably in countries with strong economic ties to China. While the USD may enjoy a significant inertia as the most important global reserve currency, the RMB's challenge to its dominance is coming up surely and gradually. Indeed, it is already here without drawing much attention.

Empirical research shows that an RMB bloc is developing in Asia, looking set to displace the USD bloc in the region (Subramanian and Kessler 2012). The subprime crisis and the following European sovereign debt crisis since 2008 have weakened the financial clout of the developed world and opened up an opportunity for the RMB to move up the leadership rank. Since 2008, the yuan has increasingly become an anchor currency in Asia for which the movement of the regional currencies have tracked closely.

China has two periods of RMB flexibility, with the first period running from June 2005 to June 2008, and the second period running from June 2010 hitherto (Figure 9.5). Since June 2010 when Beijing allowed the RMB to "float" again (within the PBoC's tolerance limits, as defined by

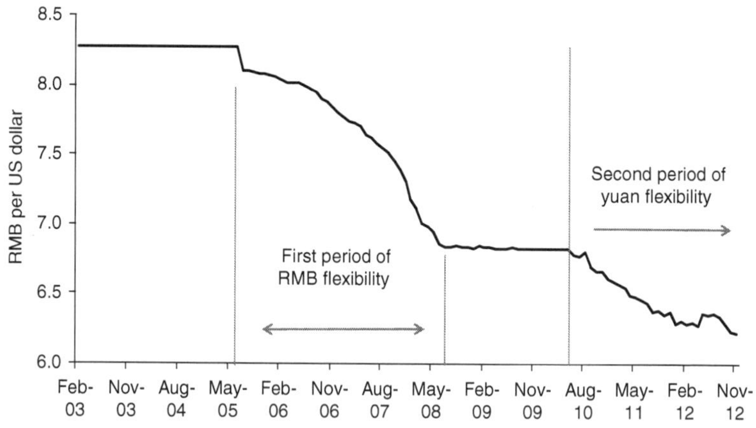

Figure 9.5 RMB/USD exchange rate
Source: Bloomberg.

the 1% trading range above and below the central rate against the USD that it sets at the beginning of each trading day), the number of Asian currencies tracking the yuan's movement has increased compared with the earlier period of flexibility between 2005 and 2008. Meanwhile, the number of Asian currencies tracking the movement of the euro and the USD has fallen since mid-2010.

Further, the correlations of the movements between the RMB and major Asian currencies have increased in the second period of RMB flexibility compared with the first period.[5] In particular, the correlations of eight out of the nine Asian currencies in our sample have increased since June 2010, suggesting that the Asian majors have been tracking the RMB's movement more closely than before. Meanwhile, the correlations with the US dollar and the euro of four out of the nine Asian majors have fallen (Figure 9.6), implying that the Asian units were tracking the G2 currencies less closely than before.

These results echo the Subramanian and Kessler 2012 research, which shows that the currencies of seven out of ten Asian major economies[6] have been tracking the RMB movement more closely than the dollar since mid-2010. A notable example is the Korean won, which has risen in tandem with the RMB against the US dollar since

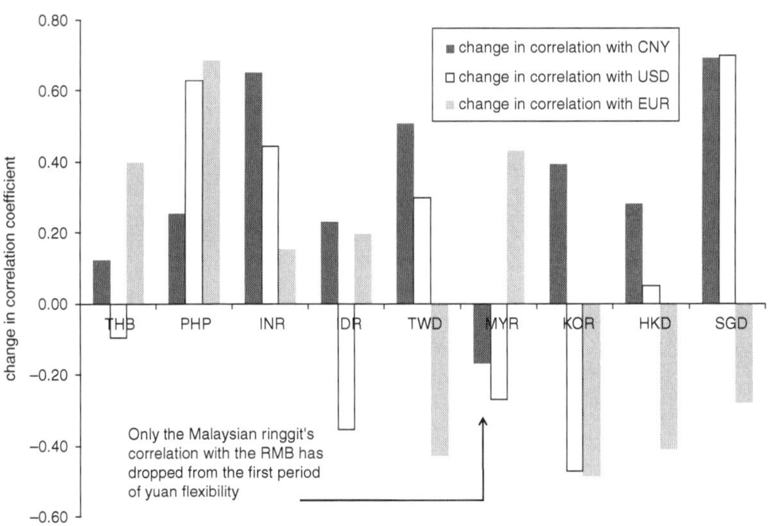

Figure 9.6 Change in correlations of Asian currencies with RMB, USD and EUR from period 1 to period 2 of RMB flexibility

Source: Bloomberg, BNPP IP Asia.

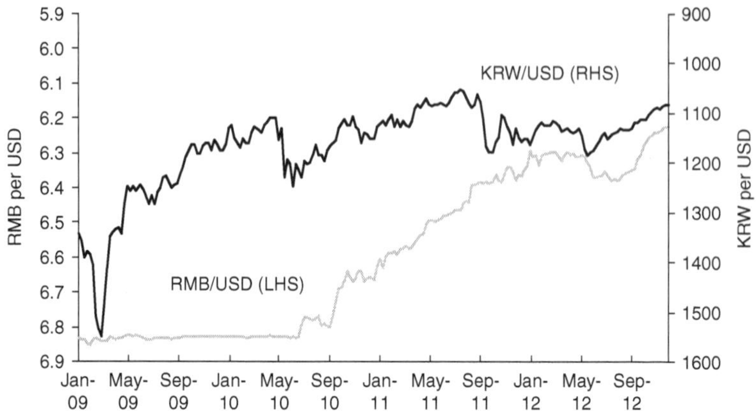

Figure 9.7 RMB and KRW have risen against the USD in tandem
Source: Bloomberg.

mid-2010 (Figure 9.7). From this perspective, Asia has effectively built a yuan bloc with more currencies moving closely together with the RMB than with the dollar.

The rise of the RMB bloc in Asia should not come as a surprise, as China's economic ties with the region have increased significantly over the past 20 years. For example, the share of China's manufacturing trade with Asia has now risen to almost a quarter of total intra-regional trade from about 2% in 1990. Its trade influence outside of the Asian region, for instance, on the other three members of the BRIC countries, has also risen significantly. Total trade (imports plus exports) between the BRIC nations has risen to 4.5% of total BRIC trade with the world from less than 1% in the 1990s. Specifically, Brazil, Russia and India's trade with China have now accounted for 17.5%, 10.6% and 9%, respectively, of their total trade values.

The point is that for countries that trade with the growing Chinese market, or are part of the supply chains centred on China, they have a strong incentive to minimise exchange rate volatility against the RMB than the USD. Further, whenever the RMB tracks the USD again, which is on a secular weakening trend despite periodic strengths, in my view, Asian currencies tracking the RMB will indirectly reap the benefit of a weakening dollar for their exports.

China's push for RMB settlement for international trade is also boosting the rise of the yuan outside Asia. For example, the currencies of India, Israel, Turkey and South Africa are now tracking the movement of the RMB more closely than before; in some cases they are tracking the yuan's movement more closely than the dollar's. It is easier for the small developing nations to accept China's request for settling trade in RMB than the major economies due to both politics and the USD's inertia in the latters' payment systems. Settling in RMB is less a leap for the small developing nations where the dollar is used as one of the foreign currencies, just like the RMB.

Here is the link from the increasing usage of the RMB by the small countries to the rise of the RMB as a reserve currency: If China were to liberalise its financial and currency markets more thoroughly, foreign demand for RMB could expand quickly through peer pressure. This, in turn, would create a feedback loop to deepen RMB internationalisation and quicken its ascent to the reserve currency status.

The emergence of the RMB bloc in Asia is an important pointer in the shift of economic power from the United States towards China. China is already the world's second-largest economy, the world's largest exporter and the world's largest net creditor. Now the RMB is rising to build a currency bloc not only to challenge the USD, but also to displace it in Asia through the RMB's influence on other Asian currencies. This is, arguably, an historic shift in the economic power balance because Asia, despite its geographical distance, has always been part of the USD bloc. Now it is changing to an RMB bloc.

Some may dispel this potential RMB challenge to the dollar's supremacy and argue that China will rise and fall the way Japan did over the past few decades. This is wrong because even during the height of the Japanese economic expansion, the JPY had never come close to rivalling the dollar as an anchor currency like the RMB does today. There was never a yen bloc in Asia. As the RMB trend develops, the gravitational force of economics will draw more and more countries towards China. Depending on the depth of China's structural reforms and economic liberalisation and rebalancing, internationalisation will give the red-back the potential to displace the green-back in the long run.

10
The Reality behind RMB-nisation

Renminbi (RMB) internationalisation is a process of opening China's capital account and integrating the country fully into the global system. But despite over 30 years of economic liberalisation, China is still unprepared for deeper integration with the world! The political system needs to be improved to get buy-in from the rest of the world to accept the RMB as a reserve currency. Political reform is imperative to eradicate moral hazard and rent seeking so that structural reforms can go deeper to support a globalised RMB. But serious incentive problems exist to hinder political changes. These are the cruel realities behind RMB-nisation.

To internationalise the yuan, it must command credibility and trust from the world, or no one will be willing to accept it. But China faces a credibility problem right from the top. Economic forces through international trade and financial transactions can only push RMB-nisation to a certain extent. Without political reform supporting deeper structural reforms, the internationalisation process would either stall or go astray. Interest rate liberalisation, exchange rate flexibility, capital account opening and domestic capital market liberalisation are all preconditions for RMB internationalisation and China's integration into the global system.

China cannot avoid political reform any longer if it wants to achieve sustainable growth and global leadership through internationalising the RMB. Its reform programme has come to a crossroads where success or failure is no longer as easily identifiable as it was before. The next generation of reforms will be more painful and difficult, as they will hit the nerve centre of the Chinese political system and vested interests. That is why deeper reforms need a stronger political system with a clearer reform vision to go forward.

However, changing the political system is easier said than done because decades of communist control has given rise to rent-seeking opportunities that benefit those in power. So there is no urgency for the Communist Party to push for political reform. Politics aside, the biggest challenge for Beijing is to support its modest international policy actions with substantial structural and financial reforms. Sequencing is crucial here. Unfortunately, there is still no policy conviction for mapping out the steps towards complete RMB-nisation.

Expecting fast and full capital account opening, interest rate liberalisation and RMB internationalisation is unrealistic. Yes, the RMB may become the third major reserve currency in a few years, overtaking the 4% global reserve allocation of the Japanese yen (JPY) and the Pound sterling (GBP) (see Chapter 9), but that is an easy first step. Gaining a bigger share in the official reserves will be very difficult, given China's credibility problem, inherent structural deficiencies, low-level financial market development and the absence of full RMB convertibility.

What is likely to happen to the RMB-nisation process in the medium term is an open capital account, but with numerous administrative controls and regulations still in place. Beijing will continue to push its currency as a global trade and finance settlement currency, but will only open up its domestic financial system in a cautious manner. It will want to retain control on capital flows along the way.

RMB internationalisation will remain the most crucial development for China and the world's monetary system in the coming decades. It is imperative for China to sort out its road map for RMB-nisation and to determine whether or how it wants to use it as a tool for pushing through deeper domestic reforms that are, in turn, needed to support currency internationalisation. The role of the RMB in the global monetary system in the post-crisis world with a weakened US leadership will depend on China's own policy choices.

Credibility problem from the top...

A look at the wealth of China's top lawmakers reveals a credibility problem for the country that is rooted in the top of the political system. Although China has a smaller number of billionaire lawmakers at the top of the government than the United States, their combined wealth is significantly larger than that of US politicians, including the US President (Bloomberg 2012). This seems to underscore the observation that rampant corruption has fattened the powers at the top, creating serious wealth inequality, which is a major fault line behind Beijing's bid to ask the world to accept the RMB as a reserve currency.

Bloomberg News, comparing data from Hurun of China (a publisher of a luxury-goods magazine that tracks China's affluent) with public data in the United States,[1] shows that the richest 70 members of the Chinese legislature, the National People Congress (NPC), had amassed total wealth of US$565.8 billion in 2011, up by US$11.5 billion from 2010. That was 75 times more than the combined net worth of US$7.5 billion of all 600 members of the US Congress, the president and his Cabinet and the nine Supreme Court justices. On a per capita basis, the richest 2% of the Chinese NPC members (60 people) had an average wealth of US$1.44 billion per person, while the richest 2% of US Congress members (11 people) only had an average wealth of US$323 million each.

In another report in June 2012, Bloomberg News reported that the extended family of then-Vice President Xi Jinping, who is now China's president, had amassed hundreds of millions of dollars in assets. In response, the Chinese government blocked all access inside the country to the Bloomberg website. Then in October 2012, the *New York Times* reported details on the billions of dollars of wealth accumulated by the family of the then Chinese premier, Wen Jiabao (The New York Times 2012), citing corporate and regulatory filings and shareholder registers as evidence, and audit reports by independent auditors. Beijing shut down the *New York Times* website in China two days after the report. This kind of government reaction raises questions about what and why they are trying to hide.

While Communist Party regulations call for top officials to disclose their wealth and that of their immediate family members, there are no laws or regulations prohibiting relatives of even the most senior officials from becoming deal makers or major investors. This is a big loophole that effectively allows them to trade on and extract profits/favours by using their political clout. Usually, the names of the official's relatives are hidden behind layers of partnerships and investment vehicles involving friends, friends of friends, work colleagues and business partners. In some cases, their ownership stakes are veiled by an intricate web of holdings as many as five layers away from the operating companies.

Complex corporate structures are not necessarily insidious. But in a system like China's, where there is no transparency and where corporate ownership and political power are closely intertwined, shell companies and complicated corporate structures do raise suspicion and magnify questions about ultimate ownership, iffy business relations and the sources of funds.

The income gain by the NPC members and other officials reflects the serious imbalances in the Chinese economy, where per capital income in 2010[2] was about US$2,400. That was even less than in Belarus, and only a fraction of the US$37,527 in the United States. These huge differences underscore the challenges that China's leadership faces in countering a rise in social unrest fuelled by rampant corruption and illegal land grabs. They also hurt the credibility of the administration that stands behind the RMB, which China is trying hard to sell to the world as a global currency.

...Hinders political reform

This credibility problem does not only hurt China's international image and foreign confidence in China's ability to manage its monetary system. It also goes deep into hindering domestic political reform, which is needed to reinforce further structural reforms. More than 30 years of easy economic reforms are now over. This also means that more than 30 years of avoidance of political change are also over. The next stage of economic reforms will be more painful and difficult, as China has moved out of the low base for structural changes, and deeper reforms require a government with a clearer vision and a stronger political will to go on. But China is facing an uphill battle in reforming its political system.

The biggest problem in the system is that politicians have made commercial interests inseparable from politics. The prevalence of billionaires in the NPC reflects the cozy relationship between the Communist Party and the rich. While the NPC only serves as a rubberstamp parliament, its 3,000-strong membership comprises some of China's most powerful politicians and executives. They wield significant power in their home turfs and decide on proposals such as tax policy, industrial development and infrastructure projects. There is a grudging acceptance by some Chinese that permitting the families of Communist Party leaders to profit excessively from the country's economic boom has been important to ensuring elite support for market reforms!

This is what creates the incentive incompatibility problem that hinders political reforms. The authorities will only make every effort to preserve the rent-seeking opportunities inherent in the political system. They have weak incentive to establish the rule of law and strengthen property rights, let alone to change the system. Meanwhile, the rich in China have strong incentive to join the system. An NPC membership grants immunity to criminal prosecution, among many other advantages, which facilitate illegal activities to get rich. So do not expect major political changes anytime soon, even though they are needed for healing the credibility deficit behind the RMB.

Unprepared for global integration

While China's economic reforms have brought millions of people out of poverty since 1978, this achievement has come from a low base. Just like a weight-loss programme, it is easy to lose the first 10 kilos of weight. But it will get harder and harder to lose more kilos after that. For China, the first 30 years of reforms were relatively easy, or from RMB-nisation's perspective, the yuan's expected climb from zero reserve allocation to over 4% to beat the JPY and GBP as the third major reserve currency (see Chapter 9) will be relatively easy. But deeper reforms that attack the vested interests and the nerve of the political system, or the RMB's further climb from 4% of global reserve allocation to, say, 8% or 10%, will be much more difficult.

Full RMB internationalisation should be a reflection of China's integration into the global system. Evidence shows that China has continued to fall short in overcoming systemic obstacles to become a major international player with long-term success. These obstacles will also hinder RMB internationalisation. Even if China were able to push RMB-nisation artificially, that would not be reflective of its global integration. Take globalisation, to which China owes its significant growth success. Many analysts have assumed that the Middle Kingdom has developed the means to meet its challenges from opening up to world trade. These means include investment in infrastructure, absorbing FDI and foreign technology and an undervalued currency.

However, strategically and structurally, the country has not been preparing itself for deeper global integration. Let us start with population. China is facing a problem of depletion within 15 years, according to the United Nation's projections. It has shown little urgency to change its one-child policy,[3] which is fundamental to creating the demographic tax in China in a few years' time. Nor has it shown any strong initiatives to scrap the *hu kou* system,[4] which impedes internal labour mobility and, hence, growth potential.

With a shrinking labour force and soon a shrinking population, Beijing lacks an immigration policy to tackle the problem. Though China is beginning to attract labour from other parts of the world, it has yet to promulgate a comprehensive legal framework that would allow the country to compete for the best talent or to deal with the complexity of international migration.

In terms of intellectual development, there are no independent domestic research entities to contribute to policy analysis and formulation. There are only government-run research institutes. Owing to political control, inadequate professional development and an educational system that stifles creativity and critical thinking, these public research entities cannot be relied upon for providing the high-quality, unbiased analysis of global issues on which sound policy making is based.

More important, over two decades of rapid growth have masked China's strategic weakness. Since China still favours state capitalism and discriminates against private firms, it lacks strong private companies that can take on Western multinational giants. Its continued discrimination against private firms has been reflected in the steady decline in bank loans to the private sector (Figure 10.1), chronically starving it of credit supply. With a few exception, such as Huawei, Lenovo and perhaps Haier (which is collectively owned and which it is debatable if it can be classified as a private company), there are no private Chinese firms with a global footprint.

All this is not to say that China had not done anything right. It has, but from a very low base when things are simple. The achievements in the past 30 years were like a rising tide raising all ships. Sailing forward, with a goal of an internationalised yuan as a global reserve currency, requires more brain power and policy vision and precision. These signs of insufficiency underscore the structural deficiency behind the RMB at this present stage. The market has been so wrong on so many occasions when forecasting and analysing the RMB-nisation trend because it sees hype most of the time and misses the fundamentals.

Figure 10.1 Discrimination against China's private sector

Source: CEIC.

Reform at a crossroads

Chinese reforms have come to a crossroads. The path going forward is going to be more difficult than in the past three decades. This means that the macro backdrop for capital account opening, interest rate liberalisation and RMB internationalisation is also going to get tougher. In recent years, competing views on the country's reform direction have emerged in domestic political and academic circles.

What is this crossroads? On the one hand, since China set up the framework of a market economy in the late 1990s, the role of the market has increased significantly. On the other hand, reforms have been stagnant in some key areas, leading to corruption, unequal wealth distribution and inefficient monopolies. In a sense, China has established a hybrid economy, with heavy government control coexisting with a market economy (which hence constrains the role of the market), or what Chinese-trained economists call "state capitalism."

In this economy, state-owned enterprises (SOEs) continue to hold monopoly positions in strategic industries, such as oil, telecommunications, railways and banking and finance. Governments at all levels have tremendous power to allocate important resources, including land and capital. The rule of law is absent. China has "rule by law" (read discretion by the politicians) in its system. Government officials at all levels have too much discretionary power to interfere in economic activities through investment approvals, administrative licensing for market access and price control.

The biggest danger that China faces under the current system, which mixes politics with commerce, is crony capitalism. China's economic evolution is path dependent. Once it travels down the government-led economic path, vested interests that benefit from rent-seeking activities will seek to push this hybrid economy into crony capitalism. As Nobel Laureate Douglas North said, once a course is set, it is hard to reverse the extreme social turmoil.[5]

During the early stage of economic liberalisation, many rent-seekers supported reforms when resource constraints were first relaxed, leading to many rent-seeking opportunities. Now they are more concerned with protecting their self-interest. Rather than continuing their reform support to establish a true market economy characterised by competition on level playing fields, they are trying to keep and expand administrative intervention and the "twin track" nature of the economy to preserve those rent-seeking opportunities.

To rectify this problem, China should eliminate the institutional basis for corruption. It should resist becoming part of what Gunnar Myrdal[6] called "Asian Drama" (Myrdal 1968). Myrdal was pessimistic about the development prospects for South and Southeast Asia, where crony capitalism was so prevalent that the power of the vested interests had overwhelmed the public power, leading to surging social inequality and, eventually, unrest. In others words, in the Myrdal world, no crony capitalist country, and by implication that includes China, would make it to the world economic power and global currency leagues.

However, eradicating corruption by strengthening government control may not succeed in China's political set-up. It could even backfire. In the Chinese system where political and commercial interests are inseparable, the expansion of government power may lead to a vicious circle where strengthening the government's hand leads to an expansion of the basis for rent seeking, which ends with more corruption, which leads to calls for more government power, more rent seeking... That is why political reform to sever the ties between politics and commerce and to establish the rule of law is imperative for building a solid foundation for the RMB to be a global currency.

Old habits die hard

In fact, the risk of increased government meddling in the economy, leading to increased rent seeking and corruption, has got bigger since the late 1990s. An indicator for that is the steady rise in China's government spending as a share of GDP since the Asian crisis in 1997–8 (Figure 10.2), which has reversed a 20-year declining trend. The Chinese authorities started using counter-cyclical fiscal policy to fight the economic shock from the Asian crisis in 1998. Since then, government spending as a share of GDP has risen steadily.

There is ample evidence from industries and sectors (including steel, cement, civil aviation, transport and the primary sector) showing an increase in state intervention in their business (Lo 2010). This trend has created fears of re-nationalisation. SOEs and firms with close political connections have been given preferred access to resources at the expense of the private firms. The return of the government's "visible hand" meddling with the market is likely to continue in the coming years, as Beijing will continue to use fiscal pump priming to counteract the aftershocks of the global financial crises. There will be more infrastructure projects, social welfare spending and fiscal support for various industries and, hence, more opportunities for rent seeking and corruption.

Crucially, although the total number of SOEs has dropped over the years, the scope of their business has expanded into sectors which were previously dominated by private firms. The strengthening of the SOEs'

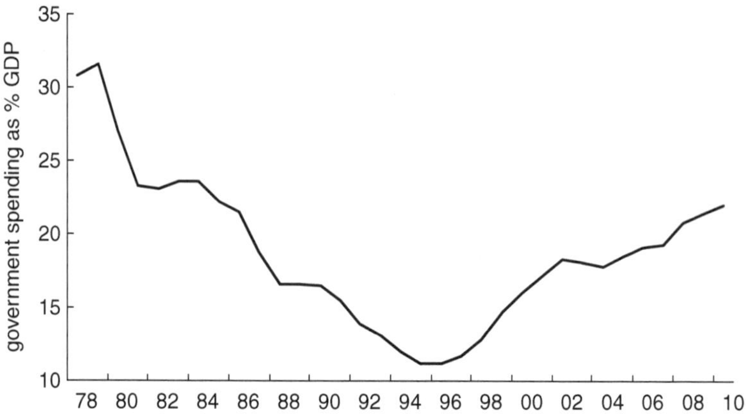

Figure 10.2 Sign of rising government intervention
Source: CEIC.

monopoly power has created insurmountable barriers to entry and competition for private firms. One of the key aspects of China's industrial policy in recent years has been the creation of "national champions" that can compete with international firms on the global stage (Lo 2007), though we have yet to see any real Chinese international conglomerates taking on the western giants.

From a macroeconomic perspective, it may not be bad for China to return to a bigger government approach, especially when many other governments in Europe, Britain, the United States and Asia are doing so to fight the global financial crisis. China's government expenditures do not seem excessive yet, as reflected by its very low public debt as a share of GDP, compared to the other major economies (Figure 10.3).

However, the implications are negative from a microeconomic perspective, where a bigger government without the rule of law most likely means more moral hazard and incentive distortions in the country. The most notable sign for this is the local government's enthusiasm in setting up cumbersome administrative approval procedures.

For example, there is a ridiculous attempt to charge fees for rain and sunshine. A township government in Central China's Henan province has a local regulation to levy a "natural-water fee" on farmers. Every farmer has to pay RMB30 for rainwater on his land (First Financial Daily 2012). Another example is a new ruling in 2012 by the local meteorological authorities in Northeast China's Heilongjiang Province that wind and solar resources are deemed state property. Any usage/assessment of

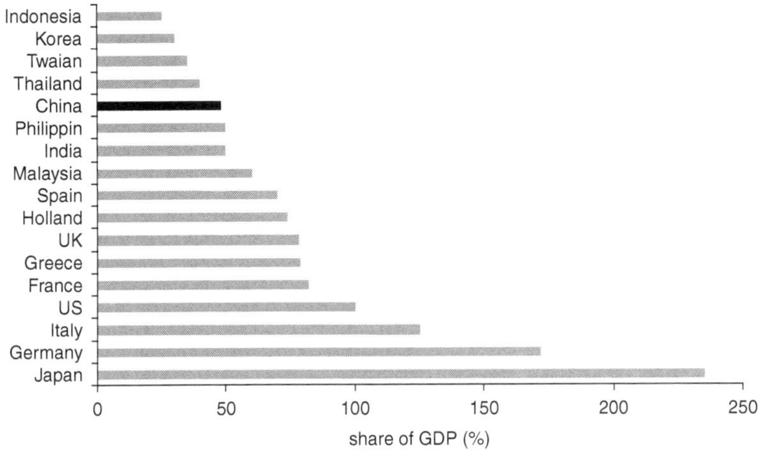

Figure 10.3 Government debt as % of GDP (2010)
Source: CEIC, author.

such resources must be approved by the meteorological officials (Global Times 2012).

The lack of transparency and supervision of the administrative agencies has resulted in rampant corruption. The central authorities know about these issues, and have even reported many cases on the government websites. But many of these reports have subsequently been removed to cover up the cases. For example, a People's Bank of China (PBoC) report on the central bank's website reported that 16,000 to 18,000 officials and SOE employees had fled China with US$120 billion between mid-1990 and 2008. These officials smuggled funds out of China through offshore bank accounts (BBC News 2012). But the report was later removed from the central bank's website.

Officially, prosecutors handled 18,464 bribery and fund embezzlement cases nationwide in 2011. These included 2,524 officials higher than county-head level, 198 at prefectural level and 7 at provincial and ministerial levels, according to the government media (Xinhua News Agency 2012). China's housing boom and the local governments' heavy reliance on land sales revenue for funding fiscal expenditure have created a hotbed for corruption in the housing sector. Shanghai's housing authorities have been involved in serious corruption cases. In August 2008, Shanghai Housing Deputy Director Yin Guoyuan was sentenced to death for taking bribes and other crimes. In June 2011, former Deputy Director of Shanghai Housing, Land and Resources Administration,

Tao Xiaoxing, was sentenced to life imprisonment for taking RMB10.5 million in bribes (Caixin 2012). The list goes on.

The lack of political reform to break the politics-commerce chain is the root cause for these problems and is stalling China's reform momentum. Political reform should not only reduce red tape and distortion in resource allocation and pricing, but it should also promote the rule of law for facilitating the market mechanism. But this is easier than done. Compared with the reforms implemented between the 1980s and 2000s, the next stage of reforms will be more painful and difficult because they will have to hit the deep-rooted problems and the political nerve of the system.

The fact that the government has the power to allocate land, credit and other resources remains the biggest obstacle to making deep changes in China. The government is too involved in economic activities that could be better undertaken by the private sector. But it fails to play an active role in the areas for which the government should be responsible, such as the provision of public goods, safety standards and a system based on rule of law.

The ball is in China's court to convince the world that it can transform its administration into a credible force that stands behind the RMB which it is trying to internationalise. The next generation of reforms should focus on redefining the role of the government in the market economy. But this will also mean reducing the power and interests of government officials, which will certainly be met with strong resistance.

Limits of state capitalism

China has so far not paid dearly for all its deficiency. Its role in the global economy remains confined to low- to medium-end processing and assembly functions. The most critical, sophisticated and profitable parts of the value chain, including research and development, logistics, marketing, servicing, product design, branding and distribution, are dominated by the Americans, Europeans, Japanese, Koreans and even Taiwanese. While these companies outsource the low- and medium-value parts of their work to China, China just "outsources" the high value-added functions to them.

China does have giant firms, as it is a development policy to build them. But they mostly remain in the hands of the government or government-controlled entities, and owe their profitability to their legal monopolies and government subsidies; the latter also takes the form of ultra-low interest-rate bank loans and an undervalued RMB. These companies may have the heft needed for global operations, but they are plagued by incentive incompatibility and rent-seeking problems that erode the motivation and ability to compete with global firms.

All these are hardly the qualities for a global RMB. Before the RMB is fully internationalised, these shortcomings must be rectified. The good news is that these problems are not insurmountable. The question is whether China can remove them under the current political system and state capitalism. The answer is likely not. This brings us back to the need for political reform.

There are limits to state capitalism which, for many Chinese-trained economists, means that state resources backed by political power enter the market and dominate private capital. And China has done exactly that. Despite more than three decades of economic reforms, China's SOEs still dominate the strategic sectors in its economy. State control has created and sustained monopolies, which undermine the function of the market mechanism, and created a hotbed for corruption and rent seeking.

Beijing did see these problems. As early as 1999, it wanted to make strategic adjustments, and ordered state-owned capital to pull out of all industries except a few sectors in which the government's presence was deemed essential. But because of their cozy ties with government officials, enterprises that deploy state-owned capital can always lobby decision makers and manipulate laws to their own advantage. They can always survive and even expand since they have easy access to financial support and government contracts. Many well-intended laws and regulations are never implemented.

For example, China has some of the best environmental laws in the world, but they are only there for foreigners to look at and admire. Just look outside the window in Beijing, the smog tells you the reality that these laws are never enforced. This is why offices inside Zhongnanhai,[7] China's political headquarters for its senior leaders, are all equipped with thousands of air purifiers, while the high officials are assuring the public of improved air quality (perhaps they mean in their private working and living environment only).

Another example is the 2004 blanket ban on golf courses. The purposes of the ban were to preserve dwindling farmland, save water and reduce the huge number of peasants displaced by the rich man's sport. There were 170 golf courses across the country at the time when the ban was announced. Today (in 2012) there are more than 600, and they are increasing!

The increasing amount of power abuse, corruption and moral hazard has led to an expanding number of financial, industrial and commercial scandals and crises that have killed tens of thousands of innocent people (including children). All these incidents have led to rising social grievances. This is indicative of the point at which China's economy has reached its limits under the existing system.

Under the current political set-up, enforcement of well-meaning policies and laws is sketchy at best and without oversight. Officials at all levels tend to hide their mistakes, play up their achievements and pander to their superiors. Whether or not China shows itself as a credible global force, its hosting a new global reserve currency, the RMB, will largely depend on its determination to restructure itself, both politically and economically. The continuation of state capitalism cannot remove the structural fault lines that are threatening the success of RMB-nisation.

The cruel reality

To put it simply, the cruel reality behind RMB internationalisation is that opening up China in true form via capital account liberalisation will expose the political dangers that could cause the demise of the Communist Party. This perhaps explains why there is no policy conviction for the road map to internationalise the RMB, no discussion on the sequencing of the internationalisation process and no intention for political reform.

In the past, the party leaders' moral legitimacy to rule China stemmed from a perceived commitment to Confucian values. Today, however, the leaders are widely seen to have lost their Confucian virtues and lack commitment to an ethical system, hence resulting in wealth inequality, power abuse and rampant corruption. Most of the public anger is directed at the lower-level corrupt officials. But the downfall of former Chongqing Communist Party chief, Bo Xilai, who was purged on corruption and other charges in 2012 (Financial Times 2012), and the exposure of the massive wealth that Beijing's senior leaders have amassed (see above) point to rot at the top.

China's leaders are also seen to be responsible for the moral state of the country, which is perceived to be in poor shape. If nothing is done to improve people's perceptions of moral collapse, the leaders risk a massive uprising calling for a wholesale change of leadership. The old reason for building up state power is now backfiring to threaten the Communist Party's legitimacy as China grows stronger. The point of strengthening the Party's power, and entrusting it to rule the country, was to secure political stability so that people could lead decent lives. It may have made sense to build up this power when China was constantly bullied by foreigners. But it is harder to justify now that the country has grown strong not only enough to protect itself but also to bully others.

These dangers are buried when the country is shut off from foreign influences. But fully opening up China through RMB-nisation and capital account liberalisation will bring in information, technology and ideological changes to the country so that the hidden political dangers cannot be buried anymore. Thus, for all the right things that China should do to ensure the success of the RMB's ascent to become a global reserve currency, including political reform, anti-corruption, deeper economic structural reforms and financial liberalisation, most of them will not come fast, if they are carried out at all.

The Communist Party fears, with good reason, that if it starts the process, it may lead to its demise. Yet the alternative of not making the needed bold and painful changes will likely lead to the same outcome. The economic, social and political contradictions at the heart of the country are unsustainable in the long term. This backdrop is hardly conducive for building a globalised RMB.

Concluding remarks

All the above are structural and political issues that will take a long time to unfold. Many unforeseen factors, benign or not, will affect the trajectory of the process and its final outcome. So they are not predictions for the demise of the RMB-nisation effort. For the foreseeable future, there is no doubt that RMB internationalisation will go on, mainly driven by the yuan's role as an international trade settlement currency in the medium term. It will acquire a major reserve currency status over the longer term. But the whole process is not going to be fast and steady as many in the financial markets have expected.

RMB-nisation should proceed as a natural economic and financial development for China. To push it artificially without making the fundamental changes behind the internationalisation process will only make the effort futile or even counterproductive. Policies aimed at promoting the RMB based on its appreciation will make the internationalisation process unsustainable, as the Japanese experience in yen internationalisation has shown (see Chapter 4).

Yuan deposits in Hong Kong, for example, shrank by 13% in September 2012 from a peak in November 2011, as RMB appreciation expectations faded in late 2011. Issuance of CNH bonds dropped by 55% in the first ten months of 2012, compared to a year earlier, because fading bets on RMB appreciation also cut demand for these bonds. All this is evidence that RMB-nisation based on currency appreciation expectation is not sustainable; once the speculation disappears, foreign non-trade demand for RMB also disappears.

As with other major reforms which China does not always undertake along a conventional path, it is internationalising the yuan in its own unique way. This means internationalising the RMB without capital account liberalisation and the RMB becoming a reserve currency (albeit in a limited number of emerging market central banks) before it is fully convertible. China's capital account liberalisation is likely to move forward in the medium term with Chinese characteristics, namely Beijing's removing "hard" controls on capital flows over time while keeping "soft" controls through administrative measures, such as the quota system. The purpose is to allow the RMB to play an increasing role in global trade and finance while keeping control over capital flows.

The bilateral currency pact that China signed with Japan in December 2011 shows China's effort to reduce its dependence on the USD. Other countries, especially in Asia, are eager to sign bilateral currency swap agreements with China because they see advantages to tighter trade and finance links with China. These agreements are soft tools for China to promote RMB-nisation. Though the shifts in global acceptance of the RMB are symbolic at present, they will develop into a critical mass over time and have the potential to transform the global monetary system.

Assuming China continues its structural reform and capital account opening efforts with the support of political reform, the RMB may become a major international currency after a decade. There is precedent to such currency shifts. The USD rose from being a currency with a limited international role to being a serious competitor to the GBP in just over a decade (Eichengreen and Flandreau 2010). The assumption of China implementing political reform to push deeper structural changes is of utmost importance here for the RMB to succeed.

In the short term, to broaden the RMB's international role without waiting for its structural reforms to catch up, China will need to make good use of the offshore RMB market as a platform. Hong Kong will lead the pack as the prime offshore RMB centre. Linking up to it are other centres around the world in a hub-and spoke model (see Chapter 8). Over the medium term, as China's capital account becomes more open and the domestic financial markets become more developed, the effort may shift onshore to Shanghai and to promoting it as an international financial centre augmenting RMB internationalisation.

Although China's large size and economic dynamism are significant advantages for promoting the RMB as an international currency, its underdeveloped financial markets and financial repression are major obstacles to the RMB's ambition to gain a global reserve currency status. The opening of the capital account with Chinese characteristics is only a temporary phenomenon on the RMB-nisation path. It is not sustainable if China wants full RMB internationalisation. Without full capital account and currency convertibility, it will be very difficult for the yuan to get even close to the euro's 25% official reserve allocation, let alone the USD's 63% global reserve share.

For the world, the RMB will rise to become a competitive international and reserve currency, eroding but not displacing the USD's, or even the euro's (assuming its continued existence), global dominance. The process of the yuan's ascent will cause potential volatility to the global monetary order. The world's monetary system will inevitably have to incorporate the RMB as a major currency in the future. For China, the big question is whether it sees RMB-nisation as an end in itself or a means to an end (to jump-start deeper domestic reforms to achieve sustainable growth).

Notes

Preface

1. The euro was virtually born in 1999, but actual circulation of its notes and coins (replacing the national currencies of the Euro zone member countries) started in January 2002.

1 Renminibi Shakes Up Global Currencies

1. The Renminbi is also known as the yuan. In the foreign exchange market, the code CNY refers to the onshore currency in China, while the code CNH refers to the renminbi circulating offshore in Hong Kong. Prior to the introduction of the CNH market, the term RMB was used somewhat interchangeably with CNY. Now CNY and CNH exclusively refer to the onshore and offshore renminbi, respectively. The abbreviation RMB is used as a general acronym to describe the Chinese currency.
2. Purchasing power parity (PPP) is an economic theory and a technique for determining the relative value of currencies, estimating the amount of adjustment needed on the exchange rate between countries in order for the exchange to be equivalent to (or on par with) each currency's purchasing power. It asks how much money would be needed to buy the same basket of goods and services in two countries, and uses that amount to calculate an implicit foreign exchange rate. Using the PPP rate, an amount of money thus has the same purchasing power in different countries.
3. The European Monetary Union (EMU) was created in 1999 with 17 member states that now use one currency, the euro. It is a subset of the European Union (EU), which has 27 member states and was created in 1993.
4. The Group of Seven, or G7, began in 1975, and includes the countries of France, Germany, Italy, Japan, the United Kingdom, the United States and Canada.
5. The Group of Ten, or G10, refers to the group of countries that have agreed to participate in the *General Arrangements to Borrow* (GAB). The GAB was established in 1962, when the governments of eight IMF members – Belgium, Canada, France, Italy, Japan, the Netherlands, the United Kingdom and the United States – and the central banks of two others, Germany and Sweden, agreed to make resources available to the IMF for drawings by participants and, under certain circumstances, for drawings by non-participants. The GAB was strengthened in 1964 by including Switzerland, then a non-member of the IMF, but the name of the G10 remained the same.
6. The 8% growth target has been moderated to between 7% and 8% since 2011, as the Chinese leadership has begun to understand that the economy is going through a maturing stage and facing capacity constraints along the way.

2 A Not-so-Mighty Yuan

1. Wenzhou is a prefecture-level city in southeastern Zhejiang province in China. As of the 2010 census, Wenzhou city proper; which includes two satellite cities and six counties, had a population of 9,122,100.
2. Back in 2007, Beijing broadened the RMB/USD daily trading range from ±0.3% to ±0.5% of the mid-point rate set by the PBoC, and the RMB/non-dollar currencies trading band from 1.5% to 3.0%.
3. Zhongnanhai is an area in central Beijing, adjacent to the Forbidden City, which serves as the central headquarters for the Communist Party of China and the State Council (Central government). The term *Zhongnanhai* is closely linked with the central government and senior Communist Party officials. It is often used as a metonym for the Chinese leadership at large (in the same sense that the term "White House" frequently refers to the President of the United States and his associates).

3 From Money to RMB-nisation

1. See Chapter 2 for the key steps of RMB internationalisation that Beijing has taken since the late 2000s.
2. If the capital base consists of assets denominated in different currencies, regular valuation of the assets in terms of the home currency will create an inherent volatility of asset values due to exchange-rate fluctuations, even though underlying asset prices may have not changed in their original currency terms.
3. The United Nations forecasts that China's working population (aged 15–64) will start shrinking in 2017, and its total population will start contracting in 2027, if other factors do not change to affect the current demographic trends.
4. In the pessimistic scenario, a multi-decade adjustment process for Europe and the United States is not unimaginable, as shown by Japan, which has gone through more than 20 years of post-bubble adjustment; and it is still not finished with the process yet.
5. The approval for using RMB as an investment currency for FDI going into China came in late 2011 as part of Beijing's effort to liberalise the capital account. Before this, FDI in China had to be denominated in foreign currencies, which would then be exchanged into RMB and invested onshore.

4 Trade Is not Enough

1. The Association of Southeast Asian Nations (ASEAN) is a geo-political and economic organisation of ten countries located in Southeast Asia. It was formed on 8 August 1967 by Indonesia, Malaysia, the Philippines, Singapore and Thailand. Since then, membership has expanded to include Brunei, Burma (Myanmar), Cambodia, Laos and Vietnam. The Association aims at accelerating economic growth, social progress and cultural development among its members, protecting regional peace and stability and providing opportunities for member countries to discuss differences peacefully.

2. This "bridge" concept was first used by Norman Chan, HKMA Chief Executive, during the China Daily Asia Leadership Roundtable, "Hong Kong's Visions and Strategies on RMB Internationalisation" held in Hong Kong on 11 July 2011.
3. Offshore RMB-denominated bonds are called CNH bonds in the financial markets, while onshore RMB-denominated bonds are referred to as CNY bonds.
4. There is no hard evidence for verifying the ultimate demand for RQFII products, because there have been no reports or data update in the market following the marketing failure of the RQFII funds to retail investors. Anecdotal evidence from market sources indicates that some RQFII quota holders still had more than three-quarters of their quota unsubscribed by autumn 2012.
5. This speculative motive is not necessarily the same as the speculative motive in the demand for money theory, which refers to investment demand for money. In the yen internationalisation perspective, this speculative motive refers to speculation on the JPY's exchange-rate movement.

5 The Next Steps for Internationalisation

1. Since the launching of the CNH market and up until the time of writing, there has been only one RMB clearing bank in the offshore market, and that is the Bank of China (BoC). China's central bank, the People's Bank of China (PBoC), grants the BoC an annual quota of RMB8 billion to facilitate offshore RMB trading and clearing processes. The PBoC is effectively controlling offshore RMB circulation through the BoC via the quota system.
2. "Sterilisation" in macroeconomics refers to the actions taken by the central bank to negate potentially harmful effects of capital inflows – such as currency appreciation and inflation – both of which can reduce export competitiveness. Consider a case in which capital inflows push up the RMB exchange rate. To weaken or stabilise the RMB against the USD, the PBoC will sell RMB and buy USD in the FX market. The increased supply of RMB would lower its exchange rate, but it would also boost domestic inflationary pressure. To sterilise this inflationary impact, the PBoC would issue RMB bills/notes/bonds to absorb the RMB that was released into the system due to FX intervention. It would do the opposite if it wanted to strengthen the RMB exchange rate in the case of capital outflow.
3. The two most commonly speculated time frames for the RMB to displace the USD as the super currency are 2015 and 2020.
4. The Society for Worldwide Interbank Financial Telecommunication (SWIFT) provides a network that enables financial institutions worldwide to send and receive information about financial transactions in a secure, standardised and reliable environment. SWIFT does not facilitate funds transfer. Rather, it sends payment orders, which must be settled by correspondent accounts that the institutions have with each other.
5. Rent-seeking activity arises when an economic agent uses his/her resources to obtain an economic gain from others without reciprocating any benefits back to society through wealth creation. In other words, rent seeking is a zero-sum game with no net wealth creation. An example is when a company

lobbies the government for loan subsidies, grants or tariff protection. These activities do not create any benefit for the society; they just redistribute resources from the taxpayers to the special-interest group.

6. Before this initiative, which was implemented in early 2012, only Chinese firms on Beijing's approved list could use RMB for foreign trade settlement with countries that were on the government's approved list.
7. In this move, China will allow Japan to make FDI in China using RMB as the investment currency, develop an RMB/yen FX market to promote trade settlement in RMB in Japan and encourage Japanese entities to issue RMB bonds in Tokyo and other offshore markets. Japan will invest in Chinese sovereign debts as reserve assets. But no timetable has been agreed on for the implementation at the time of writing.
8. Assuming the Japanese exporters are willing to settle in RMB.
9. The governments of these four cities have been lobbying Beijing ardently to develop offshore RMB centres in their jurisdictions.

6 China Ready for a Globalised RMB?

1. The Chinese banks were kept afloat due to the too-big-to-fail policy of the Chinese government, which had kept public confidence in the banks that they would never be allowed to go belly up.
2. As part of the stimulus package in late 2008 and early 2009 to fight the negative impact of the US subprime crisis on the Chinese economy, Beijing ordered banks to lend almost indiscriminately to boost investment and infrastructure projects. The expected rise in NPLs is a direct result of this lending spree.
3. In 2009, the average return on equity for Standard Chartered and HSBC was 14.3% and 5.1%, respectively; the average return on total assets was 0.8% and 0.3%, respectively. Sources: Bank annual reports.
4. Net interest margin is calculated by dividing net interest income by the average balance of total interest-earning assets.
5. Despite it being the third-largest in the world by market capitalisation, China's bond market is pretty much closed to foreign participation, except through very limited doors, such as the QFII and RQFII quota schemes. Trading in the Chinese bond market is very thin, sometimes as quiet as a morgue, as most investors (the majority of them are institutional) buy and hold the bonds through maturity.
6. See http://asianbondsonline.adb.org/china/data/bondmarket.php?code=LCY_in_GDP_Local
7. At the time of writing, Chinese regulations only allow foreign investors to invest in and trade Chinese bonds that are listed on the stock exchanges. The regulations are expected to be relaxed eventually to allow foreign participation in the inter-bank bond market. But no official timetable has been given.
8. On 3 April 2012, Beijing expanded the QFII quota by US$50 bn to a total of US$80 bn, and the RQFII quota by RMB50 bn to a total RMB70 bn.
9. In the pilot program launched in July 2009, only 365 Chinese exporters were allowed to conduct cross-border trade settlement in yuan. The programme was later expanded to 20 provincial regions in June 2010, and then to all parts

of the country in August 2011. However, only those companies enlisted in the program had the right to settle cross-border trade in yuan. This restricted list was scrapped on 3 March 2012.

10. The formal model underlying the Impossible Trinity theorem is uncovered Interest Rate Parity, which states that in the absence of a risk premium, arbitrage will ensure that the depreciation or appreciation of a country's currency against another will be equal to the nominal interest rate differential between them. Since under a currency peg, the exchange rate cannot move, the two countries' nominal interest rates must be equal so that the underlying appreciation/depreciation pressure will go away. This, in turn, implies that the pegging country has no ability to set its nominal interest rate, and hence no independent monetary policy. The only way for the country to have both a fixed exchange rate and an independent monetary policy is if it can prevent arbitrage in the FX market from taking place, that is, by instituting capital controls on international transactions (i.e. a closed capital account).
11. See endnote 5 in Chapter 5.
12. In China, private lending operates in a legal grey zone. Loans between individuals are "permitted" as long as the lending rate does not exceed four times the benchmark bank lending rate. Courts appear to uphold private lending contracts and will enforce the collection of collateral. On the other hand, loans between companies are illegal. Presumably, the intent of this prohibition is to prevent the channelling of loans through the formal banking system to the informal credit market. However, a typical Wenzhou SME is owned by a single person or a small number of people. This means that the line between a loan from an individual and from a firm can become quite blurred. Such unclear ownership and regulatory structures play into the advantage of an informal lender but not a formal lender.

7 Creeping Reforms Raise Systemic Risk

1. He was dubbed the "Chinese Paul Volker" for his hard-handed and decisive anti-inflationary policy.
2. Wenzhou is a prefecture-level city in the Southeastern Zhejiang province in China. It was a prosperous foreign treaty port, which remains well-preserved today. It is situated in a mountainous region and, as a result, has been isolated for most of its history from the rest of the country, making the local culture and language very distinct not only from the rest of China but also from the neighbouring areas. Wenzhou is also known for its emigrants who leave their native land for Europe and the United States, with a reputation for being entrepreneurs who start restaurants, retail and wholesale businesses in their adopted countries. People of Wenzhou origin make up a large number of ethnic Chinese residents of Italy, the Netherlands, France and Africa.
3. As of the first half of 2012.
4. The National Development and Reform Commission (NDRC) controls corporate bond issuance by the SOEs, the PBoC oversees commercial paper and medium-term notes issuance and the China Securities and Regulatory Commission (CSRC) manages bonds issued by listed companies and traded on the Chinese stock exchanges.

5. Approval by the NDRC could take up to a year.
6. The CSRC, for example, has fast-tracked approval for some bond applications to less than two months.
7. As of the first quarter of 2012.
8. One basis point equals one-one hundredth of one percent.
9. See endnote 5 in Chapter 5.

8 RMB-nisation Needs Offshore Market

1. The terms "offshore market(s)" and "offshore centre(s)" are often interchangeable as used by financial market players.
2. Formerly, when some firm/individual received foreign currencies from foreign trade settlement, that firm/individual just put the foreign currency receipts in the banks' foreign currency deposit accounts. But the one-way bet on RMB appreciation had prompted these agents to change their foreign currency receipts (or even switch out of other foreign currency deposits) into RMB deposits. See Chapter 4, Figure 4.4, for more details.
3. Singapore is the fourth-largest FX trading centre in the world and the second-largest in Asia after Tokyo.
4. The hub-and-spoke model is a system of connections arranged like a chariot wheel, in which all traffic moves along spokes connected to the hub at the centre. The model is commonly used in industry, in particular in transport, telecommunications and freight, as well as in distributed computing.
5. However, the fact that there are more Taiwanese tourists going to China than Chinese tourists coming to Taiwan (i.e. Taiwan runs a tourism deficit with China) is not conducive to RMB accumulation in Taiwan, though this is positive for building two-way flows of RMB between Taiwan and China.
6. This is a quota granted for overseas Chinese affiliates in Hong Kong to invest their RMB held offshore back in China's equity and fixed-income markets.
7. The only RMB-denominated stock listed on the Hong Kong Stock Exchange so far is the Hui Xian Real Estate Investment Trust (REIT) by Hong Kong billionaire Li Ka-shing. The REIT made its debut on 29 April 2011.
8. In economics, moral hazard is a situation where a party has a tendency to take risks because the costs that could incur will not be borne by the party taking the risk. Moral hazard can be present at any time when two parties come into an agreement with one another. Each party in a contract may have the opportunity to gain from acting contrary to the principles laid out by the agreement. For example, a person with insurance against automobile theft may be less cautious about locking his/her car because the negative consequences of vehicle theft are mostly borne by the insurance company.
9. See endnote 5 in Chapter 5.

9 RMB – The Third Major Reserve Currency

1. The SDR is an international reserve asset, created by the IMF in 1969 to supplement its member countries' official reserves. Its value is based on a

basket of four key international currencies: the USD, euro, JPY and GBP. SDRs can be exchanged for freely usable currencies. The SDR is neither a currency nor a claim on the IMF. Rather, it is a potential claim on the freely usable currencies of the IMF members. SDR Holders can obtain these currencies in exchange for their SDRs in two ways: first, through the arrangement of voluntary exchanges between members, and second, by the IMF designating members with strong external positions to purchase SDRs from members with weak external positions. In addition to its role as a supplementary reserve asset, the SDR serves as the unit of account of the IMF and some other international organisations.

2. In this move, China will allow Japan to make FDI in China in RMB, develop a RMB/yen FX market to promote trade settlement in RMB in Japan and encourage Japanese entities to issue RMB bonds in Tokyo and other offshore markets. Japan will invest up to US$10 billion in Chinese sovereign debt as reserve assets. But no timetable for implementation has been agreed on at the time of writing.
3. The G7 began in 1975 as the Group of Six and included France, West Germany, Italy, Japan, United Kingdom, and United States. They were joined by Canada the following year to become the G7.
4. The Chinese central bank governor made an explicit appeal, in March 2010 during a G20 meeting in London, to replace the USD by the SDR as the world reserve currency. This was the first explicit challenge by China on the USD's global dominance, less than a year after it launched the RMB internationalisation programme in June 2009.
5. We calculated the correlations of the nominal effective exchange rates (NEER) between the RMB and the Thai baht, Indian rupee, Indonesia rupiah, Malaysian ringgit, Korean won, Taiwan dollar, Hong Kong dollar, Singapore dollar and Philippine peso.
6. These seven countries include Korea, Taiwan, Malaysia, Thailand, Indonesia, the Philippines and Singapore.

10 The Reality behind RMB-nisation

1. The US data come from a database which can be downloaded from the website of the Washington-based Center for Responsive Politics.
2. This is the most recent year for which we can draw a comparison between China and other countries on their income levels. No other countries in the world are as "efficient" as China in releasing detailed GDP data within a couple of months after the year ends.
3. Introduced in 1978, China's one-child policy was initially applied to first-born children starting in 1979. It officially restricts married urban couples to having only one child, while allowing exemptions for several cases, including twins, rural couples, ethnic minorities and parents without any siblings themselves. The policy was created by the Chinese government to alleviate social, economic and environmental problems.
4. A *hu kou* is a record in the system of household registration which is required by law in mainland China. A household registration record officially identifies a person as a resident of an area and includes personal information such as name, date of birth, parents, spouse and child/children. *Hu kou* was

originally set up to limit mass migration from the country to the cities to ensure some structural stability. By regulating labour movement, it served to ensure an adequate supply of low-cost workers to the state-owned businesses. But this function has become outdated. Residents in their birthplaces enjoy preferential treatment in terms of welfare, education, housing etc. under the *hu kou* system. They lose all these benefits once they emigrate to other provinces.

5. Douglas North won the Nobel Prize in Economics in 1993 for his work on institutions. He believes that past decisions can act as a constraint on policy choices, and that institutions persist over time because of the high transaction costs involved in changing them.
6. Gunnar Myrdal won the Nobel Prize in Economics in 1974.
7. See endnote 3 in Chapter 2.

Bibliography

ANZ (2012), "RMB Internationalisation – Get Ready for the Next Big Thing," sponsor statement in AsiaMoney Renminbi Focus, May pp. 6–7.

BBC News (2012), "Chinese Officials Stole $120 Billion, Fled Mainly to the US," 17 June. http://bbc.co.uk/news/world-asia-pacific-13813688.

Bell, Daniel and Eric Li (2012), "In Defence of the Chinese Way of Picking Leaders," *Financial Times*, p. 9.

Bloomberg News (2012), "China's Billionaire Lawmakers Make US Peers Look Like Paupers," 27 February.

Caixin (2012), "Former Shanghai Urban Planning Official on Trial for Graft," 19 June. http://english.caixin.com/2012-06-19/100402432.html.

Carse, Stephen and Wood, Geoffrey (1981), "The Choice of Invoicing Currency in Merchandise Trade," *National Institute Economic Review*, 98, pp. 60–72.

CBRC (2010), China Banking Regulatory Commission 2009 Annual Report, Beijing.

China Daily (2011), "Nigeria Bank Chief Sees Yuan Becoming Reserve Currency," 6 September. http://www.chinadaily.com.cn/world/2011-09/06/content_13635209.htm.

Deutsche Bank (2006), "China's Commodity Hunger: Implications for Africa and Latin America," Deutsche Bank Research, 13 June http://www.dbresearch.com/PROD/DBR_INTERNET_EN-PROD/PROD0000000000199956.pdf.

Economist (2012) "Big Mac Index," 14 January.

Eichengreen, Barry (2009), "The Dollar Dilemma," *Foreign Affairs* Sept/Oct http://www.wright.edu/~tdung/dollar_dilemma.htm.

Eichengreen, Barry (2010), *Exorbitant Privilege: The Rise and Fall of the Dollar and the Future of the International Monetary System*, University of Oxford Press, December.

Eichengreen, Barry and Marc Flandreau (2010), "The Federal Reserve, the Bank of England and the Rise of the Dollar as an International Currency, 1914–1939," BIS Working Paper 328, Basel.

Financial Times (2012), "Bo Xilai's Downfall and China's Future," 19 March.

First Financial Daily (2012), "Gushi County in Henan Levies 'Natural Water Fee' on Farmers," 10 July (in Chinese).

Fukuda, Shin-ichi and Ji Cong (1994), "On the Choice of Invoice Currency by Japanese Exporters: The PTM Approach," *Journal of the Japanese and International Economies*, 8, pp. 511–29.

Gao, Haihong and Yu, Yongding (2009), "Internationalisation of the Renminbi," Asian Office Research, Bank of International Settlements, August.

Global Times (2012), "To Own the Sun," 2 July. http://www.globaltimes.cn/content/718532.shtml.

Grassman, Sven (1973), "A Fundamental Symmetry in International Payment Patterns," *Journal of International Economics*, 3, pp. 105–16.

Hajime Hori, eds., *Organisation, Performance and Equity: Perspectives on the Japanese Economy*, Kluwer Academic Publishers, Massachusetts, pp. 305–55.

HSBC (2011), "CNH Growth Set to Continue," in the *Global Times*, 25 May, http://business.globaltimes.cn/industries/2011-05/658922.html.

IMF (2012), "Changing Patterns of Global Trade," International Monetary Fund Departmental Paper no. 12/01, January.

Ito, Takatoshi, Satoshi Koibuchi, Kiyotaka and Junko Shimizu (2010), "Why Has the Yen Failed to Become a Dominant Invoicing Currency in Asia? A Firm-Level Analysis of Japanese Exporters' Invoicing," NEBR Working Paper 16231, National Bureau of Economic Research, July.

Kawai, Masahiro (1996), "The Japanese Yen as an International Currency: Performance and Prospects," in Ryuzo Sato, Rama Ramachandran and Hajime Hori, eds. "Organisation, Performance and Equity: Perspectives on the Japanese Economy", Kluwer Academic Publishers, pp 305–355.

Kenen, Peter (1988), "International Money and Macroeconomics," in K.A. Elliot and J. Williamson eds., "World Economic Problems," Institute for International Economics, Washington.

Kose, Ayhan, Eswar Prasad, Kenneth Rogoff and Shang-ji Wei (2009), "Financial Globalization: A Reappraisal," IMF Staff Papers, 56, no.1, pp. 8–62.

Krugman, Paul (1980), "Vehicle Currencies and the Structure of International Exchange," *Journal of Money, Credit and Banking*, 12, pp. 513–26.

Krugman, Paul (1984), "The International Role of the Dollar: Theory and Prospect," in John Bilson and Richard Marston, eds., *Exchange Rate Theory and Practice*, Chicago: University of Chicago Press, pp. 261–78.

Krugman, Paul (2010), "Capital Export, Elasticity Pessimism and the Renminbi," *The New York Times*, 16 March.

Lardy, Nicholas (1998), *China's Unfinished Economic Reform*, Washington: Brookings Institute Press.

Lardy, Nicholas (2008), "Financial Repression in China," Policy Briefs in International Economics 08–8, September. Washington: Peterson Institute for International Economics.

Lin, Yifu (2009), "Three Conditions of the RMB Internationalization," *Wen Wei Po*, 28 June.

Lo, Chi (2007), *Understanding China's Growth: Forces that Drive China's Economic Future*, Palgrave Macmillan, pp. 183–88.

Lo, Chi (2009), *Asia and the Subprime Crisis: Lift the Veil on the Financial Tsunami*, Palgrave Macmillan, chapter 9.

Lo, Chi (2010), *China After the Subprime Crisis: Opportunities in the New Economic Landscape*, Palgrave Macmillan, pp.148–53.

Lo, Chi (2012), *Thinking the Inevitable: China's Economic Superpower Aspiration in the New Paradigm*, Enrich Professional Publishing, pp. 81–5.

Ma, Guonan (2006), "Who Pays China's Bank Restructuring Bill?" CEPII Working Papers, February, no. 2006–4.

Mankiw, Gregory (2007), *Macroeconomics* (6th ed.), Worth Publishers, pp. 22–32.

Maziad, Samar, Pascal Farahmand, Shengzu Wang, Stephanie Segal, and Faisal Ahmed (2011), Internationalization of Emerging Market Currencies: A Balance between Risks and Rewards," IMF Staff Discussion Note, SDN/11/17, October.

McCauley, Robert (2011), "RMB Internationalization and China's Financial Development," *BIS Quarterly Review*, December.

McKinnon, R.I. (1979), *Money in International Exchange: The Convertible Currency System*, Oxford University Press.

Morgan Stanley Research Asia Pacific (2011), "HKMA Action to LC-Backed Trade Finance Loans," 24 November.

Mundell, Robert (1983), "The Case for a Managed International Gold Standard," in Michael Connolly eds., *The International Monetary System: Choices for the Future*, New York: Praeger, pp. 1–19.

Myrdal, Gunnar (1968), *Asian Drama: An Inquiry into the Poverty of Nations*, The Penguin Press.

New York Times (2012), "Billions in Hidden Riches for Family of Chinese Leader," 25 October.

Ogawa, E. (2001), "The Japanese Yen as an International Currency," Regional Financial Arrangements in East Asia, Korea Institute for international Economic Policy (KIEP), pp. 25–51.

Ogawa, E. and Sasaki, Y.N. (1998), "Inertia in the Key Currency," *Japan and the World Economy*, Vol.10, No.4, pp. 421–39.

Otero-Iglesias, Miguel (2010), "The Internationalisation of the Renminbi: A Strategy of Crossing the River by Feeling the Stones," paper for the International Symposium on Chinese Politics, Observatory of Chinese Politics, Galician Institute of International Analysis and Documentation, March 7–13.

Page, S (1977): "Currency of invoicing in merchandise trade", National Institute Economic Review, vol 81, no 1, pp 77–81.

Parsons, Craig and Kiyotaka Sato (2008), "New Estimates of Exchange Rate Pass-Through in Japanese Exports," *International Journal of Finance and Economics*, 13 (2), pp. 174–83.

Prasad, Eswar and Raghuram Rajan (2008), "A Pragmatic Approach to Capital Account Liberalization," *Journal of Economic Perspectives* 22, no. 3, pp. 149–72.

Prasad, Eswar, Thomas Rumbaugh and Qing Wang, "Putting the Cart Before the Horse? Capital Account Liberalisation and Exchange Rate Flexibility in China", IMF Policy Discussion Paper, International Monetary Fund.

Prasad, Eswar and Lei Ye (2010), "The Renminbi's Role in the Global Monetary System," IZA Discussion Paper Series 6335, February.

Reuters (2011), "China FX Head Proposes Adding BRICS Currencies to SDR," 5 May.

Sato, Kiyotaka (1999), "The International use of the Japanese Yen: The Case of Japan's Trade with East Asia," *The World Economy*, 22 (4), pp. 547–84

Sato, Kiyotaka (2003), "Currency Invoicing in Japanese Exports to East Asia: Implications for the Yen Internationalisation," *Asian Economic Journal*, 17 (2), pp. 129–54.

Smith, Gary (2012), "Renminbi to Shake Up Reserve Management Status Quo," *Central Banking Journal*, 16 May. http://www.centralbanking.com/central-banking-journal/feature/2175154/renminbi-shake-reserves-management-status-quo.

Subramanian, Arvind and Martin Kessler (2012), "The Renminbi Bloc is Here: Asia Down, Rest of the World to Go," Peterson Institute for International Economics Working Paper WP12–19, October.

Swoboda, Alexander (1969), "Vehicle Currencies and the Foreign Exchange Market: the Case of the Dollar," in Robert Aliber ed., *The International Market for Foreign Exchange*, New York: Praeger.

Tavlas, G.S. (1991), "On the International Use of Currencies: the Case of Deutsche Mark," Princeton Studies in International Economics, Princeton University, Issue 181of Essays in international finance.

Triffin, Robert (1961), *Gold and the Dollar Crisis: The Future of Convertibility*, rev. ed., New Haven: Yale University Press.

Van Overtveldt, Johan (2011), *The End of the Euro: The Uneasy Future of the European Union*, Agate B2.

Wall Street Journal (2011), "Japan Considers Buying Chinese Bonds," 21 December.

Xiao, Gang (2010), "Don't Blame it on the Government," 26 August, Bank of China website: http://www.boc.cn.

Xinhua News Agency (2012), "18464 Major Corruption Related Cases Were Handled in 2011," 11 March. http://news.xinhuanet.com/legal/2012–03/11/c_111637050.htm (in Chinese).

Yu, Yongding (2009),"Opinions upon RMB Internationalization," China and Global Economy Forum: Financial Crisis and Reforms of International Financial System, Shanghai, China, 13 May.

Zhao, Xijun (2009), "It is Important to Develop Domestic Financial Market for RMB Internationalization," *The Banker*, No.5, pp. 38–42.

Zhou, Xiaochuan (2005), "Rules for Developing a Financial Center and the Reform of the RMB Exchange Rate Regime," Central Banker Speeches, 10 August, Bank for International Settlements http://www.bis.org/review/r050901f.pdf

Zhou, Xiaochuan (2006), "China's Economic Development and External Financial Cooperation," Speech at the Sino-French Financial Forum, Beijing, Central Banker Speech, 21 September, Bank for International Settlements http://www.bis.org/review/r061011c.pdf

Index

Printed and bound in the United States of America